JIHAD AND THE WEST

JIHAD AND THE WEST

S M Arif

MD PUBLICATIONS PVT LTD
NEW DELHI
www.mdppl.com

Published by :

MD Publications Pvt Ltd
"MD House", 11, Darya Ganj,
New Delhi - 110 002
Phone : +91-11-41563325 (Customer Service)
+91-11-41562846 (Editorial)
E-mail (orders): order@mdppl.com
Website: www.mdppl.com

ISBN: 978-81-7533-258-4

Published and Printed by Mr. Pranav Gupta on behalf of **MD Publications Pvt Ltd** at Times Press, Delhi.

PREFACE

Jihad, an Islamic term, is also a religious duty of Muslims. In Arabic, the word jihad is a noun meaning "struggle." Jihad appears frequently in the Qur'an and common usage as the idiomatic expression "striving in the way of Allah (al-jihad fi sabil Allah)". A person engaged in jihad is called a mujahid, the plural is mujahideen. Many believe that there is no such thing as lesser jihad, and jihad by the sword is considered most important. Controversy has arisen over whether use of the term jihad without further explanation refers to jihad of the sword, and whether some have used confusion over the definition of the term to their advantage. A minority among the Sunni scholars sometimes refer to this duty as the sixth pillar of Islam, though it occupies no such official status. In Twelver Shi'a Islam, however, Jihad is one of the 10 Practices of the Religion.

It is well known that the concept of Jihad is subject to certain conditions. Jihad is meant for upholding the uprightness of the Word of Allah, for the victory of the suppressed, for safeguarding the places of worship and for defence against the aggression and atrocities of the tyrants. It is not meant for eliminating other religions, destruction of their places of worship or unwarranted massacre of Non-Muslims. For propagation and acceptance of its teachings Islam recommends interesting and suitable form of preaching, persuasion and discussion.

The concept of Jihad was not widely known in the western world before the terrorist attacks on the United States on September 11, 2001. Since then, the word has been woven into what our media and government feed us along with notions of Terrorism, Suicide Bombings, Hamas, Al-Qaeda, Osama Bin Laden, and now, Jihad. Our society hears exhortations resounding from the Middle East calling the people to rise up in Jihad and beat back the imperialist Americans. The attack on the World Trade Center in New York is a new phase in an ongoing global religious and ideological conflict. This conflict started in 1990, with the gulf war. The mother of all wars, as Saddam Hussein called it, and is unlikely to end for some time.

The objectives of Jihad as laid down in Islamic Shariah do not provide that the earth should be free from the followers of religions other than Islam. The main object of Jihad is defence against the tyrants by restraining the aggressor from continuing atrocities. Islamic Jihad is not unprovoked armed conflict of action against enemies, motivated by national sentiment or extension of domain, as projected by enemies of Islam. Under Islamic Shariah certain rules and regulations are attached to it. In addition to the conditions, Islam has laid down certain rules and limitations for Jihad. From Islamic point of view, Jihad is constructive action for ending mischief. It is not desperate action for loot, destruction and carnage.

I am very grateful to Mr Pranav Gupta, Director of MD Publications Pvt Ltd, New Delhi, for his kind cooperation and support for this book.

S M Arif

Contents

1

The Days of the Prophet

Muslims regard as prophets of Islam those non-divine humans chosen by Allah (the standard Arabic-language word for "the God") as prophets. Each prophet brought the same basic ideas of Islam, including belief in one God and avoidance of idolatry and sin. Each came to preach Islam and told of the coming of the final law-bearing prophet and messenger of God: Muhammad. Each prophet directed a message to a dif-ferent group and each prophet taught minor variations in Sharia (or the practice of religion) to a different target-aud-ience. These variations constitute applications of Islam: main-stream Muslims do not consider them discrete versions of Islam. Islamic tradition holds that God sent messengers to every nation.

In Islam, only Muhammad was sent to convey God's message to the whole world, whereas other messengers (*rasuls*) were sent to convey their messages to a specific group of people or nation. Unlike Judaism and Christianity, Islam distinguishes between a direct messenger of God (*rasul*) and a prophet (*nabi*). Both function as divinely inspired recipients of God's revelation. However, in addition, *rasuls* receive a divine message or revelation for a community in book form. While every *rasul* is a *nabi*, not every *nabi* is a *rasul*. Muslims regard Adam as the first prophet and Muhammad as the last prophet; hence Muhammad's title *Seal of the Prophets.*

Islam regards Jesus as a *rasul* (and sometimes as a *nabi*) because he received *wahi* (revelation) from God, through which

God revealed the *Injil* (Gospel) to him. Muslims believe that God has sent over 124,000 prophets all over the world as mentioned in the Sahih Hadith. Five (sometimes known as *Ulul Azmi* or the Imams-literally: "leaders"-of the *Rasuls*) receive the highest reverence for their perseverance and unusually strong commitment to God in the face of great suffering:

1. Nuh (Noah)
2. Ibrahim (Abraham)
3. Musa (Moses)
4. Isa (Jesus)
5. Muhammad

In both Arabic and Hebrew, the term *nabî* (plural forms: *nabiyyûn* and *anbiyâ*) means "prophet". These terms occur 75 times in the Qur'an. The term *nubuwwa* (meaning "prophethood") occurs five times in the Qur'an. The terms *rasûl* (plural: *rusul*) and *mursal* (plural: *mursalûn*) denote "messenger" or "apostle" and occur more than 300 times. The term for a prophetic "message", *risâla* (plural: *risâlât*) appears in the Qur'an in ten instances. The Syriac form of *rasûl Allâh* (literally: "messenger of God").

PROPHETS AND MESSENGERS IN THE BIBLE

The words "prophet" and "messenger" appear several times in the Old and New Testaments. In the Old Testament the word "prophet" (Hebrew: *nabi*) occurs more commonly, and the word "messenger" (Hebrew: *malak*) refers to angels, But the last book of the Old Testament, the Book of Malachi, speaks of a messenger that most commentators interpret as a reference to John the Baptist. In the New Testament, however, the word "messenger" becomes more frequent, sometimes in association with the concept of a prophet. "Messenger" can refer to Jesus, to his Apostles and to John the Baptist

It seems that in the New Testament messengers have a higher rank than prophets; Jesus Christ said about John the Baptist:

But what went you out for to see? A prophet? Yea, I say unto you, and more than a prophet. For this is he, of whom it is written, Behold, I send my messenger before thy face, which shall prepare thy way before thee.

PROPHETS AND MESSENGERS IN THE QUR'AN

DISTINGUISHING BETWEEN PROPHETS AND MESSENGERS

The Quran, like the New Testament, ranks a Messenger (apostle) higher than a Prophet. For example, in the Qur'an whenever both titles appear together, "messenger" comes first. According to the Muslim scholar al-Baydawi, a mes-senger esta-blishes a new religious law (*sharia*) whereas a prophet continues an old one. This would imply that prophets were more numerous than messengers and occupied a lower rank. God sends both prophets and messengers as givers of good news and as warners to their people. In the case of mes-sengers, however, it appears that a close relationship exists between them and their people (*ummah*). A messenger will become the witness that God will take from that community on the Day of Judgment. According to the Qur'an, Allah sent Muhammad to all of humanity and to the Djinn.

The Faithful distinguish between celestial and human messengers. In the Qur'anic world, God has made the angels messengers but not prophets. The human messengers, however, also function as prophets-though not every prophet serves a messenger. Angels always carry "orders" to the human prophets or messengers on what to say, what to do, and so forth. While human messengers deliver some messages about new orders to the people, prophets only reinforce previous orders by earlier messengers or prophets, but since the angels carry orders to prophets to do their duties, then all angels of revelations count as messengers.

THE STATUS OF PROPHETS

The Qur'anic verse 4:69 lists various virtuous groups of human beings, among whom prophets (which include messengers) occupy the highest rank. Verse 4:69 reads:

And whoever obeys God and the messenger, these will be [in paradise] with the prophets and the truthful and the martyrs and the righteous, upon whom God has bestowed favors".

MODES OF PROPHETIC REVELATION

Qur'an Verse: 4:157

And their saying: Surely we have killed the Messiah, Jesus son of Maryam, the apostle of Allah; and they did not kill him nor did they crucify him, but it appeared to them so (like Jesus) and most surely those who differ therein are only in a doubt about it; they have no knowledge respecting it, but only follow a conjecture, and they killed him not for sure. Verse 158. Nay! Allah took him up to Himself; and Allah is Mighty, Wise. Verse 159. And there is not one of the followers of the Book but most certainly believes in this before his death, and on the day of resurrection he (Jesus) shall be a witness against them.

Muslims believe that the Prophet Muhammad performed his greatest miracle in revealing the Holy Qur'an to mankind; Muslims regard this as the last in a series of divine revelations, one which came to him through the inspiraton of the Angel Gabriel. At the time of the revelation of the Qur'an, the Arabs who stood at the pinacle of linguistic and poetic eloquence expressed astonishment at its linguistic perfection. The Qur'an seemed even more miraculous to the Arabians of his time given the Prophet Muhammed's illiteracy (a very common state in the 7th century, especially in Arabia). Moreover, Muslims believe he had not read or written down any of the previous religious scriptures.

Muslims used this situation as an argument and evidence against those who opposed Islam during the Prophet's day, to testify to the fact that Muhammad couldn't have produced such perfect eloquence as appears in the Qur'an without divine intervention. Muslims believe that the Qur'an has survived in its original form since its compilation. Muslims up until present times have memorized it, making it the most memorized book in human history. Muslims believe that, unlike other miracles done by other prophets who came before Muhammad, all ages can witness the miracle of the Quran. With the revelation of the Holy Qur'an came a revolution in science, literature and philosophy that not only took place in the Islamic empire but worldwide.

PROPHETS AND SCRIPTURES

THE PROPHETS AND MUHAMMAD

Every single prophet from Adam to Muhammad were important. According to Islam, as mentioned in the Qu'ran, the prophets 'Isa (Jesus), Musa (Moses), Dawud (David), Ibrahim (Abraham), Saleh (Shelah), and Muhammad were responsible for ushering in their own holy scripture, given to them by Allah. 'Isa was given the Injil (Gospel), as expressed in the following verses from the Qu'ran:

(The Holy Qu'ran, Surah Maryam, Verses 27-34)

"Then she brought him (the baby) to her people, carrying him. "They said: "O Mary! Indeed you have brought a thing Fariya (an unheard mighty thing). "O sister (i.e. the like) of Harun (Aaron) [not the brother of Musa (Moses), but he was another pious man at the time of Maryam (Mary)]! Your father was not a man who used to commit adultery, nor was your mother an unchaste woman." Then she pointed to him. They said: "How can we talk to one who is a child in the cradle?" He ['Isa (Jesus)] said: Verily! I am a slave of Allah, He has given me the Scripture and made me a Prophet; and He has made me blessed wheresoever I be, and has enjoined on me Salat (prayer), and Zakat (charity), as long as I live. And dutiful to my mother, and made me not arrogant, unblest. And Salam (peace) be upon me the day I was born, and the day I die, and the day I shall be raised alive!" Such is 'Isa (Jesus), son of Maryam (Mary). (it is) a statement of truth, about which they doubt (or dispute).

However, in Islam, the Injil is believed to have been altered by the hands of men, therefore, it now cannot be considered the full truth, as it was when Allah had given it to him. Musa was given the Books of Moses, and Ibrahim the Books of

Abraham. Dawud is responsible for the Zabur (Psalms). Saleh is responsible for the Zikr, which is a practice that focuses on the remembrance God.

It often includes the repetition of the names of Allah. On the other hand, Muhammad was given the Qu'ran, which is believed by Muslims to be the purest and truest holy book of God. In Islam, it was believed to have been given to Muhammad through divine revelation by the angel Jibreel (Gabriel). Its purpose was to purfect the beliefs of the one true God, Allah, because of the turning away of the Jews and Christians from the true religion, into dogmas and doctrines.

THE SCOPE OF THE PROPHETIC MISSION

DISTINGUISHING MUHAMMAD FROM OTHER MESSENGERS

Muslims believe that Muhammad differs from other messengers in three respects:

1. Allah sent all previous messengers to a specific nation in specific region of Earth. Their teachings also applied in a limited way for a specific time and period. However, Muhammad was sent to entire mankind and his guidance is for all mankind until the end of time.
2. The teachings of all previous Islamic messengers except Muhammad have all but disappeared, and whatever remained of them has become so much altered and mixed with falsely made-up stories that it is very difficult to recognize the original teachings. Whilst the teaching of Muhammad and the Quran is preserved in its originality and Allah has promised to protect it until end of time.
3. The teachings of previous Messengers confined themselves to specific nations and times, thus their laws relating to ethics and moral code, justice, trade, financial deals, and civil law remained incomplete. Allah (swt) through his final Messenger Mohamad completed the Religion and perfected it. It includes all the teachings from previous Messengers, and abrogated what was specific to those people and time.

Most Muslims thus believe that since the days of the prophet the teaching of Muhammad remains as the only trustworthy source to reach the guidance of Allah, and that the Qur'an contains the true teachings of Moses and Jesus and the relationship between Messengers (*rusul*), Prophets (*anbiya*), the Announcement (*naba*), and The Sender (*mursil*).

The verse about the great news (awful tiding, great event, mighty tiding, mighty event, tremendous announcement, grand news, awesome tiding) reads:

Quran 78:2 AAani alnnaba-i alAAatheemi concerning the Great News.

Nabi, Naba

The word used in this verse, *naba,* relates to the word *nabi.*

- Nabi (prophet) means: one who informs others.
- Naba means: news, announcement, information.
- Anbiya represents the plural form of *nabi.*

Anbiya inform others of a coming *naba.* The Qur'an says that the *naba* is not the Qur'an itself but that it comes in the future.

Rasul, Mursil

Note that the word *rasul* relates to the word *mursil.*

- Rasul means: a messenger, a bearer of a message.
- Mursal (een) also means: a messenger, a bearer of a message.
- Mursil means: one who sends, a sender.
- Risalat means: messages.
- Rusul also represents the plural form of *rasul.*

So a *mursil* sends a *rasul* to give *risalat.* The Qur'an says that *risalat* of the *mursil* (Allah) form His *kalimat.* The Quran says that *risalatullah* cannot end.

ALL TOGETHER

Putting these together, we see that the *mursil* sent both Jesus and Muhammad (each a *rasul*) to act as a *nabi* and to inform of the *naba*. The Qur'an itself even states that the messages (*risalat*)-by definition the *kalamat* (words) of God-remain inexhaustible. Therefore the *naba* which the *anbiya* (plural of *nabi*) announced must itself precede more *risalat* (messages).

If or when the *naba* appeared, no further need exists for any more *nabi* (who give the news of the *naba*). What about *rusul* (messengers) and *risalat* (messages)? Does the *mursil* stop sending *rusul* to give his *risalat*? The Quran says no. Note that the sender of messages and messengers (*mursil*) is a *rasul* if he gives the *risalat* himself. And note that the *mursil* can send *rusul* who are not *anbiya*.

To summarize, we have four words: *nabi, naba, rasul,* and *mursil*.

- Some *rusul* (plural of *rasul*) rank as *anbiya* (prophets) if sent (*arsala*) before the *naba*.
- Some *rusul* are not *anbiya* if sent after the *naba*.
- The *naba* itself is a *risalatun*.
- The Qur'an associates the *naba* with the *mursil*.
- *Risalat* cannot be exhausted.
- The *mursil* sends *rusul* to give *risalat* even after *naba*.
- Nothing prevents a *mursil* giving *risalat* himself (and acting as a *rasul*).

Points of belief about Muhammad

The belief in Muhammad includes four points:

1. That as the Messenger of Allah he brought humankind the Book of Guidance, the *Qur'an*
2. That he brought us the *deen* (way of life, or path)-complete and perfected, which remains applicable to all mankind until the end of times
3. That he receives his guidance from Allah and that his knowledge and guidance is perfect from any defects
4. That he is the Last and Final Messenger of Allah who has perfected the *deen* (way of life, or path, or religion) of Allah, and that no further Messenger will come after

him, as the world needs none after the *deen* is completed and perfected. And the teachings of Muhammad are for the remainder of mankind.

THE RECEPTION OF THE PROPHETS

STORIES OF PROPHETS

The Story of Yusuf (Joseph), as told by Quranic verses

Quran depicts this story as the most beautiful of stories narrated in the Quran ([Qur'an 12:03]).The story of Yusuf moves in a stream from beginning to end; its substance and form are equally coherent. It documents the execution of Allah's rulings despite the challenge of human intervention (Allah has full power and control over His Affairs, but most of men know not.) This is what the story of Yusuf confirms categorically, for it ends with comfort and marvels, which is described in Quran.

The Dream

The story begins with a dream and ends with its interpretation. As the sun appeared over the horizon, bathing the earth in its morning glory, Yusuf, son of Ya'qub awoke from his sleep, delighted by a pleasant dream he had had. Filled with excitement he ran to his father and related it.

"O my father! Verily, I saw (in a dream) eleven planets and the sun and the moon, I saw them prostrating themselves to me."

His father's face lit up. He foresaw that Yusuf would be one through whom the prophecy of his grandfather, Prophet Ibrahim, would be fulfilled, in that his offspring would keep the light of Ibrahim's House alive and spread Allah's message to mankind. Therefore, it was narrated that Muhammad was asked: "Who is the most honorable amongst the people?" He replied: "The most God-fearing." The people said: "We do not want to ask you about this." He said: "The most honorable person is Yusuf, Allah's prophet, the son of Allah's prophet, the son of the faithful friend of Allah (Ibrahim)."

However, the father was well aware of the jealousy of Yusuf's brothers, (kos mother) so he warned him against telling his dream to his brothers. "O my son! Relate not your vision to your brothers, lest they arrange a plot against you. Verily! Shaitan is to man an open enemy! Thus will your Lord choose you and teach you the interpretation of dreams and perfect His Favor on you and on the offspring of Yaqub, as He perfected it on your fathers, Ibrahim, and Ishaq aforetime! Verily! your Lord is All-Knowing, All-Wise."

Yusuf heeded his father's warning. He did not tell his brothers what he had seen. It is well known that they hated him so much that it was difficult for him to feel secure telling them what was in his heart and in his dreams. Yusuf was very handsome, with a gentle temperament. He was respectful, kind and considerate. His brother Benjamin was equally pleasant. Both were from one mother, Rachel.

THE PLOT AGAINST YUSUF

Yusuf's brothers were all jealous of his talents and because they thought their father favored him above the others (but obviously didn't). They plotted to kill him, "Truly, Yusuf and his brother (Benjamin) are loved more by our father than we, but we are Usbah (a strong group). Really our father is in a plain error. Kill Yusuf or cast him out to some other land, so that the favor of your father may be given to you alone, and after that you will be righteous folk (by intending repentance before committing the sin)."

But one of the brothers felt sorry for him, and suggested they throw him into a well so that a caravan might pick him up and take him as a slave. One from among them said: "Kill not Yusuf, but if you must do something, throw him down to the bottom of a well, he will be picked up by some caravan of travellers."

They asked their father's permission to take him out to play, who granted them their request, on the condition that they would keep watch over him. The brothers proceed with their plan and dropped him in a well and left him there. They brought back Yusuf's shirt, covered with sheep's blood, to tell their father that wolves had eaten Yusuf. Ya'qub said "Nay, but your ownselves have made up a tale. So (for me), patience is most fitting.

GOD'S PLAN TO SAVE HIM

Yusuf was rescued by a passing caravan (presumably the Ishmaelite). They had stopped by the well hoping to draw water to quench their thirst and saw the boy inside begging for help. So they retrieved him and sold him into slavery in Egypt, to a rich man referred as al-Aziz in the Qur'an. The Qur'an described Yusuf as a "very attractive man." A caravan passed by, and soon sent their waterer. He let down his bucket, and then said, "How lucky! There is a boy here!" They took him along as merchandise, and Allah was fully aware of what they did.

They sold him for a cheap price - a few dirhams (units of currency used in those days) - for they did not have any need for him. The one who bought him in Egypt said to his wife, "Take good care of him. Maybe he can help us, or maybe we can adopt him." "Thus did we establish Yusuf in the land, that we might teach him the interpretation of events?" Allah's command is always done, And Allah has full power and control over His Affairs, but most people do not know. When he reached maturity, we endowed him with wisdom and knowledge. We thus reward the righteous.

And when he (Joseph) attained his full manhood, we gave him wisdom and knowledge (the Prophethood), thus we reward the doers of good. While working for al-Aziz, he was constantly approached by al-Aziz's wife (Imra'at al-Aziz) (Presumably Zulaikha), she intended to seduce him.

Joseph continuously rejecting her because he feared his Lord, until one day, she became furious and angry to the point where she plotted on trapping him in a room. Zulaikha locked the door and pleaded him to come into her but Yusuf as a man of God refuses. 'And she, in whose house she was, sought to seduce him (to do an evil act), she closed the doors and said: "come on, O you." He said: "I seek refuge in Allah (or Allah forbid)! Truly he (your husband) is my master! He made my stay agreeable! (So I will never betray him).

Verily, the Zalimun (wrong, evildoers) will never be successful." Indeed she did desire him and he would have inclined to her desire had he not seen the evidence of his Lord. Thus it was that we might turn away from evil and illegal sexual intercourse. Surely, he was one of our chosen, guided slaves.' She then tore the back of Joseph's shirt. So they raced with one another to the door, and she tore his shirt from the back. They both found her lord (her husband) at the door. Zulaikha convinced her husband that the only way to save her honor was to put Yusuf in prison; otherwise she would not be able to control herself or to safeguard his prestige. She then said (What penalty it is for those who want to harm your family except for jail or heavy torture?) Yusuf said: (she came on to me), a witness of the wife's family said: (if his shirt was torn from the front, then she is telling the truth and he is from the liars, and if the hole was from behind then she lied and he is from the truthful), then when they saw the hole being in the rear he said (this is of your schemes, indeed your (you women) scheming is grand).

Yusuf leave this matter, and you (Al-Aziz's wife) beg forgiveness, for you have been of the sinners. A few women in town said: (Al-Aziz's wife is coming on to her boy, her love for him has blinded her, and we find her in complete illusion). As when she heard of their plot, she invited them, preparing a place for each of them to sit, and gave them knives to cut the fruit. She then ordered Yusuf to go out in front of them. As soon as they saw him they thought of how beautiful and great he is, distracted by his beauty and gracefulness they repeatedly cut their hands.

They then said: (impossible it is, this is not a human, and this is but a graceful Angel!). Al-Aziz's wife soon after replied: (that is the reason for which you blamed me, and if he doesn't do what I ordered him, he will be imprisoned, or be pettily humiliated) Yusef said: (O Lord, prison is a better choice than what they (Al-Aziz's wife and the women) want me to do, and if you don't save me from it, I'll turn to their blasphemy and be from the none-believers (illiterates). His Lord then saved him from the depths of their scheme. The male authorities and master therefore thought it would be best to send Yusuf to prison for a time.

YUSUF INTERPRETED DREAMS

After being imprisoned for a few years, God granted him with the ability to interpret dreams, a power in which he became popular amongst the prisoners using. In one occasion two less fortunate royal servants were thrown into the dungeon prior to Yusuf's imprisonment. They were haunted by two ambiguous dreams and remained unaware of the dream due to the inability to interpret it until they heard about Yusuf's popularity among the citizens. They went to Yusuf to seek for his opinion and ask him if he could help them in solving the problems. Yusuf asked them about the dreams they had, and one of them described that he saw himself in the vineyard plucking grapes and pressed it into wine, and presenting it to the king (pharaoh).

The other said to have seen himself holding a basket of bread on his head whereof the birds were eating. Yusuf reminded the prisoners that his ability to interpret dreams was a favour from God based on his adherence to monotheism. Yusuf then stated that one of the men would be released from the prison and he would serve the King but warned that the other would be crucified. One day, under the order of the King of Egypt soldiers came to take the two cooks away, the King said one would be forgiven, the other will be executed. The forgiven servant then served the King. Yusuf requested the one who he knew would be released to advise the King of Joseph, but Satan caused the man to forget to advise the King, and so Yusuf remained in prison for some years.

As the days passed and everything went back to normal one night the King was echoed by a mysterious dream. He was said to have seen seven fat cows being devoured by seven skinny cows, and seven green spikes, and others shriveled. This dream haunted him every night and day turning him anxious and disoriented. When the butler heard about it, he remembered Yusuf in prison, and persuaded the king to send him to Yusuf so that he could return with an interpretation. Yusuf told the servant that Egypt would suffer famine, and that the King should be ready for it to avoid the Egyptian from great suffering. The king followed the instruction and the land was saved from the great famine.

[12:46] "Yusuf O truthful, inform us about seven fat cows being devoured by seven skinny cows, and seven green spikes, and others shriveled. I wish to go back with some information for the people." [12:47] He said, "What you cultivate during the next seven years, when the time of harvest comes, leave the grains in their spikes, except for what you eat.[12:48] "After that, seven years of drought will come, which will consume most of what you stored for them.[12:49] "After that, a year will come that brings relief for the people, and they will, once again, press juice."

YUSUF ATTAINS PROMINENCE

After the great success, Yusuf eventually turned out to become a prominent adviser to the King of Egypt. The King elected him as His Royal Treasurer due to his good record. The king said, "Bring him to me, so I can hire him to work for me." When he talked with him, he said, "Today, you have a prominent position with us." He said, "Make me the treasurer, for I am experienced in this area and know-ledgeable." We thus established Yusuf on earth, ruling as he wished. We shower our mercy upon whomever we will, and we never fail to recompense the righteous. Additionally, the reward in the Hereafter is even better for those who believe and lead a righteous life.

THE FAMILY REUNION

Later on, he would once again run into his brothers whom he would forgive. He also found that his father (Yaqub) became blind after crying so much over the disappearance his son (Yusuf). However, when Yusuf came home, his father Yaqub sensed the pleasing and familiar fragrance of Yusuf, and his vision was restored out of joy that his son was alive and back to the family. Yusuf eventually died in Egypt. Tradition holds that when Musa (English: Moses) left Egypt, he took Yusuf's coffin with him so that he would be buried alongside his ancestors in Palestine.

PROPHETS IN THE QUR'AN

"And undoubtedly, We sent many Messengers before you, of them, there are some whose story We have narrated to you, and there are some whose story We have not narrated to you, and it is not for any Messenger that he should bring any sign without Allah's permission, but when the command of Allah will come, the matter shall be decided with truth, and then the men of falsehood shall lose there." – *Qur'an,*

God sent one of the highest ranked prophets in Islam, Eisa al-Maseeh, (Jesus the Messiah) to guide the Children of Israel. The Qur'an makes it very clear that in Islam, Jesus is not the begotten (physical) son of God, but rather a *nabi* and *rasul* (messenger) of God. 'Isa performed many miracles with the permission of God, for example: raising the dead, creating a bird from clay, talking as an infant. Islamic traditions states that he abstained from drinking alcohol. It also states that he received a revelation, the Injil (Gospel), though according to Islam, it has suffered distortion. Muslims believe that no crucifixion of 'Isa took place, meaning he did not die on the cross. They believe that God raised Isa up to himself and thet Isa will return to Earth to fight the Dajjal and break the cross.

The Qur'an and Saheeh Hadeeth tell a consistent story. From the Qur'an: Ch:4, verses: 157-159 as translated: "157. And because of their saying (in boast), "We killed Messiah 'Iesa (Jesus), son of Maryam (Mary), the Messenger of Allah," - but they killed him not, nor crucified him, but the resemblance of 'Iesa (Jesus) was put over another man (and they killed that man), and those who differ therein are full of doubts. They have no (certain) knowledge, they follow nothing but conjecture. For surely; they killed him not [i.e. 'Iesa (Jesus), son of Maryam (Mary)]; 158. But Allah raised him ['Iesa (Jesus)] up (with his body and soul) unto Himself (and he is in the heavens). And Allah is Ever All-Powerful, All-Wise; 159.

And there is none of the people of the Scripture (Jews and Christians), but must believe in him ['Iesa (Jesus), son of Maryam (Mary), as only a Messenger of Allah and a human being], before his ['Iesa (Jesus) or a Jew's or a Christian's] death (at the time of the appearance of the angel of death). "And on the Day of Resurrection, he ['Iesa (Jesus)] will be a witness against them." From Hadeeth as translated: "Narrated Abu Huraira: Allah's Apostle said, 'By Him in Whose Hands my soul is, son of Mary (Jesus) will shortly descend amongst you people (Muslims) as a just ruler and will break the Cross and kill the pig and abolish the Jizya (a tax taken from the non-Muslims, who are in the protection, of the Muslim government). Then there will be abundance of money and no body will accept charitable gifts.'"{Sahih Bukhari}

Habib u'l A'zam, Imam u'l Anbiya Sayyidina Muhammad ibn 'Abdullah,(53 B.H-11 A.H; 571-632 AD) ranks as the last prophet in Islam ("seal of the Prophets"). Muslims shun idolatry of any of the prophets, as their messages from God hold the most weight. His father's name was 'Abdullah ibn 'Abd al-Muttalib and his mother's name was Amina bint Wahb az-Zuhriyya. Muhammad. Born in Mecca in 571 AD (53 AH), Muhammad spent the first part of his life as a well-travelled merchant. He would often spend his time in the mountains surrounding Mecca in prayer contemplating the situation with the city. At the age of forty, during one of those trips to the mountain, Muhammad began to, despite his illiteracy, receive and recite verses from Allah which today make up the Qur'an.

He quickly spread the message he was receiving, converting a few others in the city, including his wife. He is the last (seal) of the prophets with a message to all humanity. When oppression became intolerable for his followers, Muhammad first asked his fellow Muslims to migrate to

Medina and later himself migrated to Medina away from the oppressors in Mecca. Muhammad served not just as a prophet, but as a military leader who helped defeat the Meccans in 624 during the Battle of Badr. He continued to lead the Muslims as Islam spread across the Arabian Penin-sula. He performed the first hajj in 629 and established Islam as it is still practised by Muslims today. Others continued Muhammad's legacy after his death in 632, having been given the position of caliph (or successor) to Muhammad. The Five Pillars of Islam were established from his Hadiths after Muhammad's death.

OTHER PROPHETS

Muslims believe in other prophets other than those mentioned by name in the Qur'an. Many verses in the Quran discuss this:

- "And certainly we sent messengers (rasul) before you: there are some of them that we have mentioned to you and there are others whom we have not mentioned to you..."
- "For we assuredly sent amongst every People a messenger..."[1]

Muslims believe that God has sent 124,000 (or 224,000) prophets and 313 messengers all over the world, as mentioned by the prophet Muhammad in the Sahih Hadith. Historic narratives suggest a prophet named Khaled bin Sinan in pre-Islamic Arabia. The Qur'an mentions Al-Imran as the father of Maryam. Al-Khidr is not mentioned by name, but is traditionally assumed to be referred to in Qur'an 18:66. Biblical prophets Danyal (Daniel), Ishaia (Isaiah), Armya (Jeremiah), and Samuel are mentioned by Ibn Kathir in his book as prophets.

The Qur'an mentions Luqman in the sura named after him but does not clearly identify him as a prophet or a *wali*. According to the most widespread Shiite belief, Luqman was a wise man, not a prophet nor a wali. Legend recounts that Luqman had a dream, and in that dream he faced the choice between becoming a King and a wise man, and he chose the second. Numerous other historical figures may rank as prophets, but debate and contention surround this matter. Such figures include: Zoroaster, Gautama Buddha, Socrates, Merlin, Lao Tzu, Confucius, Krishna, (also mentioned in some books of Hadith) and Rama.

However, Muslims will argue that one cannot know this for certain, since the Qur'an does not mentioned them by name. Those in favour of counting such men as prophets often argue that they came with the word of God, but that it later became corrupted, which accounts for the differ-ences between Islam and the various religions and philo-sophies associated with which each man. Support for such claims appears in the Hadith and in the Qur'an, which state that a messenger was sent to every people.

MARYAM MOTHER OF 'ISA

A few scholars (such as Ibn Hazm) see Maryam as a nabi and a prophetess, since God sent her a message via an angel. The Qur'an, however, does not explicitly state that she is one. According to the Islamic belief, she was a holy woman, but she was not a prophet. In the Qur'an, 'Isa is usually referred to as 'Isa ibn Maryam (Jesus, son of Mary), a matronymic, and indicative of Jesus having no father. Maryam is seen as a very holy and important woman in the world of Islam. She is the only women in all of Islam that has a surah attributed to her, Surah Maryam, the nintenth surah of the Qu'ran.

Muhammad ibn 'Abdullâh is the founder of the religion of Islam and is regarded by Muslims as a messenger and prophet of God, the last and the greatest law-bearer in a series of prophets. Muslims consider him the restorer of the uncorrupted original monotheistic faith (*Islam*) of Adam, Noah, Abraham, Moses, Jesus and other prophets. He was also active as a diplomat, merchant, philosopher, orator, legis-lator, reformer, military general, and, according to Muslim belief, an agent of divine action.

Born in 570 CE in the Arabian city of Mecca, he was orphaned at a young age and brought up under the care of his uncle Abu Talib. He later worked mostly as a merchant, as well as a shepherd, and was first married by age 25. Discontented with life in Mecca, he retreated to a cave in the surrounding mountains for meditation and reflection.

According to Islamic beliefs it was here, at age 40, in the month of Ramadan, where he received his first revelation from God. Three years after this event Muhammad started preaching these revelations publicly, proclaiming that "God is One", that complete "surrender" to Him (lit. *Islam*) is the only way (*dîn*) acceptable to God, and that he himself was a prophet and messenger of God, in the same vein as other Islamic prophets.

Muhammad gained few followers early on, and was met with hostility from some Meccan tribes; he and his followers were treated harshly. To escape persecution Muhammad and his followers migrated to Medina (then known as Yathrib) in the year 622 CE. This event, the Hijra, marks the beginning of the Islamic calendar.

In Medina, Muhammad united the conflicting tribes, and after eight years of fighting with the Meccan tribes, his followers, who by then had grown to ten thousand, conquered Mecca. In 632, a few months after returning to Medina from his Farewell pilgrimage, Muhammad fell ill and died. By the time of his death, most of the Arabian Peninsula had converted to Islam; and he united the tribes of Arabia into a single Muslim religious polity.

The revelations (or *Ayat*, lit. "Signs of God") which Muhammad reported receiving until his death—form the verses of the Qur'an, regarded by Muslims as the "Word of God" and around which the religion is based. Besides the Qur'an, Muhammad's life (*sira*) and traditions (*Sunnah*) are also upheld by Muslims.

They discuss Muhammad and other prophets of Islam with reverence, adding the phrase *peace be upon him* whenever their names are mentioned. While conceptions of Muhammad in medieval Christ-endom and premodern times were largely negative, appraisals in modern times have been far less so. Besides this, his life and deeds have been debated by followers and opponents over the centuries.

NAMES AND APPELLATIONS IN THE QUR'AN

The name *Muhammad* means "Praiseworthy" and occurs four times in the Qur'an. The Qur'an addresses Muhammad in the second person not by his name but by the appellations prophet, messenger, servant of God (*'abd*), announcer (*bashir*), warner (*nathir*), reminder (*mudhakkir*), witness (*shahid*), bearer of good tidings (*mubashshir*), one who calls [unto God] (*dâ'î*) and the light-giving lamp (*siraj munir*). Muhammad is sometimes addressed by desig-nations deriving from his state at the time of the address: thus he is referred to as the enwrapped (*al-muzzammil*) in Qur'an 73:1 and the shrouded (*al-muddaththir*) in Qur'an 74:1. In the Qur'an, believers are not to distinguish between the messengers of God and are to believe in all of them (Surah 2:285). God has caused some messengers to excel above others 2:253 and in Surah 33:40 He singles out Muhammad as the "Seal of the Prophets". "The Qur'an also refers to Muhammad as *Ahmad* more praiseworthy".

SOURCES FOR MUHAMMAD'S LIFE

Muhammad's life is well documented within numerous records in historical texts, although like other premodern historical figures not every detail of his life is known. Because Muhammad is a highly influential historical figure, his life, deeds, and thoughts have been debated by followers and opponents over the centuries, which makes a biography of him difficult to write. The most trustworthy source for the historical Muhammad is the Qur'an. The Qur'an has a few allusions to Muhammad's life, revealing the salient aspects associated with him.

The Qur'an responds "constantly and often candidly to Muhammad's changing historical circumstances and contains a wealth of hidden data." In its actual form, the Qur'an is generally considered by academic scholars to record the words spoken by Muhammad, because the search for variants in Western academia has not yielded any differences of great significance. Next in importance are the historical works by writers of the third and fourth century of the Muslim era. These include the traditional Muslim biographies of Muhammad and quotes attributed to him (the *sira* and *hadith* literature), which provide further information on Muhammad's life.

The earliest surviving written *sira* (biographies of Muhammad and quotes attributed to him) is Ibn Ishaq's *Life of God's Messenger* written some 120 to 130 years after Muhammad's death. Although the original work is lost, portions of it survive in the recensions of Ibn Hisham and Al-Tabari. Another early source is the history of Muhammad's campaigns by al-Waqidi (death 207 of Muslim era), and the work of his secretary Ibn Sa'd al-Baghdadi (death 230 of Muslim era). Many scholars accept the accuracy of the earliest biographies, though their accuracy is unascertainable.

Recent studies have led scholars to distinguish between the traditions touching legal matters and the purely historical ones. In the former sphere, traditions could have been subject to invention while in the latter sphere, aside from exceptional cases, the material may have been only subject to "tendential shaping". In addition, the hadith collections are accounts of the verbal and physical traditions of Muhammad that date from several generations after his death. Hadith compilations are records of the traditions or sayings of Muhammad.

They might be defined as the biography of Muhammad perpetuated by the long memory of his community for their exemplification and obedience. Western academics view the hadith collections with caution as accurate historical sources. Scholars such as Madelung do not reject the narrations which have been complied in later periods, but judge them in the context of history and on the basis of their compatibility with the events and figures. Finally, there are oral traditions. Although usually discounted by positivist historians, oral tradition plays a major role in the Islamic understanding of Muhammad.

There are also a few non-Muslim sources that, according

to S. A. Nigosian, confirm the existence of Muhammad and are valuable for corroboration of traditional Muslim statements. The Arabian Peninsula was largely arid and volcanic, making agriculture difficult except near oases or springs.

The landscape was thus dotted with towns and cities, two prominent ones being Mecca and Medina. Medina was a large flourishing agricultural settlement, while Mecca was an important financial center for many surrounding tribes. Communal life was essential for survival in the desert conditions, as people needed support against the harsh environment and lifestyle.

Tribal grouping was encouraged by the need to act as a unit, this unity being based on the bond of kinship by blood. Indigenous Arabs were either nomadic or sedentary (or bedouins), the former constantly traveling from one place to another seeking water and pasture for their flocks, while the latter settled and focused on trade and agriculture.

Nomadic survival was also dependent on raiding caravans or oases, the nomads not viewing this as a crime. In pre-Islamic Arabia, gods or goddesses were viewed as protectors of individual tribes, their spirits being associated with sacred trees, stones, springs and wells. As well as being the site of an annual pilgrimage, the Kaaba shrine in Mecca housed 360 idol statues of tribal patron deities.

Aside from these gods, the Arabs shared a common belief in a supreme deity called Allah (literally "the god"), who was remote from their everyday concerns and thus not the object of cult or ritual. Three goddesses were associated with Allah as his daughters: al-Lât, Manât and al-'Uzzá. Monotheistic communities existed in Arabia, including Christians and Jews. Hanifs – native pre-Islamic Arab monotheists – are also sometimes listed alongside Jews and Christians in pre-Islamic Arabia, although their historicity is disputed amongst scholars. According to Muslim tradition, Muhammad himself was a Hanif and one of the descendants of Ishmael, son of Abraham.

LIFE

MUHAMMAD IN MECCA

Muhammad was born and lived in Mecca for the first 52 years of his life (570–622) which was divided into two phases, that is before and after declaring the prophecy.

CHILDHOOD AND EARLY LIFE

Muhammad was born in the month of Rabi' al-awwal in 570. He belonged to the Banu Hashim, one of the pro-minent families of Mecca, although it seems not to have been prosperous during Muhammad's early lifetime. Tradition places the year of Muhammad's birth as corresponding with the Year of the Elephant, which is named after the failed destruction of Mecca that year by the Aksumite king Abraha who had in his army a number of elephants. Recent scholarship has suggested alternative dates for this event, such as 568 or 569. Muhammad's father, Abdullah, died almost six months before he was born.

According to the tradition, soon after Muhammad's birth he was sent to live with a Bedouin family in the desert, as the desert-life was considered healthier for infants. Muhammad stayed with his foster-mother, Halimah bint Abi Dhuayb and her husband until he was two years old. Some western scholars of Islam have rejected the historicity of this tradition. At the age of six Muhammad lost his mother Amina to illness and he became fully orphaned. He was subsequently brought up for two years under the guardianship of his paternal grandfather Abd al-Muttalib, of the Banu Hashim clan of the Quraysh tribe. When Muhammad was eight, his grandfather also died. He now came under the care of his uncle Abu Talib, the new leader of Banu Hashim.

According to Watt, because of the general disregard of the guardians in taking care of weak members of the tribes in Mecca in sixth century, "Muhammad's guardians saw that he did not starve to death, but it was hard for them to do more for him, especially as the fortunes of the clan of Hashim seem to have been declining at that time." While still in his teens, Muhammad accompanied his uncle on trading journeys to Syria gaining experience in the com-mercial trade, the only career open to Muhammad as an orphan. According to tradition, when Muhammad was either nine or twelve while accompanying the Meccans' caravan to Syria, he met a Christian monk or hermit named Bahira who is said to have foreseen Muhammed's career as a prophet of God.

Little is known of Muhammad during his later youth, and from the fragmentary information that is available, it is hard to separate history from legend. It is known that he became a merchant and "was involved in trade between the Indian ocean and the Mediterranean Sea." Due to his upright character he acquired the nickname "Al-Amin", meaning "faithful, trustworthy" and was sought out as an impartial arbitrator. His reputation attracted a proposal from Khadijah, a forty-year-old widow in 595. Muhammad consented to the marriage, which by all accounts was a happy one.

BEGINNINGS OF THE QUR'AN

At some point Muhammad adopted the practice of meditating alone for several weeks every year in a cave on Mount Hira near Mecca. Islamic tradition holds that during one of his visits to Mount Hira, the angel Gabriel appeared to him in the year 610 and commanded Muhammad to recite the following verses:

Proclaim! (or read!) in the name of thy Lord and Cherisher, Who created- Created man, out of a (mere) clot of congealed blood: Proclaim! And thy Lord is Most Bountiful,- He Who taught (the use of) the pen,- Taught man that which he knew not.(Qur'an 96:1-5)

According to some traditions, upon receiving his first revelations Muhammad was deeply distressed and contemplated throwing himself off the top of a mountain but the spirit moved closer and told him that he has been chosen as a messenger of God. Muhammad returned home and was consoled and reassured by his wife, Khadijah and her

Christian cousin, Waraqah ibn Nawfal. Shia tradition maintains that Muhammad was neither surprised nor frightened at the appearance of Gabriel but rather welcomed him as if he had been expecting him. The initial revelation was followed by a pause of three years during which Muhammad gave himself up further to prayers and spiritual practices. When the revelations resumed he was reassured and commanded to begin preaching: Your lord has not forsaken you nor does he hate [you] (Qur'an 93:1-11).

According to Welch these revelations were accom-panied by mysterious seizures, and the reports are unlikely to have been forged by later Muslims. Muhammad was confident that he could distinguish his own thoughts from these messages. According to the Qur'an, one of the main roles of Muhammad is to warn the unbelievers of their eschatological punishment (Qur'an 38:70, Qur'an 6:19). Sometimes the Qur'an does not explicitly refer to the Judgment day but provides examples from the history of some extinct communities and warns Muhammad's contemporaries of similar calamities (Qur'an 41:13–16). Muhammad is not only a warner to those who reject God's revelation, but also a bearer of good news for those who abandon evil, listen to the divine word and serve God. Muhammad's mission also involves preaching monotheism: The Qur'an demands Muhammad to proclaim and praise the name of his Lord and instructs him not to worship idols apart from God or associate other deities with God.

The key themes of the early Qur'anic verses included the responsibility of man towards his creator; the resurrection of dead, God's final judgment followed by vivid descriptions of the tortures in hell and pleasures in Paradise; and the signs of God in all aspects of life. Religious duties required of the believers at this time were few: belief in God, asking for forgiveness of sins, offering frequent prayers, assisting others particularly those in need, rejecting cheating and the love of wealth (considered to be significant in the commercial life of Mecca), being chaste and not to kill newborn girls.

OPPOSITION

According to Muslim tradition, Muhammad's wife Khadija was the first to believe he was a prophet. She was soon followed by Muhammad's ten-year-old cousin Ali ibn Abi Talib, close friend Abu Bakr, and adopted son Zaid. Around 613, Muhammad began his public preaching (Qur'an 26:214). Most Meccans ignored him and mocked him, while a few others became his followers. There were three main groups of early converts to Islam: younger brothers and sons of great merchants; people who had fallen out of the first rank in their tribe or failed to attain it; and the weak, mostly unprotected foreigners.

According to Ibn Sad, the opposition in Mecca started when Muhammad delivered verses that condemned idol worship and the Meccan forefathers who engaged in polytheism. However, the Qur'anic exegesis maintains that it began as soon as Muhammad started public preaching. As the number of followers increased, he became a threat to the local tribes and the rulers of the city, whose wealth rested upon the Kaaba, the focal point of Meccan religious life, which Muhammad threatened to overthrow. Muh-ammad's denunciation of the Meccan traditional religion was especially offensive to his own tribe, the Quraysh, as they were the guardians of the Ka'aba.

The powerful merchants tried to convince Muhammad to abandon his preaching by offering him admission into the inner circle of merchants, and establishing his position therein by an advantageous marriage. However, he refused. Tradition records at great length the persecution and ill-treatment of Muhammad and his followers. Sumayyah bint Khabbab, a slave of Abu Jahl and a prominent Meccan leader, is famous as the first martyr of Islam, having been killed with a spear by her master when she refused to give up her faith. Bilal, another Muslim slave was tortured by Umayya ibn khalaf who placed a heavy rock on his chest to force his conversion. Apart from insults, Muhammad was protected from physical harm as he belonged to the Banu Hashim clan.

In 615, some of Muhammad's followers emigrated to the Ethiopian Aksumite Empire and founded a small colony there under the protection of the Christian Ethiopian emperor Ac%ama ibn Abjar. An early hadith known as "The Story of the Cranes" was propagated by two Islamic scholars, Ibn Kathir al Dimashqi and Ibn Hijir al Masri, where the former has strengthened it and the latter called it fabricated. The hadith describes Muhammad's involvement at the time of migration in an episode which historian William Muir called the "Satanic Verses."

The account holds that Muhammad pronounced a verse acknowledging the existence of three Meccan goddesses considered to be the daughters of Allah, praising them, and appealing for their intercession. According to this account, Muhammad later retracted the verses at the behest of Gabriel. Islamic scholars have weakened the hadith and have denied the historicity of the incident as early as the tenth century CE. In any event, relations between the Muslims and their pagan fellow-tribesmen were already deteriorated and worsening. In 617 the leaders of Makhzum and Banu Abd-Shams, two important Quraysh clans, declared a public boycott against Banu Hashim, their commercial rival, to pressurize it into withdrawing its protection of Muhammad. The boycott lasted three years but eventually collapsed as it failed in its objective.

LAST YEARS IN MECCA

Muhammad's wife Khadijah and his uncle Abu Talib both died in 619, the year thus being known as the "year of sorrow." With the death of Abu Talib, the leadership of the Banu Hashim clan was passed to Abu Lahab, an inveterate enemy of Muhammad. Soon afterwards, Abu Lahab with-drew the clan's protection from Muhammad. This pla-ced Muhammad in danger of death since the withdrawal of clan protection implied that the blood revenge for his killing would not be exacted. Muhammad then visited Ta'if, an-other important city in Arabia, and tried to find a pro-tector for himself there, but his effort failed and further brought him into physical danger. Muhammad was forced to return to Mecca. A Meccan man named Mut'im b. Adi (and the protection of the tribe of Banu Nawfal) made it possible for him safely to re-enter his native city.

Many people were visiting Mecca on business or as pilgrims to the Kaaba. Muhammad took this opportunity to look for a new home for himself and his followers. After several unsuccessful negotiations, he found hope with some men from Yathrib (later called Medina). The Arab population of Yathrib was familiar with monotheism because a Jewish community existed there.

Converts to Islam came from nearly all Arab tribes in Medina, such that by June of the subsequent year there were seventy-five Muslims coming to Mecca for pilgrimage and to meet Muhammad. Meeting him secretly by night, the group made what was known as the "*Second Pledge of al-`Aqaba*", or the "*Pledge of War*" Following the pledges at Aqabah, Muhammad encouraged his followers to emigrate to Yathrib. As with the migration to Abyssinia, the Quraysh attempted to stop the emigration. However, almost all Muslims managed to leave.

ISRA AND MI'RAJ

Islamic tradition relates that in 620, Muhammad experienced the *Isra and Mi'raj*, a miraculous journey said to have occurred with the angel Gabriel in one night. In the first part of the journey, the *Isra*, he is said to have travelled from Mecca to "the farthest mosque" (in Arabic: *masjid al-aqsa*), which Muslims usually identify with the Al-Aqsa Mosque in Jerusalem. In the second part, the *Miraj*, Muhammad is said to have toured heaven and hell, and spoken with earlier prophets, such as Abraham, Moses, and Jesus. Ibn Ishaq, author of the first biography of Muhammad, presents this event as a spiritual experience whereas later historians like Al-Tabari and Ibn Kathir present it as a physical journey.

Some western scholars of Islam hold that the oldest Muslim tradition identified the journey as one traveled through the heavens from the sacred enclosure at Mecca to the celestial *al-Baytu l-Mamur* (heavenly prototype of the Kaaba); but later tradition identified Muhammad's journey from Mecca to Jerusalem.

MUHAMMAD IN MEDINA

HIJRA

A delegation consisting of the representatives of the twelve important clans of Medina, invited Muhammad as a neutral outsider to Medina to serve as chief arbitrator for the entire community. There was fighting in Yathrib mainly involving its Arab and Jewish inhabitants for around a hundred years before 620. The recurring slaughters and disagreements over the resulting claims, especially after the Battle of Bu'ath in which all clans were involved, made it obvious to them that the tribal conceptions of blood-feud and an eye for an eye were no longer workable unless there was one man with authority to adjudicate in disputed cases.

The delegation from Medina pledged themselves and their fellow-citizens to accept Muhammad into their community and physically protect him as one of themselves. Muhammad instructed his followers to immigrate to Medina until virtually all his followers left Mecca. Being alarmed at the departure of Muslims, according to the tradition, the Meccans plotted to assassinate Muhammad. With the help of Ali, Muhammad fooled the Meccans who were watching him, and secretly slipped away from the town with Abu Bakr. By 622, Muhammad immigrated to Medina, a large agricultural oasis. Those who migrated from Mecca along with Muhammad became known as *muhajirun* (emigrants).

ESTABLISHMENT OF A NEW POLITY

Among the first things Muhammad did in order to settle down the longstanding grievances among the tribes of Medina was drafting a document known as the Con-stitution of Medina, "establishing a kind of alliance or fede-ration" among the eight Medinan tribes and Muslim emi-grants from Mecca, which specified the rights and duties of all citizens and the relationship of the different com-munities in Medina (including that of the Muslim com-munity to other communities, specifically the Jews and other "Peoples of the Book"). The community defined in the Constitution of Medina, *Ummah*, had a religious outlook but was also shaped by practical considerations and substantially preserved the legal forms of the old Arab tribes. It effectively established the first Islamic state.

The first group of pagan converts to Islam in Medina was the clans who had not produced great leaders for themselves but had suffered from warlike leaders from other clans. This was followed by the general acceptance of Islam by the pagan population of Medina, apart from some exceptions. According to Ibn Ishaq, this was influenced by the conversion of Sa'd ibn Mu'adh (a prominent Medinan leader) to Islam. Those Medinans who converted to Islam and helped the Muslim emigrants find shelter became known as the *ansar* (helpers). Then Muhammad instituted brotherhood between the emigrants and the helpers and he chose Ali as his own brother.

With the early general conversion of the pagans, the pagan opposition was never of prime importance in the affairs of Medina. Those remaining pagans were very bitter about the advance of Islam and in particular, Asma bint Marwan and Abu 'Afak had composed verses taunting and insulting the Muslims. These two were assassinated and Muhammad did not disapprove of it. No one dared take vengeance on them, and some members of Asma bint Marwan's clan who previously converted to Islam in secret, now professed Islam openly. This ended overt opposition to Muhammad among the pagans.

BEGINNINGS OF ARMED CONFLICT

Following the emigration, the Meccans seized the properties of the Muslim emigrants in Mecca. Economically uprooted and with no available profession, the Muslim migrants turned to raiding Meccan caravans as an act of war, deliberately initiating armed conflict between the Muslims and Mecca. Muhammad delivered Qur'anic verses permitting the Muslims to fight the Meccans. These attacks pressured Mecca by interfering with trade, and allowed the Muslims to acquire wealth, power and prestige while working towards their ultimate goal of inducing Mecca's submission to the new faith. In March of 624, Muhammad led some three hundred warriors in a raid on a Meccan merchant caravan.

The Muslims set an ambush for them at Badr. Aware of the plan, the Meccan caravan eluded the Muslims. Meanwhile, a force from Mecca was sent to protect the caravan, continuing forward to confront the Muslims upon hearing that the caravan was safe. The Battle of Badr began in March of 624. Though outnumbered more than three to one, the Muslims won the battle, killing at least forty-five Meccans with only fourteen Muslims dead. They also suc-ceeded in killing many Meccan leaders, including Abu Jahl. Seventy prisoners had been acquired, many of whom were soon ransomed in return for wealth or freed. Muhammad and his followers saw in the victory a confirmation of their faith.

The Qur'anic verses of this period, unlike the Meccan ones, dealt with practical problems of government and issues like the distribution of spoils. Muhammad expelled from Medina the Banu Qaynuqa, one of three main Jewish tribes. Following the Battle of Badr, Muhammad also made mutual-aid alliances with a number of Bedouin tribes to protect his community from attacks from the northern part of Hijaz.

CONFLICT WITH MECCA

The attack at Badr committed Muhammad to total war with Meccans, who were now anxious to avenge their defeat. To maintain their economic prosperity, the Meccans needed to restore their prestige, which had been lost at Badr. In the ensuing months, Muhammad led expeditions on tribes allied with Mecca and sent out a raid on a Meccan caravan. Abu

Sufyan subsequently gathered an army of three thousand men and set out for an attack on Medina. A scout alerted Muhammad of the Meccan army's presence and numbers a day later. The next morning, at the Muslim conference of war, there was dispute over how best to repel the Meccans.

Muhammad and many senior figures suggested that it would be safer to fight within Medina and take advantage of its heavily fortified strongholds. Younger Muslims argued that the Meccans were destroying their crops, and that huddling in the strongholds would destroy Muslim prestige. Muhammad eventually conceded to the wishes of the latter, and readied the Muslim force for battle. Thus, Muhammad led his force outside to the mountain of Uhud (where the Meccans had camped) and fought the Battle of Uhud on March 23. Although the Muslim army had the best of the early encounters, indiscipline on the part of strategically placed archers led to a Muslim defeat, with 75 Muslims killed including Hamza, Muhammad's uncle and one of the best known martyrs in the Muslim tradition.

The Meccans did not pursue the Muslims further, but marched back to Mecca declaring victory. They were not entirely successful, however, as they had failed to achieve their aim of completely destroying the Muslims. The Muslims buried the dead, and returned to Medina that evening. Questions accumulated as to the reasons for the loss, and Muhammad subsequently delivered Qur'anic verses which indicated that their defeat was partly a punishment for disobedience and partly a test for stead-fastness. Abu Sufyan now directed his efforts towards another attack on Medina. He attracted the support of nomadic tribes to the north and east of Medina, using pro-paganda about Muhammad's weakness, promises of booty, memories of the prestige of the Quraysh and use of bribes.

Muhammad's policy was now to prevent alliances against him as much as he could. Whenever alliances of tribesmen against Medina were formed, he sent out an expedition to break them up. When Muhammad heard of men massing with hostile intentions against Medina, he reacted with severity. One example is the assassination of Ka'b ibn al-Ashraf, a chieftain of the Jewish tribe of Banu Nadir who had gone to Mecca and written poems that helped rouse the Meccans' grief, anger and desire for rev-enge after the Battle of Badr. Around a year later, Muham-mad expelled the Banu Nadir from Medina. Muhammad's attempts to prevent formation of a confede-ration against him were unsuccessful, though he was able to increase his own forces and stop many potential tribes from joining his enemies.

SIEGE OF MEDINA

With the help of the exiled Banu Nadir, the Quraysh military leader Abu Sufyan had mustered a force of 10,000 men. Muhammad prepared a force of about 3000 men and adopted a new form of defense unknown in Arabia at that time: the Muslims dug a trench wherever Medina lay open to cavalry attack. The idea is credited to a Persian convert to Islam, Salman the Persian. The siege of Medina began on March 31 627 and lasted for two weeks. Abu Sufyan's troops were unprepared for the fortifications they were confronted with, and after an ineffectual siege lasting several weeks, the coalition decided to go home.

The Qur'an discusses this battle in verses Qur'an 33:9-33:27. During the battle, the Jewish tribe of Banu Qurayza, located at the south of Medina, had entered into negotiations with Meccan forces to revolt against Muhammad. Although they were swayed by suggestions that Muhammad was sure to be overwhelmed, they desired reassurance in case the confederacy was unable to destroy him. No agreement was reached after the prolonged negotiations, in part due to sabotage attempts by Muhammad's scouts. After the coalition's retreat, the Muslims accused the Banu Qurayza of treachery and besieged them in their forts for 25 days.

The Banu Qurayza eventually surrendered and all the men, apart from a few who converted to Islam, were beheaded, while the women and children were enslaved. In the siege of Medina, the Meccans exerted their utmost strength towards the destruction of the Muslim com-munity. Their failure resulted in a significant loss of prestige; their trade with Syria was gone.

Following the Battle of the Trench, Muhammad made two expeditions to the north which ended without any fighting. While returning from one of these (or some years earlier according to other early accounts), an accusation of adultery was made against Aisha, Muhammad's wife. Aisha was exonerated from the accusations when Muhammad announced that he had received a revelation confirming Aisha's innocence and directing that charges of adultery be supported by four eye-witnesses.

TRUCE OF HUDAYBIYYA

Although Muhammad had already delivered Qur'anic verses commanding the Hajj, the Muslims had not performed it due to the enmity of the Quraysh. In the month of Shawwal 628, Muhammad ordered his followers to obtain sacrificial animals and to make preparations for a pilgrimage (*umrah*) to Mecca, saying that God had promised him the fulfillment of this goal in a vision where he was shaving his head after the completion of the Hajj.

Upon hearing of the approaching 1,400 Muslims, the Quraysh sent out a force of 200 cavalry to halt them. Muhammad evaded them by taking a more difficult route, thereby reaching al-Hudaybiyya, just outside of Mecca. According to Watt, although Muhammad's decision to make the pilgrimage was based on his dream, he was at the same time demonstrating to the pagan Meccans that Islam does not threaten the prestige of their sanctuary, and that Islam was an Arabian religion.

Negotiations commenced with emissaries going to and from Mecca. While these continued, rumors spread that one of the Muslim negotiators, Uthman bin al-Affan, had been killed by the Quraysh. Muhammad responded by calling upon the pilgrims to make a pledge not to flee (or to stick with

Muhammad, whatever decision he made) if the situation descended into war with Mecca. This pledge became known as the "Pledge of Acceptance" or the "Ple-dge under the Tree." News of Uthman's safety, how-ever, allowed for negotiations to continue, and a treaty scheduled to last ten years was eventually signed between the Muslims and Quraysh. The main points of the treaty included the cessation of hostilities; the deferral of Muhammad's pilgrimage to the following year; and an agreement to send back any Meccan who had gone to Medina without the permission of their protector.

Many Muslims were not satisfied with the terms of the treaty. However, the Qur'anic sura "Al-Fath" (The Victory) (Qur'an 48:1-29) assured the Muslims that the expedition from which they were now returning must be considered a victorious one. It was only later that Muhammad's followers would realise the benefit behind this treaty. According to Welch, these benefits included the inducing of the Meccans to recognise Muhammad as an equal; a cessation of military activity posing well for the future; and gaining the admiration of Meccans who were impressed by the incorporation of the pilgrimage rituals.

After signing the truce, Muhammad made an expe-dition against the Jewish oasis of Khaybar, known as the Battle of Khaybar. This was possibly due to it housing the Banu Nadir, who was inciting hostilities against Muham-mad, or to regain some prestige to deflect from what appeared to some Muslims as the inconclusive result of the truce of Hudaybiyya.

According to Muslim tradition, Muhammad also sent letters to many rulers of the world, asking them to convert to Islam (the exact date is given variously in the sources). Hence he sent messengers (with letters) to Heraclius of the Byzantine Empire (the eastern Roman Empire), Khosrau of Persia, and the chief of Yemen and to some others. In the years following the truce of Hudaybiyya, Muhammad sent his forces against the Arabs on Transjordanian Byzantine soil in the Battle of Mu'tah, in which the Muslims were defeated.

FINAL YEARS

CONQUEST OF MECCA

The truce of Hudaybiyya had been enforced for two years. The tribe of Banu Khuza'a had good relations with Muhammad, whereas their enemies, the Banu Bakr, had an alliance with the Meccans. A clan of the Bakr made a night raid against the *Khuz'aah*, killing a few of them. The Meccans helped the Banu Bakr with weapons and, according to some sources; a few Meccans also took part in the fighting. After this event, Muhammad sent a message to Mecca with three conditions, asking them to accept one of them. These were that either the Meccans paid blood money for those slain among the Khuza'ah tribe; or, that they should disavow themselves of the Banu Bakr; or, that they should declare the truce of Hudaybiyya null.

The Meccans replied that they would accept only the last condition. However, soon they realized their mistake and sent Abu Sufyan to renew the Hudaybiyya treaty, but now his request was declined by Muhammad. Muhammad began to prepare for a campaign. In 630, Muhammad marched on Mecca with an enormous force, said to number more than ten thousand men. With minimal casualties, Muhammad took control of Mecca. He declared an amnesty for past offences, except for ten men and women who had mocked and ridiculed him in songs and verses. Some of these were later pardoned. Most Meccans converted to Islam and Muhammad subsequently destroyed all the statues of Arabian gods in and around the Kaaba. The Qur'an discusses the conquest of Mecca.

CONQUEST OF ARABIA

Soon after the conquest of Mecca, Muhammad was alarmed by a military threat from the confederate tribes of Hawazin who were collecting an army twice the size of Muhammad's. The Banu Hawazin were old enemies of the Meccans. They were joined by the Banu Thaqif (inhabiting the city of Ta'if) who adopted an anti-Meccan policy due to the decline of the prestige of Meccans. Muhammad defeated the Hawazin and Thaqif tribes in the Battle of Hunayn. In the same year, Muhammad made the expedition of Tabuk against northern Arabia because of their previous defeat at the Battle of Mu'tah as well as reports of the hostile attitude adopted against Muslims. Although Muhammad did not make contact with hostile forces at Tabuk, he received the submission of some local chiefs of the region.

A year after the Battle of Tabuk, the Banu Thaqif sent emissaries to Medina to surrender to Muhammad and adopt Islam. Many bedouins submitted to Muhammad in order to be safe against his attacks and to benefit from the booties of the wars. However, the bedouins were alien to the system of Islam and wanted to maintain their independence, their established code of virtue and their ancestral traditions. Muhammad thus required of them a military and political agreement according to which they "acknowledge the suzerainty of Medina, to refrain from attack on the Muslims and their allies, and to pay the Zakat, the Muslim religious levy."

FAREWELL PILGRIMAGE AND DEATH

At the end of the tenth year after the migration to Medina, Muhammad carried through his first truly Islamic pilgrimage, thereby teaching his followers the rites of the annual Great Pilgrimage (Hajj). After completing the pilgrimage, Muhammad delivered a famous speech known as The Farewell Sermon. In this sermon, Muhammad advised his followers not to follow certain pre-Islamic customs such as adding intercalary months to align the lunar calendar with the solar calendar. Muhammad abolished all old blood feuds and disputes based on the former tribal system and asked for all old pledges to be returned as implications of the creation of the new Islamic community. Commenting on the vulnerability of women in his society, Muhammed asked his male followers to "Be good to women; for they are powerless captives (awan) in your households.

You took them in God's trust, and legitimated your sexual relations with the Word of God, so come to your senses people, and hear my words ...". He also told them that they were entitled to discipline their wives but should do so with kindness. Muhammad also addressed the issue of inheritance by forbidding false claims of paternity or of a client relationship to the deceased and also forbidding his followers to leave their wealth to a testamentary heir. He also upheld the sacredness of four lunar months in each year. According to Sunni tafsir, the following Qur'anic verse was delivered in this incident: "Today I have perfected your religion, and completed my favours for you and chosen Islam as a religion for you."(Qur'an 5:3)

According to Shia tafsir, it refers to appointment of Ali ibn Abi Talib at the pond of Khumm as Muhammad's successor, this occurring a few days later when Muslims were returning from Mecca to Medina. A few months after the farewell pilgrimage, Muhammad fell ill and suffered for several days with head pain and weakness. He died on Monday, June 8, 632, in Medina. He is buried where he died which was in his wife Aisha's house and is now housed within the Mosque of the Prophet in Medina. Next to Muhammad's tomb, there is another empty tomb that Muslims believe awaits Jesus.

AFTERMATH

Muhammad united the tribes of Arabia into a singular Arab Muslim religious polity in the last years of his life. With Muhammad's death, disagreement broke out over who would succeed him as leader of the Muslim community. Umar ibn al-Khattab, a prominent companion of Muhammad, nominated Abu Bakr, Muhammad's friend and collaborator. Others added their support and Abu Bakr was made the first caliph. This choice was disputed by some of Muhammad's companions, who held that Ali ibn Abi Talib, his cousin and son-in-law, had been designated the successor by Muhammad at Ghadir Khumm. Abu Bakr's immediate task was to make an expedition against the Byzantine (or Eastern Roman Empire) forces because of the previous defeat, although he first had to put down a rebellion by Arab tribes in an episode referred to by later Muslim historians as the Ridda wars, or "Wars of Apostasy".

The pre-Islamic Middle East was dominated by the Byzantine and Sassanian empires. The Roman-Persian Wars between the two had devastated the inhabitants, making the empires unpopular amongst local tribes. Furthermore, most Christian Churches in the lands to be conquered by Muslims such as Nestorians, Monophysites, Jacobites and Copts were under pressure from the Christian Orthodoxy who deemed them heretics. Within only a decade, Muslims conquered Mesopotamia and Persia, Roman Syria and Roman Egypt and established the Rashidun Empire.

WIVES AND CHILDREN

Muhammad's life is traditionally defined into two periods: pre-hijra (emigration) in Mecca (from 570 to 622), and post-hijra in Medina (from 622 until 632). Muhammad is said to have had thirteen wives or concubines (there are dif-fering accounts on the status of some of them as wife or concubine) All but two of his marriages were contracted after the migration to Medina. At the age of 25, Muhammad married Khadijah bint Khuwaylid. The marriage lasted for 25 years and was a happy one. Muhammad relied upon Khadija in many ways and did not enter into marriage with another woman during this marriage.

After the death of Khadija, it was suggested to Muhammad by Khawla bint Hakim, that he should marry Sawda bint Zama, a Muslim widow, or Aisha, the young daughter of Abu Bakr. Muhammad is said to have asked her to arrange for him to marry both. Later, Muhammad married additional wives nine of whom survived him. Aisha, who became known as Muhammad's favourite wife in Sunni tradition, survived him by many decades and was instrumental in helping to bring together the scattered sayings of Muhammad that would form the Hadith literature for the Sunni branch of Islam.

After migration to Medina, Muhammad (who was now in his fifties) married several women. These marriages were contracted mostly for political or humanitarian reasons, these wives being either widows of Muslims who had been killed in the battles and had been left without a protector, or belonging to important families or clans whom it was necessary to honor and strengthen alliances. Muhammad did his own household chores and helped with housework, such as preparing food, sewing clothes and repairing shoes. Muhammad is also said to have had accustomed his wives to dialogue; he listened to their advice, and the wives debated and even argued with him.

Khadijah is said to have borne Muhammad four daughters (Ruqayyah bint Muhammad, Umm Kulthum bint Muhammad, Zainab bint Muhammad, Fatimah Zahra) and two sons (Abd-Allah ibn Muhammad and Qasim ibn Muhammad) who both died in childhood. All except two of his daughters, Fatimah and Zainab, died before him. Shi'a scholars contend that Fatimah was Muhammad's only daughter. Maria al-Qibtiyya bore him a son named Ibrahim ibn Muhammad, but the child died when he was two years old. Muhammad's descendants through Fatimah are known as *sharifs, syeds* or *sayyids*. These are honorific titles in Arabic, *sharif* meaning 'noble' and *sayed* or *sayyid* meaning 'lord' or 'sir'. As Muhammad's only descendants, they are respected by both Sunni and Shi'a, though the Shi'as place much more emphasis and value on their distinction.

LEGACY

REFORMS

According to William Montgomery Watt, for Muhammad, religion was not a private and individual matter but rather "the total response of his personality to the total situation in which he found himself. He was responding [not only]... to the religious and intellectual aspects of the situation but also to the economic, social, and political pressures to which contemporary Mecca was subject." Bernard Lewis says that there are two important political traditions in Islam - one that views Muhammad as a statesman in Medina, and another that views him as a rebel in Mecca. He sees Islam itself as a type of revolution that greatly changed the societies into which the new religion was brought.

Historians generally agree that Islamic social reforms in areas such as social security, family structure, slavery and the rights of women and children improved on the status quo of Arab society. For example, according to Lewis, Islam "from the first denounced aristocratic privilege, rejected hierarchy, and adopted a formula of the career open to the talents". Muhammad's message transformed the society and moral order of life in the Arabian Peninsula through reorientation of society as regards to identity, world view, and the hierarchy of values. Economic reforms addressed the plight of the poor, which was becoming an issue in pre-Islamic Mecca. The Qur'an requires payment of an alms tax (zakat) for the benefit of the poor, and as Muhammad's position grew in power he demanded that those tribes who wanted to ally with him implement the zakat in particular.

SUNNAH

The Sunnah represents the actions and sayings of Muhammad (preserved in reports known as Hadith), and covers a broad array of activities and beliefs ranging from religious rituals, personal hygiene, burial of the dead to the mystical questions involving the love between humans and God. The Sunnah is considered a model of emulation for pious Muslims and has to a great degree influenced the Muslim culture. The greeting that Muhammad taught Muslims to offer each other, "may peace be upon you" is used by Muslims throughout the world. Many details of major Islamic rituals such as daily prayers, the fasting and the annual pilgrimage are only found in the Sunnah and not the Qur'an.

The Sunnah also played a major role in the development of the Islamic sciences. It contributed much to the development of Islamic law, particularly from the end of the first Islamic century. Muslim mystics, known as sufis, who were seeking for the inner meaning of the Qur'an and the inner nature of Muhammad, viewed the prophet of Islam not only as a prophet but also as a perfect saint. Sufi orders trace their chain of spiritual descent back to Muhammad.

TRADITIONAL VIEWS

MUSLIM VENERATION

Following the attestation to the oneness of God, the belief in Muhammad's prophethood is the main aspect of the Islamic faith. Every Muslim proclaims in the *Shahadah* that "I testify that Muhammad is a messenger of Allah". The Shahadah is the basic creed or tenet of Islam. Ideally, it is the first words a newborn will hear, and children are taught as soon as they are able to understand it and it will be recited when they die. Muslims must repeat the shahadah in the call to prayer (*adhan*) and the prayer itself. Non-Muslims wishing to convert to Islam are required to recite the creed. Muslims have traditionally expressed love and veneration for Muhammad. Stories of Muhammad's life, his intercession and of his miracles (particularly "Splitting of the moon") have permeated popular Muslim thought and poetry.

The Qur'an refers to Muhammad as "a mercy (*rahmat*) to the worlds" (Qur'an 21:107). The association of rain with mercy in Oriental countries has led to imagining Muhammad as a rain cloud dispensing blessings and stretching over lands, reviving the dead hearts, just as rain revives the seemingly dead earth. Muhammad's birthday is celebrated as a major feast throughout the Islamic world, excluding Wahhabi-dominated Saudi Arabia where these public celebrations are discouraged. Muslims experience Muhammad as a living reality, believing in his ongoing significance to human beings as well as animals and plants.

According to historian Denis Gril, the Qur'an does not overtly describe Muhammad performing miracles, and the supreme miracle of Muhammad is finally identified with the Qur'an itself. However, Muslim tradition credits Muhammad with several supernatural events. For example, many Muslim commentators and some Western scholars have interpreted the Surah 54:1-2 as referring to Muhammad splitting the Moon in view of the Quraysh when they began persecuting his followers. When Muslims say or write the name of Muhammad or any other prophet in Islam, they usually follow it with *Peace be upon him* (Arabic: *sallAllahu 'alayhi wa sallam*).

EUROPEAN AND WESTERN VIEWS

The biographical knowledge about Muhammad in the learned, Latin circles of the middle Ages in Europe was remarkably precise to some extent and a good amount of concrete data about his life was known. Learned European circles of the time interpreted the data in such a way that Muhammad was viewed as a charlatan driven by ambition and eagerness for power, and who seduced the Saracens into his submission under a religious guise. This knowledge about Muhammad's life in Latin theological texts was not reflected in the popular literature of the middle Ages, in which Muhammad was viewed as an idol or one of the heathen gods.

Some medieval Christians said he died in 666, alluding to the number of the beast, instead of 632; others changed his name from Muhammad to Mahound, the "devil incarnate". Bernard Lewis writes "The development of the concept of Mahound started with considering Muhammad as a kind of demon or false god worshipped with Apollyon and Termagant in an unholy trinity." A later medieval work, *Livre dou Tresor* represents Muhammad as a former monk and cardinal. Dante's *Divine Comedy* (Canto XXVIII) puts Muhammad, together with Ali, in Hell "among the sowers of discord and the schismatics, being lacerated by devils again and again."

After the reformation, Muhammad was no longer viewed as a god or idol, but as a cunning, ambitious, and self-seeking impostor. Guillaume Postel was among the first to present a more positive view of Muhammad. Boulainvilliers described Muhammad as a gifted political leader and a just lawmaker. Gottfried Leibniz praised Muhammad because "he did not deviate from the natural religion". Friedrich Bodenstedt (1851) described Muhammad as "an ominous destroyer and a prophet of murder." Later Western works, many of which from the 18th century onward, distanced themselves from the polemical histories of earlier Christian authors.

These more historically-oriented treatments, which generally reject the prophethood of Muhammad, are coloured by the Western philosophical and theological framework of their authors. Many of these studies reflect much historical research, and most pay more attention to human, social, economic, and political factors than to religious, theological, and spiritual matters. It was not until the latter part of the 20th century that Western authors combined rigorous scholarship as understood in the modern West with empathy toward the subject at hand and, especially, awareness of the religious and spiritual realities involved in the study of the life of the founder of a major world religion.

According to Watt and Richard Bell, recent writers have generally dismissed the idea that Muhammad deliberately deceived his followers, arguing that Muhammad "was absolutely sincere and acted in complete good faith". Watt says that sincerity does not directly imply correctness: In contemporary terms, Muhammad might have mistaken his own subconscious for divine revelation. Although Muhammad's image in the west is much less unfavorable than in the past, prejudicial folk beliefs remain. Watt and Lewis argue that viewing Muhammad as a self-seeking impostor makes it impossible to understand the development of Islam. Welch holds that Muhammad was able to be so influential and successful because of his firm belief in his vocation. Muhammad's readiness to endure hardship for his cause when there seemed to be no rational basis for hope shows his sincerity.

Other religious traditions:

- Bahá'ís venerate Muhammad as one of a number of prophets or "Manifestations of God", but consider his teachings to have been superseded by those of Bahá'u'lláh.
- Muhammad is regarded as one of the Saints of Ecclesia Gnostica Catholica.
- The Church of Jesus Christ of Latter-day Saints considers Muhammad, along with Confucius, the Reformers, as well as philosophers including Socrates, Plato, and others, to

have received a portion of God's light and that moral truths were given to them to enlighten nations and bring a higher level of understanding to individuals.

- Guru Nanak, the founder of Sikhism, viewed Muhammad as an agent of the Hindu Supreme Being Brahman.
- The Roman Catholic Church does not regard Muhammad as a prophet. According to Pope John Paul II, Muhammad's teachings "completely reduces Divine Revelation" and sets aside "all the richness of God's self-revelation, which constitutes the heritage of the Old and New Testaments". He then explained that the God of the Qur'an is "ultimately a God outside of the world, a God who is only Majesty, never Emmanuel, God-with-us. Islam is not a religion of redemption. There is no room for the Cross and the Resurrection. [...] For this reason not only the theology but also the anthropology of Islam is very distant from Christianity." Pope John Paul II adds that nevertheless Muslims' fidelity to prayer deserves admiration.

2

Islam Beyond Arabia

Late in the six year A.H., on his return from Hudaibiyah, the Prophet decided to send messages to the kings beyond Arabia calling them to Islam. In order to authenticate the credentials of his envoys, a silver seal was made in which were graven the words: "*Muhammad the Messenger of Allâh*" in the following formation: [Sahih Al-Bukhari 2/872,873]

Envoys were chosen on the basis of their experience and knowledge, and sent on their errands in Muharram in the year 7 A.H., a few days before heading for Khaibar. [Rahmat-al-lil'alameen 1/171]

DEPUTATION TO ABYSSINIA (ETHIOPIA)

Negus, king of Abyssinia (Ethiopia), his name was Ashama bin Al-Abjar, received the Prophet's message, despatched by Amr bin Omaiyah Ad-Damari, which At-Tabari referred to, either late in the sixth year or early in the seventh year A.H. Deep scrutiny into the letter shows that it was not the one sent after Al-Hudaibiyah event. Wording of the letter rather indicates that it was sent to that king when Ja'far and his companions immigrated to Abyssinia (Ethiopia) during the Makkan period. One of its sentences read "I have despatched my cousin, Ja'far with a group of Muslims, to you. Do be generous towards them and give up haughtiness."

Al-Baihaqi, on the authority of Ibn Ishaq, gave the following narration of the Prophet's letter sent to Negus:

"This letter is sent from Muhammad, the Prophet to Negus Al-Ashama, and the king of Abyssinia (Ethiopia).

Peace be upon him who follows true guidance and believes in Allâh and His Messenger. I bear witness that there is no god but Allâh Alone with a associate, He has taken neither a wife nor a son, and that Muhammad is His slave and Messenger. I call you unto the fold of Islam; if you embrace Islam, you will find safety,

> "Say (O Muhammad): 'O people of the Scripture (Jews and Christians), come to a word that is just between us and you, that we worship none but Allâh, and that we associate no partners with Him, and that none of us shall take others as lords besides Allâh.' Then, if they turn away, say: 'Bear witness that we are Muslims.' "[Al-Qur'an 3:64]

Should you reject this invitation, then you will be held responsible for all the evils of the Christians of your people."

Dr. Hameedullah (Paris), a reliable verifier, has adduced a version of the above letter disclosed only a short time ago and identical to Ibn Al-Qaiyim's narration. Dr. Hameedullah exerted painstaking effort and used all means of modern technology to verify the text of the letter, which reads as follows:

"In the Name of Allâh, the Most Beneficent, the Most Merciful.

From Muhammad the Messenger of Allâh to Negus, king of Abyssinia (Ethiopia).

Peace be upon him who follows true guidance. Salutations, I entertain Allâh's praise, there is no god but He, the Sovereign, the Holy, the Source of peace, the Giver of peace, the Guardian of faith, the Preserver of safety. I bear witness that Jesus, the son of Mary, is the spirit of Allâh and His Word which He cast into Mary, the virgin, the good, the pure, so that she conceived Jesus. Allâh created him from His spirit and His breathing as He created Adam by His Hand. I call you to Allâh Alone with no associate and to His obedience and to follow me and to believe in that which came to me, for I am the Messenger of Allâh. I invite you and your men to Allâh, the Glorious, and the All-Mighty. I hereby bear witness that I have communicated my message and advice. I invite you to listen and accept my advice. Peace be upon him who follows true guidance." [Za'd Al-Ma'ad 3/60]

The text of this letter is doubtlessly authentic, but to maintain that it was written after Al-Hudaibiyah event is still a question lacking in definite evidence. When 'Amr bin Omaiyah Ad-Damari communicated the Apostolic letter to Negus, the latter took the parchment and placed it on his eye, descended to the floor, confessed his faith in Islam and wrote the following reply to the Prophet :

"In the Name of Allâh, the Most Beneficent, the Most Merciful.

From Negus Ashama to Muhammad, the Messenger of Allâh. Peace be upon you, O Messenger of Allâh! and mercy and blessing from Allâh beside Whom there is no god. I have received your letter in which you have mentioned about Jesus and by the Lord of heaven and earth; Jesus is not more than what you say. We fully acknowledge that with which you have been sent to us and we have entertained your cousin and his companions.

I bear witness that you are the Messenger of Allâh, true and confirming (those who have gone before you), I pledge to you through your cousin and surrender myself through him to the Lord of the worlds." [Za'd Al-Ma'ad 3/61]

The Prophet had asked Negus to send Ja'far and his companions, the emigrants to Abyssinia (Ethiopia), back home. They came back to see the Prophet in Khâibar. Negus later died in Rajab 9 A.H. shortly after Tabuk *Ghazwa.*

The Prophet announced his death and observed prayer in absentia for him. Another king succeeded Negus to the throne and another letter was sent to him by the Prophet but whether or not he embraced Islam is still a question not answered yet. [Sahih Muslim 2/99]

LETTER TO THE VICEGERENT OF EGYPT CALLED (MUQAWQAS)

The Prophet wrote to Juraij bin Matta [Rahmat-al-lil'alameen 1/178; Dr. Hamidullah said that his name was Binyamin], called Muqawqas, vicegerent of Egypt and Alexandria saying:

"In the Name of Allâh, the Most Beneficent, the Most Merciful.

From Muhammad slave of Allâh and His Messenger to Muqawqas, vicegerent of Egypt. Peace be upon him who follows true guidance. Thereafter, I invite you to accept Islam. Therefore, if you want security, accept Islam. If you accept Islam, Allâh, the Sublime, shall reward you doubly. But if you refuse to do so, you will bear the burden of the transgression of all the Copts.

Hatib bin Abi Balta'a, who was chosen to communicate the message, requested an audience with Muqawqas before imparting the contents of the letter. He addressed Egypt's vicegerent saying: "There used to be someone before you, who had arrogated the status of the Supreme Lord, so Allâh punished him and made an example of him in the Hereafter, and in this life; therefore, take warning and never set a bad example to others." Muqawqas answered: "We are in no position to relinquish our religion except for a better one." Hatib resumed: "We invite you to embrace Islam, which will suffice you all what you may lose. Our Prophet has called people to profess this Faith, Quraish and the Jews stood against him as bitter enemies, whereas Christians stood closest to his Call.

Upon my life, Moses's news about Christ is identical to the latter's good tidings about the advent of Muhammad; likewise, this invitation of ours to you to embrace Islam is similar to your invitation to the people of Torah to accept the New Testament. Once a Prophet rises in a nation, he is eligible for positive response; hence you are subject to the same Divine Law. Bear in mind that we have not come to dissuade you from religion of Christ but rather bidding you to adhere to its tenets." Muqawqas meditated over the contents of the letter deeply and said: "I have come to the conviction that this Prophet bids nothing abominable; he is neither a straying magician nor a lying soothsayer. He bears the true manifest seeds of Prophethood, and so I will consider the affair deeply." He took the parchment and ordered that it be kept in an ivory casket. He called a scribe to write the following reply in Arabic:

"In the Name of Allâh, the Most Beneficent, the Most Merciful.

From Muqawqas to Muhammad bin 'Abdullah.

Peace be upon you. I have read your letter and understood its contents, and what you are calling for. I already know that the coming of a Prophet is still due, but I used to believe he would be born in Syria. I am sending you as presents two maids, who come from noble Coptic families; clothing and a steed for riding on. Peace be upon you." It is noteworthy that Muqawqas did not avail himself of this priceless opportunity and he did not embrace Islam. The presents were accepted; Maria, the first maid, stayed with the Prophet, and gave birth to his son Ibrahîm; the other Sirin, was given to Hassan bin Thabit Al-Ansari.

LETTER TO CHOSROES, EMPEROR OF PERSIA

"In the Name of Allâh, the Most Beneficent, the Most Merciful.

From Muhammad, the Messenger of Allâh to Chosroes, king of Persia.

Peace be upon him who follows true guidance, believes in Allâh and His Messenger and testifies that there is no god but Allâh Alone with no associate, and that Muhammad is His slave and Messenger. I invite you to accept the religion of Allâh. I am the Messenger of Allâh sent to all people in order that I may infuse fear of Allâh in every living person, and that the charge may be proved against those who reject the Truth. Accept Islam as your religion so that you may live in security, otherwise, you will be responsible for all the sins of the Magians."

'Abdullah bin Hudhafa As-Sahmi was chosen to carry the letter. This envoy carried it to the king of Bahrain but we do not know as yet if the latter despatched to Chosroes by one of his men or chose 'Abdullah himself.

The proud monarch was enraged by the style of the letter as the name of the Prophet had been put above his own name. He tore the letter into shreds and forthwith dictated a command to his viceroy in Yemen to send a couple of troopers to arrest the Prophet and bring him to his presence. The governor, Bazan by name, immediately sent two men to Madinah for the purpose. As soon as the men reached Madinah, the Prophet was informed by a Divine Revelation that Pervez, the emperor of Persia, had been murdered by his son.

The Prophet disclosed to them the news and they were stunned. He added asking them to tell their new monarch that Islam would prevail everywhere and outstrip the sovereignty of Chosroes himself. They hurried back to Bazan and communicated to him what they heard. Meanwhile, Sherweh, the new monarch sent a letter to Bazan confirming the news and bidding him to stop any procedures as regards the Prophet till further notice. Bazan, together with the Persians in Yemen, went into the folds of Islam, and gladly signified his adhesion to the Prophet. [Fath Al-Bari 8/127,128]

THE ENVOY TO CAESAR, KING OF ROME

Al-Bukhari gave a long narration of the contents of the letter sent by the Prophet to Hercules, king of the Byzantines: "In the Name of Allâh, the Most Beneficent, and the Most Merciful.

From Muhammad, the slave of Allâh and His Messenger to Hercules, king of the Byzantines blessed are those who follow true guidance. I invite you to embrace Islam so that you may live in security. If you come within the fold of Islam, Allâh will give you double reward, but in case you turn your back upon it, then the burden of the sins of all your people shall fall on your shoulders.

"Say (O Muhammad): 'O people of the Scripture (Jews and Christians), come to a word that is just between us and you, that we worship none but Allâh, and that we associate no partners with Him, and that none of us shall take others as lords besides Allâh.' Then, if they turn away, say: 'Bear witness that we are Muslims.' "[Al-Qur'an 3:64] [Sahih Al-Bukhari 1/4, 5]

The Muslim envoy, Dihyah bin Khalifah Al-Kalbi, was ordered to hand the letter over to king of Busra, who would in turn, send it to Caesar. Incidentally, Abu Sufyan bin Harb, who by that time had not embraced Islam, was summoned to the court and Hercules asked him many questions about Muhammad and the religion which he preached. The testimony which this avowed enemy of the Prophet gave regarding the personal excellence of the Prophet's character and the good that Islam was doing the human race left Hercules wonder-struck.

Al-Bukhâri, on the authority of Ibn Abbas, narrated that Hercules sent for Abu Sufyan and his companions, who happened to be trading in Ash-Sham, Jerusalem. That was during the truce that had been concluded between the polytheists of Quraish and the Messenger of Allâh. Hercules, seated amongst his chiefs of staff, asked, "Who amongst you is the nearest relative to the man who claims to be a Prophet?" "I (Abu Sufyan) replied: 'I am the nearest relative to him from amongst the group.' So they made me sit in front of him and made my companions sit behind me. Then he called upon his translator and said (to him). 'Tell them (i.e. Abu Sufyan's companions) that I am going to ask him (i.e. Abu Sufyan) regarding that men who claims to be a Prophet. So if he tells a lie, they should contradict him (instantly)'.

By Allâh had I not been afraid that my companions would consider me a liar, I would have told lies", Abu Sufyan later said. Abu Sufyan's testimony went as follows: "Muhammad descends from a noble family. No one of his family happened to assume kingship. His followers are those deemed weak with numbers ever growing. He neither tells lies nor betrays others, we fight him and he fights us but with alternate victory. He bids people to worship Allâh Alone with no associate, and abandon our fathers' beliefs. He orders us to observe prayer, honesty, and abstinence and maintain strong family ties."

"Hercules, on hearing this testimony, turned to his translator bidding him to communicate to us his following impression which reveals full conviction in the truthfulness of Muhammad's Prophethood: 'I fully realize that Prophets come from noble families; he does not affect any previous example of Prophethood. Since none of his ancestors was a monarch, we cannot then allege that he is a man trying to reclaim his father's monarchy. So long as he does not tell lies to people, he is for the more reason, immune to telling lies as regards Allâh.

Concerning his followers being those deemed weak with numbers ever growing, it is something that goes in agreement with questions of Faith until this latter assumes its full dimensions geographically and demographically. I have understood that no instance of apostasy has as yet appeared among his followers and this points to the bliss of Faith that finds its abode in the human heart. Betrayal, as I see, is alien to him because real Prophets hold betrayal in abhorrence. Bidding worship of Allâh with no associates, observance of prayer, honesty and abstinence and prohibition of paganism are traits bound to subject to him all my possessions. I have already known that a Prophet must arise but it has never occurred to me that he will be an Arab from among you. If I was sure I would be faithful to him, I might hope to meet him, and if I were with him, I would wash his feet.'

Hercules then requested that the Prophet's letter be read. The observations of the emperor and finally the definite and clear-cut exposition of the Islamic message could not but create a tense atmosphere amongst the clergy present at the court. We were ordered to go out." Abu Sufyan said, "While coming out, I said to my companions, 'The matter of Ibn Abi Kabshah (i.e. Muhammad) has become so prominent that even the king of Banu Al-Asfar (i.e. the Romans) is afraid of him.'

So I continued to believe that Allâh's Messenger would be victorious, till Allâh made me embrace Islam." The king did not embrace Islam-for it was differently ordained. However, the Muslim envoy was returned to Madinah with the felicitations of the emperor.

On his way back to Madinah, Dihyah Al-Kalbi was intercepted by people from Judham tribe in Hasmi, who looted the presents sent to the Prophet. Zaid bin Haritha at the head of five hundred men was despatched to that spot, inflicted heavy losses on those people and captured 1000 camels, 5000 of their cattle and a hundred women and boys.

The chief of Judham who had embraced Islam filed a complaint with the Prophet, who gave a positive response to the former's protest, and ordered that all the spoils and captives be returned.

LETTER TO MUNDHIR BIN SAWA, GOVERNOR OF BAHRAIN

The Prophet despatched 'Al-'Ala' bin Al-Hadrami to the governor of Bahrain, carrying a letter inviting him to embrace Islam. In reply, Al-Mundhir bin Sawa wrote the following letter:

"Allâh's Messenger! I received your injunctions. Prior to this, I read your letter, which you wrote to the people of Bahrain extending to them an invitation to Islam. Islam appealed to some of them and they entered the fold of Islam, while others did not find it appealing. In my country, there live Magians and Jews, and therefore you may inform me of the treatment to be extended to them."

The Prophet wrote the following letter in reply to his:

"In the Name of Allâh, the Most Beneficent, the Most Merciful.

From Muhammad, Messenger of Allâh to Mundhir bin Sawa.

Peace be on you! I praise Allâh with no associate, and I bear witness that Muhammad is His slave and Messenger. Thereafter, I remind you of Allâh, the Mighty, and the

Glorious. Whoever accepts admonition does it for his good. Whoever follows my messengers and acts in accordance with their guidance, he, in fact, accepts my advice. My messengers have highly praised your behaviour. You shall continue in your present office. Give the new Muslims full chance to preach their religion. I accept your recommendation regarding the people of Bahrain, and I pardon the offences of the offenders; therefore, you may also forgive them. Of the people of Bahrain whoever wants to go on in their Jewish or Magian faith, should be made to pay *Jizya* (poll-tax)."[Za'd Al-Ma'ad 3/61, 62]

LETTER TO HAUDHA BIN 'ALI, GOVERNOR OF YAMAMA

"In the Name of Allâh, the Most Beneficent, the Most Merciful.

From Muhammad, Messenger of Allâh to Haudha bin 'Ali. Peace be upon him who follows true guidance. Be informed that my religion shall prevail everywhere. You should accept Islam, and whatever under your command shall remain yours."

The envoy chosen was Sulait bin 'Amr Al-'Amiri, who after communicating his message carried back the following reply to the Prophet:

"The Faith, to which you invite me, is very good. I am a famous orator and poet, the Arabs highly respect me and I am of account among them. If you include me in your government, I am prepared to follow you."

The governor then bestowed a reward on Sulait and presented him with clothes made of Hajr fabric. Of course, he put all those presents in the trust of the Prophet. The Prophet did not accept Haudha's demand. He usually turned down such peremptory tone, and would say that the whole matter was in the Hand of Allâh, Who gave His land to whoever He desired. Gabriel later came with the Revelation that Haudha had died. The Prophet, in the context of his comment on this news, said: "Yamama is bound to give rise to a liar who will arrogate Prophethood to himself but he will subsequently be killed." In reply to a question relating to the identity of the killer, the Prophet said "It is one of you, followers of Islam."[Za'd Al-Ma'ad 3/63]

LETTER TO HARITH BIN ABI SHAMIR AL-GHASSANI, KING OF DAMASCUS

"In the Name of Allâh, the Most Beneficent, the Most Merciful.

From Muhammad, Messenger of Allâh to Al-Harith bin Abi Shamir. Peace be upon him who follows true guidance, believes in it and regards it as true. I invite you to believe in Allâh Alone with no associate, thenceafter your kingdom will remain yours."

Shuja' bin Wahab had the honour of taking the letter to Harith, who upon hearing the letter read in his audience, was madly infuriated and uttered: "Who dares to disposs me of my country, I'll fight him (the Prophet)," and arrogantly rejected the Prophet's invitation to the fold of Islam.[Za'd Al-Ma'ad 3/62; Muhadarat Tareekh Al-Umam Al-Islamiyah 1/146]

LETTER TO THE KING OF 'OMAN, JAIFER, AND HIS BROTHER 'ABD AL-JALANDI

"In the Name of Allâh, the Most Beneficent, the Most Merciful.

From Muhammad bin 'Abdullah to Jaifer and 'Abd Al-Jalandi.

Peace be upon him who follows true guidance; thereafter I invite both of you to the Call of Islam. Embrace Islam. Allâh has sent me as a Prophet to all His creatures in order that I may instil fear of Allâh in the hearts of His disobedient creatures so that there may be left no excuse for those who deny Allâh. If you two accept Islam, you will remain in command of your country; but if you refuse my Call, you've got to remember that all your possessions are perishable. My horsemen will appropriate your land, and my Prophethood will assume preponderance over your kingship." 'Amr bin Al-'As, who was chosen to carry the letter, narrated the following story that happened before he was admitted into the audience of Jaifer.

"When I arrived in 'Oman I contacted 'Abd, who was known to be more mild-tempered than his brother:

'Amr: I am the messenger of Allâh's Prophet coming to see both, you and your brother.

'Abd: You have to see my brother and read to him the letter you are carrying. He is my senior in both age and kingship. Incidentally, what is the purport of your mission?

'Amr: The Prophet calls upon you to believe in Allâh Alone with no associate discard any other deities and testify to the slavehood and Messengership of Muhammad.

'Abd: O 'Amr! You come from a noble family, but first of all, tell me what was your father's attitude concerning this Faith? You know, we used to follow his steps.

'Amr: Death overtook him before believing in Muhammad's mission; I wish now he had embraced Islam and been truthful to it before his death. I myself had adopted the same attitude until Allâh guided me towards Islam.

'Abd: When did you embrace Islam?

'Amr: When I was at Negus's court. By the way, the latter did also enter into the fold of Islam.

'Abd: What was his people's reaction?

'Amr: They approved of him and followed his steps.

'Abd: The bishops and monks?

'Amr: They did the same.

'Abd: Beware 'Amr of lying for this soon betrays man.

'Amr: I never tell lies; moreover, our religion never allows it.

'Abd: Has Hercules been informed of the Islamization of Negus?

'Amr: Yes, of course.

'Abd: How did you happen to know that?

'Amr: Negus used to pay land tax to Hercules, but when the former embraced Islam, he swore he would discontinue that tax. When this news reached Hercules, his courtiers urged him to take action against Negus but he refused and added that he himself would do the same if he were not sparing of his kingship.

'Abd: What does your Prophet exhort you to do?

'Amr: He exhorts us to obey Allâh, the All-Mighty, and the All-Glorious, be pious and maintain good ties with family kin; he forbids disobedience, aggression, adultery, wine, idolatry and devotion to the cross.

'Abd: Fair words and fair beliefs are those you are calling for. I wish my brother would follow me to believe in Muhammad and profess his religion, but my brother is too sparing of his kingship to become a subordinate.

'Amr: Should your brother surrender himself to Islam, the Prophet would give him authority over his people and take alms tax from the wealthy people to be given to the needy.

'Abd: That is fair behaviour. But what is this alms tax you have mentioned?

'Amr: It is a Divine injunction that alms tax be taken from the well-to-do people who have surplus wealth and be distributed to the poor.

'Abd: I doubt if this can work among our people.

'Amr stayed for some days to be admitted into Jaifer's court until he was finally granted this permit. "He asked me to hand him the letter to read it. After that he asked me how Quraish reacted and I answered that they had followed him, some out of their own freewill and others overpowered by military fighting. Now, people have chosen Islam in preference to other creeds, and have realized through their mental insight that they had been straying in darkness. None, except you, is now out of the domain of Islam, so I advise you to embrace Islam so that you can provide security to yourself and your country."

Here, he asked me to call on him the following day. The following day he showed some reluctance in receiving me but his brother, 'Abd, interceded and I was given the chance to see him again but this time to address me in a threatening arrogant tone. However, after a private talk with his brother and reconsidering the whole situation, both brothers embraced Islam and proved to be true to Islam that had begun to make its way into this new area.

The context of this story reveals that this letter was sent at a much later date than the others, most likely after the conquest of Makkah. Through these letters, the Prophet managed to communicate his Message to most monarchs at that time; some believed, while others remained obdurate and persisted in their disbelief. However, the idea of embracing Islam, and the advent of a new Prophet preoccupied all of them.

DHU QARAD INVASION

It was in fact not a battle but rather a skirmish carried out against a platoon of Bani Fazarah. The place by which it was fought is known as Dhu Qarad, a reservoir of water at a day's journey from Madinah. According to the majority of scholars, this incident took place three days before the battle of Khaibar. It has been narrated on the authority of Salamah bin Al-Akwa', the hero of this battle, that the Messenger of Allâh sent his hireling Rabah, with his camels to a nearby pasture. I, taking Talhah's horse, went there for the same purpose.

When the day dawned, 'Abdur Rahman Al-Fazari made a raid, drove away all the camels, and killed the man who looked after them. I told Rabah to ride the horse, take it to Talhah and inform the Messenger of Allâh that the polytheists had made away with his camels. Then I stood upon a hillock and turning my face to Madinah, shouted thrice: "Come to our help!" After that I set out in pursuit of the raiders, shooting at them with arrows and chanting (self-eulogatory) verse:

I am the son of Al-Akwa'

Today is the day of defeat for the mean.

By Allâh, I continued shooting at them and hamstringing their animals. Whenever a horseman turned upon me, I would come to a tree (hid myself) sitting at its base, shoot at him and hamstring his horse. At last they entered a narrow mountain gorge. I ascended that mountain and held them at bay throwing stones at them. I continued to chase them in this way until I got all the camels released with no one left with them. They fled in all directions and I following and shooting at them continually until they dropped more than thirty mantles and thirty lances, lightening their burden. On everything they dropped, I put a mark with a stone so that the Messenger of Allâh and his Companions might recognize them (that it was booty left by the enemy). They went on until they came to a narrow valley. They sat down to eat something, and I sat on the top of a tapering rock.

Four of them ascended the mountain coming towards me. When they were near enough to hear me, I shouted: "Do you recognize me?" They said: "No. Who are you?" I said: "I am Salamah son of Al-Akwa'. I can kill anyone of you I like but none of you can kill me." So they returned. I did not move from my place until I saw the horsemen of the Messenger of Allâh, who came riding through the trees. The foremost among them was Akhram, behind him was Abu Qatadah Al-Ansari followed by Al-Miqdad bin Al-Aswad. Akhram and 'Abdur Rahman Al-Fazari met in combat. Akhram hamstrung 'Abdur Rahman's horse but the latter managed to strike him with his lance and kill him. 'Abdur Rahman turned around riding Akhram's horse. Abu Qatadah, seeing this, got engaged in fierce combat with 'Abdur Rahman smote him with his lance and it was fatal.

The polytheists consequently fled away and I was in their pursuit until before sunset they reached a valley with a spring of water called Dhu Qarad. They rested there to have a drink. I however, running in hot pursuit, turned them out of the valley before they could drink a drop of water. Later on, the Prophet, along with his Companions, overtook me. I addressed him saying: Messenger of Allâh let me select from our people one hundred men and I will follow the marauders and finish them. In reply, the Prophet said: "Ibn Al-Akwa', you have taken enough and so now you have to show magnanimity; now they have reached the habitation of Ghatfan where they are being feted." He added saying: "Our best horseman today is Abu Qatadah, and our best footman today is Salamah." He allotted me two shares of the booty - the share meant for the horseman and the other meant for the footman, and combined both of them for me. Intending to return to Madinah, he made me mount behind him on his she-camel called Al-'Adba'.

CONQUEST OF KHAIBAR (IN MOHARRAM, 7A.H.)

Khaibar was a spacious strongly fortified territory, studded with castles and farms, lying at a distance of 60-80 miles north of Madinah, now a village known for its uncongenial climate. After Al-Hudaibiyah Treaty, the major party of the anti-Islam tripartite coalition -Quraish, the bedouin horde of Najd tribes and the Jews-was neutralized, therefore, the Prophet deemed it an appropriate time to settle his affairs with the other two wings-the Jews and the Najd tribes-in order that peace and security could prevail and the Muslims may devote their time and effort in propagating the Message of Allâh and calling people to embrace it. Khaibar itself had always remained a hotbed of intrigue and conspiracy, and the Jews had always constituted it a source of military provocations and war instigation centre, so it was given a top priority on the agenda of the Prophet's compelling exigencies.

The Jews of Khaibar had united by an ancient alliance with the Confederates, triggered Bani Quraiza to practise treachery, maintained contacts with Ghatfan and the Arabians and they even devised an attempt at the Prophet's life. In fact, the continual afflictions that the Muslims had sustained were primarily attributable to the Jews. Envoys were repeatedly sent to them for peaceful settlement, but all in vain. Consequently the Prophet came to the conclusion that a military campaign was a must in order to forestall their hostilities.

Interpreters of the Noble *Quran* suggest that capturing Khaibar had been a Divine promise implied in Allâh's Words:

> "Allâh has promised you abundant spoils that you will capture, and He has hastened for you this." [Al-Quran 48:20] i.e., Al-Hudaibiyah Peace Treaty and the surrender of Khaibar.

The hypocrites and people weak of heart had hung back from joining the true Muslims in Al-Hudaibiyah campaigns, so now Allâh, the All-Mighty inculcated the following words in His Prophet's ears:

> "Those who lagged behind will say, when you set forth to take the spoils, 'Allow us to follow you.' They want to change Allâh's Words. Say: 'You shall not follow us; thus Allâh has said beforehand.' Then they will say: 'Nay, you envy us.' Nay, but they understand not except a little." [Al-Qur'an 48:15]

For this reason, the Prophet invited only those who were willing to fight in the cause of Allâh to accompany him in his march against Khaibar and 1400 men only, who had sworn allegiance in response to his call.

Meanwhile, Siba'bin 'Arfatah Al-Ghifari was chosen to run the affairs of Madinah. Another incident of high significance is noteworthy, namely the Islamization of Abu Huraira, a venerable Muslim scholar and an authentic narrator of the Prophetic traditions. The hypocrites of Arabia took notice of the fresh Islamic intentions so they began to alert the Jews to the imminent military activities. Their chief, 'Abdullah bin Ubai delegated an envoy to the Jews of Khaibar warning them against the dangers approaching, and nerving them to resist the Muslims as they outnumbered the latter and were better equipped. On hearing the news the Jews despatched Kinanah bin Abi Al-Huqaiq and Haudha bin Qais to their former allies, the tribe of Ghatfan requesting military assistance, promising to grant them half the yield of the fruit that their farms could yield if they managed to beat the Muslims.

The Prophet marched by way of Isra Mountain and then went forward with the army till he halted in a valley called Ar-Raji', encamping between Khaibar and Ghatfan so as to prevent the latter from reinforcing the Jews. The guides accompanying him led him to an intersection from which branched out three roads with different designations; all leading to his destination. He abstained from following the first two roads on grounds of their ominous designation and chose the third for its propitious indications.

It is noteworthy that some interesting incidents featured the Muslims' march towards Khaibar; of which we mention the following:

1. It has been narrated on the authority of Salamah bin Al-Akwa', who said: We marched upon Khaibar with the Messenger of Allâh. We journeyed during the night. One of the men said to my brother 'Amir: Won't you recite to us some of your verses, 'Amir? So he began to chant his verses to urge the camels, reciting:

O Allâh, if You had not guided us,

We would have neither been guided rightly nor practised charity, nor offered prayers.

We wish to lay down our lives for You; so forgive You our lapses,

And keep us steadfast when we encounter (our enemies).

Bestow upon us peace and tranquility,

Behold, when with a cry they called upon us to help.

The Messenger of Allâh said: "Who is this driver (of the camels)?" They said: "It is 'Amir." He said: "Allâh will show mercy to him." A man said: "Martyrdom is reserved for him; O Messenger of Allâh would that you had allowed us to benefit ourselves from his life."[Sahih Al-Bukhari 2/603; Sahih Muslim 2/115] The Prophet's Companions had already known that he would never invoke Allâh's mercy upon a close Companion but to single him out for martyrdom. [Sahih Muslim 2/115]

2. On their way down a valley, the Muslims began to entertain Allâh's Greatness: shouting at the top of their voices: "Allâh is Great, Allâh is Great, and there is no god but Allâh." The Prophet asked them to lower down their voices saying: "The One you are invoking is neither absent nor deaf; He is close to you, All-hearing.[Sahih Al-Bukhari 2/605]"
3. In a spot called As-Sahba', not far from Khaibar, the Prophet observed the afternoon prayer, and then he called his Companions to have whatever food provisions they had. What they brought was too scanty to satisfy them all. The Prophet took it by his hand and it immediately grew in quantity, so they all ate to their fill. Shortly afterward, he and the others rinsed their mouths and performed the evening prayer without ablution [Sahih Al-Bukhari 2/603]; he did the same for the night prayer [Maghazi Al-Waqidi p.112].

The following morning, at sunrise, the Muslims encountered the Jews when they had come out about their jobs with their axes, spades and strings driving their cattle along. They began to shout in surprise: "Muhammad has come along with his force!" The Messenger of Allâh said: "Allâh is Great, Khaibar shall face destruction. Behold! When we descend in the city centre, it will be a bad day for those who have been warned (but have not taken heed). [Sahih Al-Bukhari 2/603, 604]"

For encampment, the Prophet had chosen a certain plot of land he deemed suitable to serve as the headquarters of his army. However, a veteran fighter of his called Hubab bin Al-Mundhir suggested that they, under the exigencies of war requirements and for the sake of providing maximum logistic facilities, shift to another place. On approaching the vicinity of Khaibar, the Prophet ordered his troops to halt, and began to invoke his Lord saying: "O Allâh! Lord of the seven heavens and what they harbour beneath, Lord of the seven earths and what lies in their wombs, Lord of devils and whomsoever they have led astray; we beseech You to grant us the good of this village (Khaibar), the good of its inhabitants and the good that lies in it. We seek refuge with You from the evil of this village, the evil of its inhabitants, and the evil that lies in it." Then he ordered, "Now march (towards the village) in the Name of Allâh." [Ibn Hisham 2/329]

"The banner", the Prophet declared "would be entrusted to a man who loves Allâh and His Messenger and they (Allâh and His Messenger) love him." All the Muslims came forward in the following morning hoping to be granted the honour of carrying the banner. The Prophet called for 'Ali bin Abi Talib whose eyes used to hurt, and handed it to him. 'Ali, on his part, pledged he would fight the enemies until they embraced Islam. The Prophet answered him saying: "Take things easy and invite them to accept Islam and brief them on their duties towards Allâh. I swear by Allâh that if only one should be guided through your example that would surely outweigh the best of our camels." [Sahih Al-Bukhari 2/505, 606]

Khaibar, it seems, was split into two parts with five forts in the first: Na'im, As-Sa'b bin Mu'adh, the castle of Az-Zubair, 'Abi Castle, and An-Nizar in Ash-Shiqq; three others were in part two: Al-Qamus, Al-Wateeh and As-Salalim.

THE ACTUAL OPERATION BEGINS

The Prophet began the campaign by reducing the minor strongholds one after the other. The first fort he was to attack was Na'im, the first defence line with a formidable strategic position. Marhab, the leader of the fort, invited 'Amr bin Al-Akwa' to meet him in combat and the latter responded; when 'Amr struck the Jew, his sword recoiled and wounded his knee, and he died of that wound. The Prophet later said:

"For him ('Amir) there is a double reward in the Hereafter."

He indicated this by putting two of his fingers together. 'Ali bin Abi Talib then undertook to meet Marhab in combat, and managed to kill him. Yasir, Marhab's brother, then turned up challenging the Muslims to a fight. Az-Zubair was equal to it and killed him on the spot. Real fighting then broke out and lasted for a few days. The Jews showed courage and proved to be too formidable even to the repeated rushes of the veteran soldiers of Islam. However, they later realized the futility of resistance and began to abandon their positions in An-Na'im and infiltrate into the fortress of As-Sa'b.

Al-Hubab bin Al-Mundhir Al-Ansari led the attack on As-Sa'b fortress and laid siege to it for three days after which the Muslims stormed it with a lot of booty, provisions and food to fall to their lot therein. This victory came in the wake of the Prophet's invocation to Allâh to help Banu Aslam in their relentless and daring attempts to capture that fort. During the process of the war operations, extreme hunger struck the Muslims. They lit fires, slaughtered domestic asses and began to cook them and when the Prophet inquired about the fires and cooking, he ordered that they throw away the meat and wash the cooking pots, forbidding the practice of eating such meat.

The Jews, meanwhile, evacuated An-Natat and barricaded themselves in Az-Zubair fort, a formidable defensive position inaccessible to both cavalry and infantry. The Muslims besieged it for three days, but in vain. A Jew spy told the Prophet about a subterranean water source that provided them with water, and advised that it be cut off in order to undermine their resistance. The Prophet did that so the Jews got out to engage with the Muslims in fierce fighting during which some Muslims and ten Jews were killed, but the fort was eventually conquered.

Shortly after this battle, the Jews moved to 'Abi Castle and barricaded themselves inside. The same events recurred; the Muslims besieged the new site for three days and then the great Muslim hero Abu Dujanah Sammak bin Kharshah Al-Ansari-of the red ribbon-led the Muslim army and broke into the castle, conducted fierce military operations within and forced the remaining Jews to flee for their lives into another fort, An-Nizar.

An-Nizar was the most powerful fort, and the Jews came to the established conviction that it was too immune to be stormed, so they deemed it a safe place for their children and women. The Muslims, however, were not dismayed but dragged on the siege, but because standing at a commanding top, the fort was impregnable. The Jews inside were too cowardly to meet the Muslims in open fight but rather hurled a shower of arrows and stones on the attackers. Considering this situation, the Prophet ordered that rams be used and these proved effective and caused cracks in the ramparts providing an easy access into the heart of the fort, where the Jews were put to rout and fled in all directions leaving behind their women and children. With these series of military victories, the first division of Khaibar was totally reduced, and the Jews in the other minor fortresses evacuated them and fled to the second division.

THE SECOND PART OF KHAIBAR CONQUERED

When the Prophet, along with his army, moved to this part of Khaibar, Al-Katiba, he laid a heavy siege to it for fourteen days with the Jews barricading themselves inside their forts. When he was about to use the rams, the Jews realized that they would perish, therefore, they asked for a negotiable peace treaty. There is one controversial point in this context. Was this part of Khaibar (with its three forts) conquered by force? Ibn Ishaq clearly stated that Al-Qamus fort was conquered by force. Al-Waqidi, on the other hand, maintained that the three forts were taken through peace negotiations, and force, if any, was resorted to only to hand the fort over to the Muslims; the two other forts surrendered without fighting.

NEGOTIATIONS

Ibn Abi Al-Huqaiq was despatched to the Messenger of Allâh to negotiate the surrender treaty. The Prophet agreed to spare their lives on condition they evacuate Khaibar and the adjacent land, leaving whatever gold and silver they had in their possession. However, he stipulated that he would disavow any commitment if they concealed anything. Shortly afterwards, the forts were handed over to the Muslims and all Khaibar was reduced and brought under the sway of Islam.

This treaty notwithstanding, Abi Al-Huqaiq's two sons concealed a leather bag full of jewels, and money belonging to Huyai bin Al-Akhtab, who carried it with him when Banu Nadir had been banished. Kinanah bin Ar-Rabi', who had hidden the musk somewhere, was obdurate in his denial and so he was killed when the musk was discovered and his dishonesty was proven. Abi Al-Huqaiq's two sons were killed in recompense for breaching the covenant, and Safiyah, Huyai's daughter was taken as a captive.

DISTRIBUTION OF SPOILS

In accordance with the agreement already concluded, the Jews would be obliged to evacuate Khaibar, but they were anxious to keep on cultivating the rich soil and fine orchard for which Khaibar was famous. They, therefore, approached the Prophet with the request that they be allowed to cultivate their lands and they would give half of the produce to the Muslims. Muhammad was kind enough to accede to their request.

The Messenger divided the land of Khaibar into two: one half to provide the food to be stored in case of any accidental calamity that might befall the Muslims, and for entertaining the foreign delegates who started to frequent Madinah a lot; the other half would go to the Muslims who had witnessed Al-Hudaibiyah event whether present or absent. The total number of shares came to 36, of which 18 were given to the people above-mentioned. The army consisted of 1400 men of whom were 200 horsemen. The horseman was allotted 3 shares and the footman one. [Za'd Al-Ma'ad 2/137, 138]

The spoils taken at Khaibar were so great that Ibn 'Umar said: "We never ate our fill until we had conquered Khaibar." 'Aishah [R] is narrated to have said: "Now we can eat our fill of dates." [Sahih Al-Bukhari 2/609]

On their return to Madinah, the Emigrants were able to return to the Helpers of Madinah all the gifts they had received. All of this affluence came after the conquest of Khaibar and the great economic benefits that the Muslims began to reap. [Za'd Al-Ma'ad 2/148; Sahih Muslim 2/96]

The conquest of Khaibar coincided with the arrival of the Prophet's cousin Ja'far bin Abi Talib and his companions along with Abi Musa Al-Ash'ari and some Muslims from Abyssinia (Ethiopia).

Abu Musa Al-Ash'ari narrated that he and over fifty companions, while in Yemen, took a ship which landed them in Abyssinia (Ethiopia) and they happened to meet there Ja'far and his companions. He said, "We stayed together until the Prophet sent an envoy asking us to come back. When we returned, we found out that he had already conquered Khaibar, yet he gave us our due shares of the spoils." The advent of those men came at the request made by the Messenger of Allâh to Negus, king of Abyssinia (Ethiopia), through a Prophetic deputy, 'Amr bin Omaiya Ad-Damari. Negus sent them back, 16 men altogether with their wives and children on two boats. The rest of emigrants had arrived in Madinah earlier. [Muhadarat Tareekh Al-Umam Al-Islamiyah 1/128]

In the same context, Safiyah, whose husband Kinanah bin Abi Al-Huqaiq was killed for treachery, was taken as a captive and brought along with other prisoners of war. After the permission of the Prophet was sought, Dihyah Al-Kalbi chose one of them and she happened to be Safiyah. The other Muslims, however, advised that Safiyah, being the daughter of the chief of Bani Quraiza and Bani Nadir, should be married to the Prophet, who agreed to their opinion, invited her to Islam, freed and took her as wife on her embracing Islam. The wedding feast consisted of dates and fat, and was held on his way back to Madinah at a spot called Sadd As-Sahba'.

After the conquest of Khaibar, a Jewish woman called Zainab bint Al-Harith offered the Prophet a roasted sheep she had poisoned. He took a mouthful, but it was not to his liking so he spat it out. After investigation, the woman confessed that she had stuffed the food with poison alleging that if the eater were a king, she would then rid herself of him, but should he be a Prophet, then he would be bound to learn about it. The Prophet, however, connived at her treacherous attempt, but ordered that she be killed when Bishr bin Al-Bara' died of that poison.

The number of Muslims who were martyred was controversial, but it ranged between 16 and 18, while the number of Jews killed came to 93. The rest of Khaibar also fell to the Muslims. Allâh cast fear into the hearts of the people of Fadak, a village standing to the north of Khaibar, and they hastened to ask for peace, and be allowed to leave in safety, and give up their wealth in return for that. The Prophet en-tered into an agreement with them similar to the previous one with the people of Khaibar. Fadak was exclusively the Prophet's because neither Muslim cavalry nor camelry were involved in fight thereby.

No sooner had the Prophet discharged the affair of Khaibar than he started a fresh move towards Wadi Al-Qura, another Jewish colony in Arabia. He mobilized his forces and divided them into three regiments with four banners entrusted to Sa'd bin 'Ubada, Al-Hubab bin Mundhir, 'Abbad bin Bishr and Sahl bin Haneef. Prior to fighting, he invited the Jews to embrace Islam but all his words and exhortations fell on deaf ears. Eleven of the Jews were killed one after another and with each one newly killed; a fresh call was extended inviting those people to profess the new faith. Fighting went on ceaselessly for approximately two days and resulted in full surrender of the Jews. Their land was conquered, and a lot of booty fell in the hands of the Muslims.

The Prophet stayed in Wadi Al-Qura for four days, distributed the booty among the Muslim fighters and reached an agreement with the Jews similar to that of Khaibar. [Za'd Al-Ma'ad 2/146, 147]

The Jews of Taima', hearing beforehand about the successive victories of the Muslim army and the defeats that their brethren, the Jews, had sustained, showed no resistance when the Prophet reached their habitation. On the contrary, they took the initiative and offered to sign a reconciliation treaty to the effect that they receive protection but pay tribute in return. Having achieved his objective and subdued the Jews completely, the Prophet made his way back home and arrived in Madinah in late Safar or early Rabi' Al-Awwal 7 A.H.

It is noteworthy that the Prophet, being the best amongst war experts, realized quite readily that evacuating Madinah after the lapse of the prohibited months (Muharram, Dhul Qa'da and Dhul Hijja) would not be wise at all with the presence of the desert bedouins roaming in its vicinity. Such a careless attitude, the Prophet believed, would tempt the undisciplined mob to practise their favourite hobby of plundering, looting and all acts of piracy. This premonition always in mind, the Prophet despatched Aban bin Sa'id at the head of a platoon to deter those bedouins and forestall any attempt at raiding the headquarters of the nascent Islamic state during his absence in Khaibar. Aban achieved his task successfully and joined the Prophet in Khaibar after it had been conquered.

THE EXPEDITION OF DHAT-UR-RIQA

Having subdued two powerful sides of the Confederates coalition, the Prophet started preparations to discipline the third party, i.e. the desert bedouins, who took Najd for habitation, and continued in their usual practices of looting and plundering. Unlike the Jews of Khaibar and people of Makkah, they had a liking for living in the wilderness dispersed in scattered spots, hence the difficulty of bringing them under control, and the futility of carrying out deterrent campaigns against them. However, the Prophet was determined to put an end to this unacceptable situation and called the Muslims around him to get ready to launch a decisive campaign against those harassing rebels.

Meanwhile it was reported to him that Bani Muharib and Banu Tha'lbah of the Ghatfan tribe were gathering army in order to encounter the Muslims. The Prophet proceeded towards Najd at the head of 400 or 700 men, after he had mandated Abu Dhar - in another version, 'Uthman bin 'Affan - to dispose the affairs of Madinah during his absence. The Muslim fighters penetrated deep into their land until they reached a spot called Nakhlah where they came across some bedouins of Ghatfan, but no fighting took place because the latter had agreed to go into reconciliation with the Muslims. The Prophet led his followers that day in a prayer of fear.

Al-Bukhari, on the authority of Abu Musa Al-Ash'ari, narrated that they set out on an expedition with the Messenger of Allâh. "We were six in number and had (with us) only one camel which we rode turn by turn. Our feet were injured. My feet were so badly injured that my nails came off. We, therefore, bandaged our feet with rags, so this expedition was called *Dhat-ur-Riqa'*(i.e. the expedition of rags.)" [Sahih Al-Bukhari 2/592; Sahih Muslim 2/118]

Jabir narrated: In the course of *Dhat-ur-Riqa'*expedition, we came to a leafy tree where the Prophet sat shading himself off the burning sun. The others dispersed here and there seeking shelter from heat. The Prophet had a short nap after he had hung his sword on the tree. A polytheist, meanwhile came, seized the sword and unsheathed it.

The Prophet woke up to find his sword drawn in the man's hand. The bedouin here asked the Prophet (unarmed then): "Who would hold me back from killing you now?" The Prophet then answered: "It is Allâh." In another version, it was reported that the Prophet took the sword when it had fallen down and the man said: "You (the Prophet) are the best one to hold a sword." The Prophet asked the man if he would testify to the Oneness of Allâh and the Messengership of Muhammad. The Arabian answered that he would never engage in a fight against him, nor would he ally people fighting the Muslims. The Prophet set the man free and let him go to his people to say to them that he had seen the best one among all people. [Mukhtasar Seerat Ar-Rasool p.264; Fath Al-Bari 7/416]

A woman from the Arabians was taken prisoner in the context of this battle. Her husband, on hearing the news, swore he would never stop until he had shed the blood of a Muslim. Secretly at night, he approached the camp of the Muslims when he saw two sentries stationed there to alert the Muslims against any emergency. He shot the first one, Abbad bin Bishr, who was observing prayer, with an arrow but he did not stop prayer, he simply pulled it out. Then he was shot by three other arrows but would not interrupt his prayer. After he had done the closing salutations, he awakened his companion 'Ammar bin Yasir, who remons-trated that he should have alerted him to which the latter replied that he was half way through a Chapter and did not like to interrupt it. [Za'd Al-Ma'ad 2/112; Ibn Hisham 2/203-209]

The victory at the expedition of *Dhat-ur-Riqa'*had a tremendous impact on all the Arabians. It cast fear into their hearts and rendered them too powerless to antagonize the Muslim society in Madinah. They began to acquiesce in the prevailing situation and resigned themselves to new geo-political conditions working in favour of the new religion. Some of them even embraced Islam and took an active part in the conquest of Makkah and the battle of Hunain, and received their due shares of the war booty.

From that time onward, the anti-Islam tripartite coalition had been subdued, and peace and security prevailed. The Muslims, then started to redress any political imbalance and fill in the small gaps that still triggered unrest here and there in the face of the great drive of Islamization that enveloped the whole area. We could in this context mention some of these incidental skirmishes which pointed markedly to the ever-growing power of the Muslim society.

1. A platoon headed by Ghalib bin 'Abdullah Al-Laithi in Safar or in Rabi'Al-Awwal 7 A.H. was despatched to muffle the provocative behaviour of Bani Al-Muluh. The Muslims managed to kill a large number of the enemy soldiers and captured a great deal of booty. A large army of polytheists rushed in their heel but floods hindered the pursuit, and the Muslims managed to withdraw in safety.
2. 'Umar bin Al-Khattab, at the head of a 30-soldier group, set out to a spot called Turbah in Sha'ban 7 A.H. to discipline the people of Hawazin. He no longer arrived at their habitation that they fled for their lives.
3. Thirty men with Basheer bin Sa'd Al-Ansari headed for Bani Murrah in Sha'ban 7 A.H. in Fadak area. He killed a large number of the enemy and seized a lot of their camels and cattle. On his way back, the enemy gathered up forces and overtook the Muslims at night. They showered Basheer and his men with arrows, and killed all the Muslims except Basheer, who took refuge in Fadak and stayed with the Jews there until his wounds healed.
4. Ghalib bin 'Abdullah Al-Laithi at the head of a platoon of 130 men launched an attack against Bani 'Awâl and Bani 'Abd bin Tha'lbah in Ramadan 7 A.H. They killed some of the enemy's men and captured their cattle and camels. 'Usama bin Zaid killed Mardas bin Nahik, a polytheist, but after he had pronounced the testimony of Allâh's Oneness to which incident the Prophet commented addressing his Companions: "Would you rip open his heart to discern whether he is truthful or a liar?"
5. A thirty-horseman group headed by 'Abdullah bin Rawaha marched towards Khaibar on reports that Aseer (or Basheer bin Razam) was rallying the ranks of Bani Ghatfan to attack the Muslims: They managed to persuade that Jew to follow them to Madinah encouraging him that the Prophet would institute him as a ruler of Khaibar. On their way back occurred a sort of misunderstanding that gave rise to fierce fighting between the two parties resulting in the death of Aseer and the

thirty men with him.

6. In Shawwal 7 A.H., Basheer bin Sa'd Al-Ansari marched towards Yemen and Jabar at the head of 300 Muslim fighters to subdue a large mob of polytheists who gathered to raid the outskirts of Madinah. Basheer and his men used to march at night and lurk during the day until they reached their destination. Having heard about the advent of the Muslims, the polytheists fled away leaving behind them a large booty and two men who later embraced Islam on arrival in Madinah.
7. In the year 7 A.H., shortly before the Compensatory *'Umrah* (lesser pilgrimage), a man called Jashm bin Mu'awiyah came to a spot called Ghabah where he wanted to gather the people of Qais and entice them into fighting the Muslims. The Prophet, on hearing these reports, despatched Abu Hadrad with two men to see to the situation. Abu Hadrad, through a clever strategy, managed to rout the enemy and capture a lot of their cattle. [Za'd Al-Ma'ad 2/149, 150; Rahmat-ul-lil'alameen 2/229, 230; Mukhtasar Seerat Ar-Rasool p.322-324]

COMPENSATORY 'UMRAH (LESSER PILGRIMAGE)

When Dhul Qa'da month approached towards the close of the seventh year A.H., the Prophet ordered his people, and the men who witnessed Al-Hudaibiyah Truce Treaty in particular, to make preparations to perform *'Umrah* (lesser pilgrimage). He proceeded with 2000 men besides some women and children [Fath Al-Bari 7/700], and 60 camels for sacrifice, to visit the Holy Sanctuary in Makkah. The Muslims took their weapons with them fearing the treachery of the Quraishites, but left them with a party of two hundred men at a place some eight miles from Makkah.

They entered the city with the swords in their scabbards [Za'd Al-Ma'ad 2/151; Fath Al-Bari 7/700], with the Prophet at their head on his she-camel, Al-Qaswa', while the surrounding Companions attentively focusing their look on him, all saying: "Here I am! at Your service O Allâh!" The Quraishites had left the place and retired to their tents on the adjoining hills. The Muslims performed the usual circumambulation vigorously and briskly; and on recommendation by the Prophet they did their best to appear strong and steadfast in their circumambulation as the polytheists had spread rumours that they were weak because the fever of Yathrib (Madinah) had sapped their strength. They were ordered to run in the first three rounds and then walk in the remaining ones.

The Makkans meanwhile aligned on the top of Qu'aiqa'an Mount watching the Muslims, tongue-tied at witnessing their strength and devotion. When they entered the Holy Sanctuary, 'Abdullah bin Rawaha walked before the Prophet reciting:

"Get out of his way, you disbelievers, makes way, we will fight you about its revelation with strokes that will remove heads from shoulders and make friend unmindful of friend."

After ritual walking and running between the two hills of Makkah, Safa and Marwah, the Prophet with the Muslims halted at the latter spot to slaughter the sacrificial animals and shave their heads. The main body of the pilgrims had now performed the basic rites of the lesser pilgrimage, but there remained those who were entrusted the charge of the weapons. The Prophet had these relieved, and they went through the same devotions as the others did. On the morning of the fourth day of the pilgrimage, the notables of Quraish asked 'Ali bin Abi Talib to tell the Prophet to leave Makkah along with his Companions. He, of course, could not conceive of violating the terms of Al-Hudaibiyah Treaty, therefore he ordered his men to depart for a village called Sarif where he stayed for some time.

It was during this visit of the Prophet to Makkah for pilgrimage that his uncle 'Abbas offered the hand of his sister-in-law, Maimuna-the daughter of Harith, to him. The Prophet was kind enough to accept this offer since it was an effective step towards cementing the ties of relationship between the Prophet and the influential men of Makkah. The wedding took place in Sarif. [Za'd Al-Ma'ad 2/152] Narrators attached different designations to this lesser pilgrimage. Some called it the compensatory lesser pilgrimage, performed instead of that uncompleted of Hudaibiyah; and the other one, given preponderance by jurists, is the lesser pilgrimage consequent on certain terms of a treaty already agreed upon.

On the whole, compensatory, judicial consent, retribution and reconciliation are all terms applicable to that visit. Some military operations, directed against some still obdurate desert Arabians, took place at the conclusion of the lesser pilgrimage, of which we could mention:

1. A platoon of 50 men led by Ibn Abi Al-'Awja' was despatched by the Prophet to the habitations of Bani Saleem inviting them to embrace Islam, but all the words fell on deaf ears. Fierce fighting erupted between both parties during which the Muslim leader was wounded, and two of the enemy were captured.
2. Ghalib bin 'Abdullah at the head of 200 men was despatched to Fadak where they killed some rebels and a lot of booty fell to their lot.
3. Banu Quda'a had gathered a large number of men to raid the Muslim positions. On hearing the news, the Prophet despatched Ka'b bin 'Umair Al-Ansari at the head of 15 men to deal with this situation. They encountered the army, and called them to enter into the fold of Islam but the rebels gave a negative response and showered the Muslims with arrows killing all of them except one who was carried back home later seriously wounded. [Rahmat-ul-lil'alameen 2/231]

There was also an insignificant skirmish that occurred in Rabi' Al-Awwal 8 A.H. Shuja' bin Wahab Al-Asadi, along with 25 men, marched towards Bani Hawazin tribe where they encountered no resistance but managed to gain some booty. [Talqeeh Fuhoom Ahl Al-Athar p.33; Rahmat-ul-lil'alameen 2/231]

THE BATTLE OF MU'TAH

It was the most significant and the fiercest battle during the lifetime of the Messenger of Allâh, a preliminary and a prelude to the great conquests of the land of the Christians. It took place in Jumada Al-Ula 8 A.H. / September 629 A.D. Mu'tah is a village that lies on the borders of geographical Syria. The Prophet had sent Al-Harith bin 'Umair Al-Azdi on an errand to carry a letter to the ruler of Busra. On his way, he was intercepted by Sharhabeel bin 'Amr Al-Ghassani, the governor of Al-Balqa' and a close ally to Caesar, the Byzantine Emperor. Al-Harith was tied and beheaded by Al-Ghassani.

Killing envoys and messengers used to be regarded as the most awful crime, and amounted to the degree of war declaration. The Prophet was shocked on hearing the news and ordered that a large army of 3000 men be mobilized and despatched to the north to discipline the transgressors. [Za'd Al-Ma'ad 2/155; Fath Al-Bari 7/511] It was the largest Muslim army never mobilized on this scale except in the process of the Confederates Battle. Zaid bin Haritha was appointed to lead the army. Ja'far bin Abi Talib would replace him if he was killed, and 'Abdullah bin Rawaha would succeed Ja'far in case the latter fell.[Sahih Al-Bukhari 2/611] A white banner was raised and handed over to Zaid. [Mukhtasar Seerat Ar-Rasool p.327]

The Prophet recommended that they reach the scene of Al-Harith's murder and invite the people to profess Islam. Should the latter respond positively, then no war would ensue, otherwise fighting them would be the only alternative left.

He ordered them:

> "Fight the disbelievers in the Name of Allâh, neither breaches a covenant nor entertain treachery, and under no circumstances a new-born, woman, an ageing man or a hermit should be killed; moreover neither trees should be cut down nor homes demolished. [Mukhtasar Seerat Ar-Rasool p.327; Rahmat-ul-lil'alameen 2/271]"

At the conclusion of the military preparations, the people of Madinah gathered and bade the army farewell. 'Abdullah bin Rawaha began to weep at that moment, and when asked why he was weeping, he swore that it was not love for this world nor under a motive of infatuation with the glamour of life but rather the Words of Allâh speaking of Fire that he heard the Prophet reciting:

> "There is not one of you but will pass over it (Hell); this is with your Lord, a Decree which must be accomplished." [Al-Qur'an 19:71]

The Muslim army then marched northward to Ma'ân, a town bordering on geographical Syria. There news came to the effect that Heraclius had mobilized a hundred thousand troops together with another hundred thousand men of Lakham, Judham and Balqain-Arabian tribes allied to the Byzantines. The Muslims, on their part had never thought of encountering such a huge army.

They were at a loss about what course to follow, and spent two nights debating these unfavourable conditions. Some suggested that they should write a letter to the Prophet seeking his advice. 'Abdullah bin Rawaha was opposed to them being reluctant and addressed the Muslims saying: "I swear by Allâh that this very object which you hold in abhorrence is the very one you have set out seeking, martyrdom. In our fight we don't count on number of soldiers or equipment but rather on the Faith that Allâh has honoured us with. Dart to win either of the two, victory or martyrdom." In the light of these words, they moved to engage with the enemy in Masharif, a town of Al-Balqa', and then changed direction towards Mu'tah where they encamped. The right flank was led by Qutba bin Qatadah Al-'Udhari, and the left by 'Ubadah bin Malik Al-Ansari. Bitter fighting started between the two parties, three thousand Muslims against an enemy fiftyfold as large.

Zaid bin Haritha, the closest to the Messenger's heart, assumed leadership and began to fight tenaciously and in matchless spirit of bravery until he fell, fatally stabbed. Ja'far bin Abi Talib then took the banner and did a miraculous job. In the thick of the battle, he dismounted, hamstrung his horse and resumed fighting until his right hand was cut off. He seized the banner with his left hand until this too was gone. He then clasped the banner with both arms until a Byzantine soldier struck and cut him into two parts. he was posthumously called "the flying Ja'far" or "Ja'far with two wings" because Allâh has awarded him two wings to fly wherever he desired there in the eternal Garden. Al-Bukhari reported fifty stabs in his body, none of them in the back. [Sahih Al-Bukhari 2/611]

'Abdullah bin Rawaha then proceeded to hold up the banner and fight bravely on his horseback while reciting enthusiastic verses until he too was killed. Thereupon a man, from Bani 'Ajlan, called Thabit bin Al-Arqam took the banner and called upon the Muslims to choose a leader. The honour was unanimously granted to Khalid bin Al-Waleed, a skilled brave fighter and an outstanding strategist. It was reported by Al-Bukhari that he used nine swords that broke while he was relentlessly and courageously fighting the enemies of Islam. He, however, realizing the grave situation the Muslims were in, began to follow a different course of encounter, revealing the super strategy-maker, that Khalid was rightly called. He reshuffled the right and left flanks of the Muslim army and introduced forward a division from the rear in order to cast fear into the hearts of the Byzantine by deluding them that fresh reinforcements had arrived. The Muslims engaged with the enemies in sporadic skirmishes but gradually and judiciously retreating in a fully organized and well-planned withdrawal.

The Byzantines, seeing this new strategy, believed that they were being entrapped and drawn in the heart of the desert. They stopped the pursuit, and consequently the Muslims managed to retreat back to Madinah with the slightest losses. [Fath-Al-Bari 7/513, 514; Za'd Al-Ma'ad 2/156]

The Muslims sustained twelve martyrs, whereas the number of casualties among the Byzantines was unknown although the details of the battle point clearly to a large number. Even though the battle did not satisfy the Muslims' objective, namely avenging Al-Harith's murder, it resulted in a far-ranging impact and attached to the Muslims a great reputation in the battlefields. The Byzantine Empire, at that time, was a power to be reckoned with, and mere thinking of antagonizing it used to mean self-annihilation, let alone a three-thousand-soldier army going into fight against 200,000 soldiers far better equipped and lavishly furnished with all luxurious conveniences. The battle was a real miracle proving that the Muslims were something exceptional not then familiar.

Moreover, it gave evidence that Allâh backed them and their Prophet, Muhammad, was really Allâh's Messenger. In the light of these new strategic changes, the archenemies among the desert bedouins began to reconcile themselves with the new uprising faith and several recalcitrant tribes like Banu Saleem, Ashja', Ghatfan, Dhubyan, Fazarah and others came to profess Islam out of their own sweet free will. Mu'tah Battle, after all, constituted the forerunner of the blood encounter to take place with the Byzantines subsequently. It pointed markedly to a new epoch of the Islamic conquest of the Byzantine Empire and other remote countries, to follow at a later stage.

DHAT AS-SALASIL CAMPAIGN

Dhat As-Salasil is a spot situated ten days' walk north of Madinah. The Muslims are said to have encamped in a place with a well of water called Salsal, hence the terminology *Dhat As-Salasil.* In view of the alliance between the Arabian tribes on the borders of Syria and the Byzantines, the Prophet deemed it of top urgency to carry out a wisely-planned manoeuvre that might bring about a state of rapport with those bedouins, and would at the same time detach them from the Byzantines. For the implementation of this plan, he chose 'Amr bin Al-'As, whose paternal grandmother came from Bali, a tribe dwelling in that area. This motive in mind, combined with provocative military movements, by Bani Quda'a, precipitated this preemptive strike which started in Jumada Ath-Thaniya, 8 A.H.

'Amr bin Al-'As was awarded a white flag with a black banner to go with it. He set out at the head of 300 Emigrants and Helpers assisted by a cavalry of 30 men, and was recommended to seek help from Bali, 'Udhra and Balqain tribes. He used to march at night and lurk during the day. On approaching the enemy lines and realizing the large build up of men, he sent for reinforcements from Madinah, and these arrived on the spot headed by Abu 'Ubaidah bin Al-Jarrah leading further 200 men as well as other including Abu Bakr and 'Umar bin Al-Khattab. All of them were given strict orders to cooperate, work in harmony and never leave any area for disagreement.

At noon, Abu 'Ubaidah wanted to lead the Muslims in prayer but 'Amr objected on grounds that the former came only to assist and the leadership in prayer was given to 'Amr.

The Muslim army reached the habitations of Quda'a and penetrated deep in their land, destroyed the enemies and obliged the others to flee for their lives in different directions. At the conclusion of the military operations, a courier was despatched to the Messenger of Allâh to brief him on the developments of events and the ultimate victory achieved.

KHADRAH CAMPAIGN

In Sha'ban month 8 A.H., news reached the Prophet of amassing troops by Bani Ghatfan, still outside the domain of Islam. He urgently summoned Abu Qatadah and sent him at the head of fifteen men to discipline those outlaws. It took fifteen days to teach them an unforgettable lesson. Some were killed, others captured and all their property confiscated. [Rahmat-ul-lil'alameen 2/233; Talqeeh Fuhoom Ahl Al-Athar p.33] commanded to seek help from Bali, Udhra and Balqain tribes. He used to march at night and halt during the day. On approaching the enemy lines and realizing the large number of them, he sought reinforcement from Madinah and [illegible] arrived on the spot headed by Abu Ubaidah bin al-Jarrah leading further 200 men as well as [illegible] including Abu Bakr and Umar bin Al-Khattab. All of them were given strict orders to cooperate, work in harmony and never leave any room for disagreement.

[illegible] Abu Ubaidah wanted to lead the Muslims in prayer but Amr objected on grounds that the former came only to assist and the leadership in prayer [illegible] Amr.

The Muslim army reached the habitations of Quda'ah and penetrated deep in their land, defeated the enemies and obliged the others to flee [illegible]. At the conclusion of the military operations, a courier was despatched to the Messenger of Allah to brief him on the developments and the ultimate victory achieved.

KHADRAH CAMPAIGN

In Sha'ban 8 A.H. [illegible] the Prophet [illegible] by Bani Ghatafan [illegible] Islam. [illegible] fifteen men [illegible] the head of [illegible] to discipline those [illegible] fifteen days to teach them an unforgettable lesson [illegible] [Zad al-Ma'ad 2/389; Talqeeh [illegible] p.33]

3

The Conquest of Makkah

Ibn Al-Qaiyim described the conquest of Makkah as the greatest one by which Allâh honoured His religion, Messenger, soldiers and honest party. He thereby rescued the Sacred House, whose guidance all people seek. It was the greatest propitious event in heaven and on earth. It was the most significant prelude to a new era that was to witness the great march of Islamization and the entry of people into the fold of Islam in huge hosts. It provided an ever shining face and a most glowing source of inspiration to the whole earth. [Za'd Al-Ma'ad 2/160]

PRE-CONQUEST EVENTS

According to the terms of the treaty of Hudaibiyah, the Arab tribes were given the option to join either of the parties, the Muslims or Quraish, with which they desired to enter into treaty alliance. Should any of these tribes suffer aggression, then the party to which it was allied would have the right to retaliate. As a consequence, Banu Bakr joined Quraish, and Khuza'ah joined the Prophet. They thus lived in peace for sometime but ulterior motives stretching back to pre-Islamic period ignited by unabated fire of revenge triggered fresh hostilities.

Banu Bakr, without caring a bit for the provisions of the treaty, attacked Banu Khuza'ah in a place called Al-Wateer in Sha'ban, 8 A.H. Quraish helped Banu Bakr with men and arms taking advantage of the dark night. Pressed by their enemies, the tribesmen of Khuza'ah sought the Holy Sanctuary, but here too, their lives were not spared, and, contrary to all accepted traditions, Nawfal, the chief of Banu Bakr, chasing them in the sanctified area-where no blood should be shed-massacred his adversaries.

When the aggrieved party sought justice from their Muslim allies, the Prophet , as their leader, demanded an immediate redress for not only violating the treaty but also slaying men allied to him in the sanctified area. Three demands were made, the acceptance of any one of them was imperative:

a. To pay blood money for the victims of Khuza'ah,
b. To terminate their alliance with Banu Bakr; or
c. To consider the truce to have been nullified.

This behaviour on the part of Quraish was clearly a breach of the treaty of Al-Hudaibiyah and was obviously an act of hostility against the allies of the Muslims, i.e. Banu Khuza'ah. Quraish immediately realized the grave situation and feared the horrible consequences looming on the horizon. They immediately called for an emergency meeting and decided to delegate their chief Abu Sufyan to Madinah for a renewal of the truce. He directly headed for the house of his daughter Umm Habiba (the Prophet's wife). But as he went to sit on the Messenger's carpet, she folded it up. "My daughter," said he, "I hardly knew if you think the carpet is too good for me or that I am too good for the carpet." She replied, "It is the Messenger of Allâh's carpet, and you are an unclean polytheist."

Being disgusted at the curt reply of his daughter, Abu Sufyan stepped out of her room and went to see the Prophet, but the latter was well aware of his tricks and did not hold him any assurance. He then approached Abu Bakr, but the latter too declined to interfere. He contacted 'Umar to intercede but this great Companion made a point-blank refusal. At last he saw 'Ali bin Abi Talib and began begging him in the most humble words, cunningly alluding to the prospects of mastery over all the Arabs if he were to intercede for the renewal of the treaty. 'Ali also briefly regretted his inability to do anything for him.

Abu Sufyan turned his steps back to Makkah in a state of bitter disappointment and utter horror. There he submitted a report of his meeting with his daughter, Abu Bakr, 'Umar and 'Ali's reaction and the meaningful silence of the Prophet. The Makkans were dismayed, but did not expect imminent danger.

PREPARATIONS FOR THE ATTACK ON MAKKAH

On the authority of At-Tabari, the Messenger of Allâh asked 'Aishah [R], his spouse three days prior to receiving news relating to breaching of covenant, to make preparations peculiar to marching out for war. Abu Bakr, meanwhile, came in and asked 'Aishah [R] what the matter was, showing surprise at the preparations being made as it was not, as he said, the usual time for war. She replied that she had no idea. On the morning of the third day 'Amr bin Sâlim Al-Khuza'i arrived in the company of forty horsemen to brief the Prophet on the plight of his people and seeking the Muslims' help for retaliation. People of Madinah then got to know that Quraish had breached the covenant. Budail followed 'Amr, and then Abu Sufyan and the news was unequivocally confirmed.

With view of securing a complete news black-out concerning his military intentions, the Prophet despatched an eight-men platoon under the leadership of Qatadah bin Rab'i in the direction of Edam, a short distance from Madinah, in Ramadan 8 A.H., in order to divert the attention of people and screen off the main target with which he was preoccupied.

There was so much dread and fear everywhere that Hatib, one of the most trusted followers of the Prophet secretly despatched a female messenger with a letter to Makkah containing intimation of the intended attack. The Prophet received news from the heaven of Hatib's action and sent 'Ali and Al-Miqdad with instructions to go after her. They overtook the messenger, and after a long search discovered the letter carefully hidden in her locks.

The Prophet summoned Hatib and asked him what had induced him to this act. He replied, "O Messenger of Allâh! I have no affinity of blood with Quraish; there is only a kind of friendly relationship between them and myself. My family is at Makkah and there is no one to look after it or to offer protection to it. My position stands in striking contrast to that of the refugees whose families are secure due to their blood ties with Quraish. I felt that since I am not related to them, I should, for the safety of my children, earn their gratitude by doing well to them. I swear by Allâh that I have not done this act as an apostate, forsaking Islam. I was prompted only by the considerations I have just explained."

'Umar wanted to cut his head off as a hypocrite, but the Prophet accepted his excuse and granted him pardon, then addressed 'Umar saying: "Hatib is one of those who fought in the battle of Badr. How do you know that he is a hypocrite? Allâh is likely to look favourably on those who participated in that battle. Turning then, to Hatib, he said: "Do as you please, for I have forgiven you."

After making full preparation, the Prophet proceeded to Makkah at the head of ten thousand soldiers on the 10th of Ramadan, 8 A.H. He mandated Abu Ruhm Al-Ghifari to dispose the affairs of Madinah during his absence and when they reached Al-Juhfa, Al-'Abbas bin 'Abdul Muttalib and his family came to join the Prophet. At Al-Abwa', the Muslims came across Abu Sufyan bin Al-Harith and 'Abdullah bin Omaiyah, the Prophet's cousins, but, on account of the harm they had inflicted, and their satiric language, on the believers, they were not welcomed. 'Ali addressed Abu Sufyan to go and beseech the Prophet for pardon and confess his ill-behaviour in a manner similar to that of Yusuf's (the Prophet Joseph) brothers:

> "They said: 'By Allâh! Indeed Allâh has preferred you above us, and we certainly have been sinners.'" [Al-Qur'an 12:91]

Abu Sufyan observed 'Ali's counsel, to which the Prophet quoted Allâh's Words:

> "He said: 'No reproach on you this day, may Allâh forgive you, and He is the Most Merciful of those who show mercy!'" [Al-Qur'an 12:92]

Abu Sufyan recited some verses paying a generous tribute to the Prophet and professing Islam as his only religion.

The Muslims then marched on in a state of fasting until they reached a place called Al-Qadeed where water was available. There they broke fast [Sahih Al-Bukhari 2/613] and resumed their movement towards Mar Az-Zahran. The Quraishites were quite unaware of the development of affairs, but the Prophet did not like to take them by surprise. He, therefore, ordered his men to kindle fire on all sides for cooking purposes. The idea behind this was that Quraish should be afforded full opportunity to assess the situation in which they were pitchforked correctly, and should not endanger their lives by leaping blindly in the battlefield. 'Umar bin Al-Khattab was entrusted with the guard duty. In the meanwhile, Abu Sufyan along with Hakim bin Hizam and Budail bin Warqua', two terrible polytheists, went out to reconnoiter. Before they got near the camp, they met 'Abbas, the Prophet's uncle. He apprised Abu Sufyan of the situation and advised him to accept Islam and persuade his people to surrender before Muhammad; otherwise, his head would be struck off.

Under the prevailing compelling circumstances, Abu Sufyan went in the company of 'Abbas seeking the Prophet's audience. The Muslims were furious to see Abu Sufyan and wanted to kill him on the spot. But the two men managed, not without difficulties, to see the Messenger of Allâh who advised that they see him the following day. The Prophet addressed Abu Sufyan saying: "Woe to you! Isn't it time for you to bear witness to the Oneness of Allâh and Prophethood of Muhammad?" Here, the archenemy of Islam began to beseech the Prophet in the most earnest words that testify to the Prophet's generosity and mild temper begging for pardon and forgiveness, and professing wholeheartedly the new faith.

On request by 'Abbas, the Prophet , in the context of the general amnesty he proclaimed, gave Abu Sufyan, who had a liking for bragging, a special privilege, saying: "He who takes refuge in Abu Sufyan's house is safe; whosoever confines himself to his house, the inmates thereof shall be in safety, and he who enters the Sacred Mosque is safe."

On the morning of Tuesday, 17th Ramadan, 8 A.H., the Prophet left Mar Az-Zahran. He ordered Al-'Abbas to detain Abu Sufyan at a commanding gorge that could afford a full view of the Muslim army parading on its way towards Makkah, and hence give him the chance to see the great and powerful soldiers of Allâh. The different tribes successively passed with their banners flown up, until at last the battalion of the Emigrants and Helpers with the Prophet at their head heavily armed marched by. Abu Sufyan began to wonder who those people were, to which Al-'Abbas told him that they were Muhammad and his Companions.

Abu Sufyan said that no army however powerful could resist those people and addressing Al-'Abbas, he said: "I swear by Allâh that the sovereignty of your brother's son has become too powerful to withstand." Al-'Abbas answered, "It is rather the power of Prophethood," to which the former agreed. Sa'd bin 'Ubadah carried the flag of the Helpers. When he passed by Abu Sufyan, he said "Today will witness the great fight, you cannot seek sanctuary at Al-Ka'bah. Today will witness the humiliation of Quraish." Abu Sufyan complained about this to the Prophet who got angry and said "Nay, today Al-Ka'bah will be sanctified, and Quraish honoured," and quickly ordered that Sa'd should be stripped off the flag, and that it should be entrusted to his son Qais, in another version, to Az-Zubair.

Al-'Abbas urged Abu Sufyan to hasten into Makkah and warn the Quraishites against any aggressive behaviour towards the Muslims. There in Makkah, he shouted at the top of his voice and warned against any hostilities advising them to seek safety in his house. His wife got indignant and tugged at his moustache cursing him and abusing his cowardly stance.

The people within Makkah mocked Abu Sufyan and dispersed in different directions, some into their houses, others into the Holy Sanctuary while some undisciplined reckless ruffians led by 'Ikrimah bin Abi Jahl, Safwan bin Omaiyah and Suhail bin 'Amr encamped themselves in a place called Khandamah, with a murderous intent in their minds.

The Prophet, on his part, was quite modestly and calmly drawing the final touches for the military breakthrough awaiting the Muslims, by Allâh's Will. He appointed Khalid bin Al-Waleed as a leader of the right flank of the army with Aslam, Sulaim, Ghifar, Muzainah and Juhainah tribes under his command to enter Makkah through its lower avenues. Az-Zubair bin 'Awwam was to lead the left flank and would storm Makkah from the upper side holding up the Messenger's banner. Abu 'Ubaidah took command of the in-fantry and was to penetrate into the city via a side valley. They were given full and decisive orders not to kill unless in self defence and in that case they would exterminate any aggressive elements and quell any opposition.

The Muslim battalions marched out each in its already drawn route to fulfill the missions they were supposed to carry out. Khalid bin Al-Waleed worked his way into the heart of the town quite successively killing twelve of the ruffians and sustaining two martyrs. Az-Zubair set out and reached the fixed destination where he planted the banner at Al-Fath (conquest) Mosque and waited there for the arrival of the Prophet. A tent was pitched for him where he offered prayers of thanks to the All-Mighty Allâh, Who, out of His immense grace, had granted him a splendid victory. But he did not repose long. He, in the company of the Helpers and Emigrants, got up and proceeded towards Al-Ka'bah, the Sacred House, which is an emblem of the Oneness and Supremacy of Allâh. It was unfortunately infested with idols that numbered 360. He knocked them down with his bow while reciting the verse of the Noble *Quran*:

> "And Say: 'Truth (i.e. Islamic Monotheism or this *Quran* or *Jihâd* against polytheists) has come and *Batil* (falsehood, i.e. Satan or polytheism, etc.) has vanished. Surely! *Batil* is ever bound to vanish.'" [Al-Qur'an 17:81]

And Allâh further said:

> "Say (O Muhammad): "The Truth (the *Quran* and Allah's Inspiration) has come, and *Al-Batil* (falsehood - *Iblis*) can neither create anything nor resurrect (any thing)." [Al-Qur'an 34:49]

He then started the usual circumambulation on his ride. He was not in a state of *Ihram* (ritual consecration) then. On completion, he called for 'Uthman bin Talhah, the janitor of *Al-Ka'bah,* from whom he took the key. He went in and saw images of Prophets Ibrahim and Ishmael, [AWS], throwing divination arrows. He denounced these acts of Quraish and ordered that all idols be dismantled, images and effigies deleted. He then entered the sacred hall to face the wall opposite the door and there again performed devout prostrations, and went around acclaiming Allâh's Greatness and Oneness. Shortly afterwards, he returned to the door-way and standing upon its elevated step, gazed in thankfulness on the thronging multitude below and delivered the following celebrated address:

"There is no god but Allâh Alone. He has no associates. He made good His Promise that He held to His slave and helped him and defeated all the Confederates along. Bear in mind that every claim of privilege, whether that of blood, or property, is under my heel, except that of the custody of *Al-Ka'bah* and supplying of water to the pilgrims. Bear in mind that for anyone who is slain, even though semi-deliberately, with club or whip, for him the blood-money is very severe: a hundred camels, forty of them to be pregnant.

> "O people of Quraish! Surely Allâh has abolished from you all pride of the pre-Islamic era and all conceit in your ancestry, (because) all men are descended from Adam, and Adam was made out of clay."

He then recited to them the verse:

> "O mankind! We have created you from a male and a female, and made you into nations and tribes, that you may know one another. Verily, the most honourable of you near Allâh is that (believer) who has *At-Taqwa* [i.e. one of the *Muttaqûn*: i.e. pious and righteous persons who fear Allâh much (abstain from all kinds of sins and evil deeds which He has forbidden), and love Allâh much (perform all kinds of good deeds which He has ordained)]. Verily, Allâh is All-Knowing, All-Aware." [Al-Qur'an 49:13]

He further added:

"O you people of Quraish! What do you think of the treatment that I am about to accord to you?"

They replied:

"O noble brother and son of noble brother! We expect nothing but goodness from you."

Upon this he said:

"I speak to you in the same words as Yusuf (the Prophet Joseph) spoke unto his brothers: He said: "No reproach on you this day," [Al-Qur'an 12:92] go your way, for you are freed ones."

As for the door-keeping of Al-Ka'bah and supplying of water to pilgrims, the Prophet ordered that these jobs remain in the hand of 'Uthman bin Talhah and that the key will stay with him and his descendants for ever.

When time for prayer approached, Bilal ascended Al-Ka'bah and called for prayer. Abu Sufyan bin Harb, 'Itab bin Usaid and Al-Harith bin Hisham were meanwhile sitting in the yard. 'Itab bin Usaid commented on the new situation (Bilal ascending Al-Ka'bah and calling for prayer) saying that Allâh honoured Usaid (his father) having not heard such words. The Prophet approached and assisted by Divine Revelation told them that he had learnt about what they had spoken of. Al-Harith and 'Itab, taken by incredible surprise, immediately professed Islam and bore witness to the Messengership of Muhammad adding that "We swear by Allâh that none had been with us to inform you."

On that very day, the Prophet entered 'Umm Hani's house where he washed and offered prayers of victory. 'Umm Hani had sheltered two Makkan relatives of hers in her house in which act she was granted support by the Prophet.

Shedding blood of nine arch-criminals was declared lawful even under the curtains of Al-Ka'bah. Nevertheless, only four of them were killed while the others were pardoned for different reasons. As for those who were killed, mention could be made of 'Abdul 'Uzza bin Khatal who had become a Muslim and then deputed to collect alms-tax in the company of a Helper. They had also a slave with them. 'Abdullah, in a fit of rage, killed the Helper's slave on account of a mere trifling dispute, and joined the pagan Arabs as an apostate. He was never repentant at this heinous crime but rather employed two women singers and incited them to sing satirically about the Prophet.

The other man who was put to death was Miqyas bin Sababa. He was a Muslim. A Helper accidently killed his brother Hisham. The Prophet had arranged the payment of blood money to him, which he had accepted. His revengeful nature, however, was never appeased, so he killed the Helper and went to Makkah as an apostate. Similarly; Huwairith and one woman singer went to death.

On the other hand, every attempt was made to grant pardon to the people. 'Ikrimah bin Abu Jahl, who had attacked Khalid's detachment at the time of the entry into Makkah, was forgiven. To Wahshi, the murderer of Hamzah, the Prophet's uncle, and to Hind, who had chewed his liver, was also extended his generous clemency. The same generous treatment was accorded to Habar who had attacked the Prophet's daughter with a spear, while on her way from Makkah to Madinah, so grievously that she ultimately died of the fatal injuries.

In the same context of magnanimity peculiar to Muhammad, two chiefs of Quraish were pardoned once they had embraced Islam. They were Safwan bin Omaiyah and Fudalah bin 'Umair. The latter had attempted to assassinate the Prophet while circumambulating in the Holy Sanctuary. The Prophet's matchless tolerance and broad-mindedness instigated by his mission as 'A mercy to all people', converted a terrible hypocrite into a faithful devout believer.

On the second day of the great conquest, the Prophet stood up and addressed the people in matters relating to the holy status of Makkah. After entertaining Allâh's praise, he proclaimed that Makkah was a holy land and would remain so till the Day of Judgement. No bloodshed was allowed therein. Should anyone take the liberty of fighting within Makkah on grounds derived from the events that characterized the conquest, he should remember that it had been a licence granted temporarily to the Prophet, and virtually does not go for others. Ibn 'Abbas [R] narrated: The Prophet said: "Allâh has made Makkah, a sanctuary, so it was a sanctuary before me and will continue to be a sanctuary after me. It was made legal for me (i.e. I was allowed to fight in it) for a few hours of a day. It is not allowed to uproot its shrubs or to cut its trees, or to chase (or disturb) its game, or to pick up its fallen things except by a person who would announce that (what has found) publicly." Al-'Abbas said: "O Allâh's Mes-senger! Except the lemon grass (for it is used) by our goldsmiths and for our homes." The Prophet then said: "Except the lemon grass."

In this context, out of the spirit of revenge, the tribesmen of Khuza'ah killed a man from Laith Tribe. Here the Prophet was indignant and ordered Khuza'ah to stop those pre-Islamic practices. He, moreover, gave the family of anyone killed the right to consider either of two options, blood-money or just retribution (the killer is killed).

After having delivered his address, the Prophet rode to a small hill, Safa, not far from Al-Ka'bah. Turning his face towards the Sacred House, amidst a vast admiring and devotional multitude, he raised his hand in fervent prayer to Allâh. The citizens of Madinah who had gathered round him entertained fear, as Allâh had given him victory over his native city, he might choose to stay here. He insisted on explanation of their fear and so they spoke openly. He immediately dispelled their fears and assured them that he had lived with them and would die with them.

Immediately after the great conquest, the Makkans came to realize that the only way to success lay in the avenue of Islam. They complied with the new realities and gathered to pledge fealty to the *Prophet*. The men came first pledging full obedience in all areas they can afford. Then the women to follow the men's example. The Prophet with 'Umar bin Al-Khattab receiving the pledge of fealty and communicating to them for him. Hind bint 'Utbah, Abu Sufyan's wife, came in the trail of women disguised lest the Prophet should recognize and account for her, having chewed the liver of Hamzah, his uncle. The Prophet accepted their allegiance on condition that they associate none with Allâh, to which they immediately agreed.

He added that they should not practise theft. Here Hind complained that her husband, Abu Sufyan, was tight-fisted. Her husband interrupted granting all his worldly possessions to her. The Prophet laughed and recognized the woman. She implored him to extend his pardon to her and efface all her previous sins. Some other conditions were appended including the prohibition of adultery, infanticide or forging falsehood. To all these orders, Hind replied positively swearing that she would not have come to take an oath of allegiance if she had had the least seed of disobedience to him. On returning home, she broke her idol admitting her delusion as regards stone-gods.

The Messenger of Allâh stayed in Makkah for 19 days. During that period he used to define the way to Islam, guide people to the orthodox path. He ordered Abu Usaid Al-Khuza'i to restore the pillars of the Holy Sanctuary, sent missions to all quarters inviting them to adopt Islam and break down the graven images still lying in the vicinity of Makkah, and he did have all of them scrapped, inculcating in the believers' ears his words:

> "Whoever believes in Allâh and the Hereafter is supposed to scrap out the idols that should happen to be in his house."

Shortly after the great conquest, the Prophet began to despatch platoons and errands aiming at eliminating the last symbols reminiscent of pre-Islamic practices.

He sent Khalid bin Al-Waleed in Ramadan 8 A.H. to a spot called Nakhlah where there was a goddess called Al-'Uzza venerated by Quraish and Kinanah tribes. It had custodians from Bani Shaiban. Khalid, at the head of thirty horsemen arrived at the spot and exterminated it. On his return, the Prophet asked him if he had seen anything there, to which Khalid gave a negative answer. Here, he was told that it had not been destroyed and he had to go there again and fulfill the task. He went back again and there he saw a black woman, naked with torn hair. Khalid struck her with his sword into two parts. He returned and narrated the story to the Prophet, who then confirmed the fulfillment of the task.

Later, in the same month, 'Amr bin Al-'As was sent on an errand to destroy another idol, venerated by Hudhail, called Suwa'. It used to stand at a distance of three kilometres from Makkah. On a question posed by the door-keeper, 'Amr said he had been ordered by the Prophet to knock down the idol. The man warned 'Amr that he would not be able to do it. 'Amr was surprised to see someone still in the wrong, approached the idol and destroyed it, and then he broke the casket beside it but found nothing. The man immediately embraced Islam.

Sa'd bin Zaid Al-Ashhali was also sent in the same month and on the same mission to Al-Mashallal to destroy an idol, Manat, venerated by both Al-Aws and Al-Khazraj tribes. Here also a black woman, naked with messy hair appeared wailing and beating on her chest. Sa'd immediately killed her, destroyed the idol and broke the casket and returned at the conclusion of his errand.

Khalid bin Al-Waleed at the head of 350 horsemen of Helpers, Emigrants and Bani Saleem was despatched once again in the same year 8 A.H. to the habitation of Bani Khuzaimah bedouins to invite them to the fold of Islam. He was instructed to carry out his mission with peace and goodwill. There, the people were not articulate enough to communicate their intentions, so Khalid ordered his men to kill them and take the others as captives. He even had in mind to kill the captives but some of the Companions were opposed to his plan.

News of bloodshed reached the *Prophet.* He was deeply grieved and raised his hands towards the heaven, uttering these words: "O Allâh! I am innocent of what Khalid has done," twice. [Sahih Al-Bukhari 1/450, 2/622] He immediately sent 'Ali to make every possible reparation to the tribes who had been wronged. After a careful inquiry, 'Ali paid the blood-money to all those who suffered loss. The remaining portion was also distributed amongst the members of the tribe in order to alleviate their suffering. Khalid, due to his irrational behaviour, had a row with 'Abdur Rahman bin 'Awf. Hearing this, the Prophet got angry, and ordered Khalid to stop that altercation adding that his Companions (meaning 'Abdur Rahman bin 'Awf) were too high in rank to be involved in such arguments.

That is the story of the conquest of Makkah and the decisive battle that exterminated paganism once and for all. The other tribes in the Arabian Peninsula were waiting and closely watching the final outcome of the bitter struggle between the Muslims and idolaters, already convinced that the Holy Sanctuary would not fall but in the hands of the righteous party. It had been a conviction deeply established in their minds ever since the elephant army of Abraha Al-Ashram advanced from Yemen intending to destroy the Sacred House 50 years before.

Al-Hudaibiyah Peace Treaty was the natural prelude to this great victory in which people believed deeply and over which people talked a lot. The Muslims in Makkah, who had feared to declare their Faith in public, began to appear and work ardently for this new approach of life. People began to convert into Islam in hosts, and the Muslim army that numbered 3000 only in the previous *Ghazwah,* now came to reach 10,000 in number. In fact, this decisive change provided people with the keen insight to perceive things and the world around them as a whole in a different perceptive.

The Muslims were then to steer the whole political and religious affairs of all Arabia. They had monopolised both the religious supremacy and temporal power. The whole post-Hudaibiyah phase had been well-fledged in favour of the new Islamic movement. Streams of the desert Arabians began to pour in paying full homage to the Messenger of Allâh, embracing the new faith and then carrying it to different quarters for propagation.

THE THIRD STAGE

The third and last stage of the life of the Messenger embodies the fruitful results of his call to Islam, which were the consequences of long-timed holy fights in the way of Allâh (*Jihad*), troubles, toil, disturbances, trials and a lot of bloody conflicts and battles, which lasted for over twenty years.

The conquest of Makkah was considered the most serious profit achieved by Muslims during those years. For it affected the course of events and consequently altered the Arabs' whole life. It was a decisive distinction between preconquest and post-conquest periods. For Quraish, at that time, was in the eyes of Arabs the defenders and helpers of Arabs. Other Arabs are only their ancillaries. The submission of Quraish is, therefore, estimated to be a final elimination of paganism in the Arabian Peninsula.

This stage can be divided into two main phases:

The phase of:

1. Holy wars and fighting.
2. The tribes and people's race to embrace Islam.

Being so close and rather inseparable, the two phases of this stage intervene in such a way that a happening of one phase occurs during the progress of the other. However, we have preferred - for expository purposes - to deal with these two phases distinctively. The fighting phase was given the priority in order, due to the fact that it is more intimate and fit than the other.

HUNAIN GHAZWAH

The conquest of Makkah which came forth as a consequence of a swift blow astounded both the Arabs and other tribes who realized that they were doomed and had to submit to the new situation as a *fait accompli*. Some of the fierce, powerful proud tribes did not submit and favoured resistance. Ahead of these were the septs of Hawazin and Thaqif. Nasr, Jashm and Sa'd bin Bakr and people of Bani Hilal-all of whom of Qais 'Ailan. They thought that they were too mighty to admit or surrender to such a victory. So they met Malik bin 'Awf An-Nasri and made up their mind to proceed fighting against the Muslims.

ENEMY'S MARCH AND THEIR ENCAMPMENT AT AWTAS

When Malik bin 'Awf-the general leader-decided to march and fight the Muslims, he made his countrypeople take their wealth, women and children with them to Awtas-which is a valley in Hawazin land and is quite near Hunain. It differs from Hunain in its being adjacent to Dhi-Al-Majaz which is around ten miles from Makkah in 'Arafat's direction.

THE WAR-EXPERIENCED MAN WRONGS THE LEADER'S JUDGEMENT

As soon as they had camped in Awtas, people crowded round Malik. The old sane Duraid bin As-Simmah, who was well-known as a war-experienced man, and who was among those who gathered round Malik, asked: "What valley are we in?" "In Awtas," they said. "What a good course it is for horses! It is neither a sharp pointed height nor a loosed soiled plain. What? Why do I hear camels' growling, the donkeys' braying, the children's cries and the sheep bleating?" asked Duraid. They said: "Malik bin 'Awf had made people bring their women, properties and children with them." So he called Malik and asked him what made him do such a thing.

Malik said that his aim was to have everybody's family and properties around them so that they fight fiercely to protect them." "I swear by Allâh that you are nothing but a shepherd," answered Duraid, "Do you believe that there is anything whatsoever, can stand in the way of a defeated one or stop him from fleeing? If you win the battle you avail nothing but a man with a sword and a spear; but if you lose you will bring disgrace on your people and properties," then he resumed his talk and went on wondering about some septs and their leaders. "O Malik, thrusting the distinguished people of Hawazin into the battlefield will avail you nothing. Raise them up to where they can be safe. Then make the young people mount their horses and fight. If you win, those whom you tarried will follow you, but if you were the loser it would be a loss of a battle, but your kinsmen, people and properties would not be lost."

But Malik, the general leader, refused this suggestion. "By Allâh," he said, "I will not do such a thing. You must have grown a senile. Hawazin have to obey me, or else I will lean my body against this sword so that it penetrates through my back." He rejected any sort of contribution of Duraid's in that concern. "We obey you," said his people, Duraid consequently said: "Today is a day that I have not missed but surely I will not be tempted to witness."

RECONNOITERING THE WEAPONS OF THE MESSENGER OF ALLÂH

The spies that Malik had already dispatched to spy Muslim forces, returned with their limbs cut off. "Woe unto you! What happened to you?" Said Malik. They said: "We have seen distinguished people on spotted horsebacks. What you see, would not have happened if we had been firmly together."

RECONNOITERING THE ENEMY'S WEAPONS

News about the enemy's marching were conveyed to the Messenger of Allâh , so he sent out Al-Aslami with orders to mix with people, stay with them so that he would be able to know their news and to convey it to the Messenger of Allâh when he turns back. That was exactly what he managed to do.

THE MESSENGER OF ALLÂH LEAVES MAKKAH FOR HUNAIN

On Shawwal, the nineteenth, the captive day, the Messenger of Allâh left Makkah accompanied by twelve thousand Muslims. Ten thousand of those had previously shared in Makkah Conquest. A great number of the other two thousand, who were Makkans, had recently embraced Islam. That march was on the nineteenth day of his conquest to Makkah. He borrowed a hundred armours with their equipment from Safwan bin Omaiyah.

He appointed 'Itab bin Usaid as a governor over Makkah. When it was evening time, a horseman came to the Messenger of Allâh and said: "I have climbed up so and so mountains and came across Hawazin with their riding camels, livestock and sheep. Hawazin wholly were gathered together there." The Messenger of Allâh smiled then and said: "They will all be Muslims' spoils tomorrow, if Allâh will." That night Anas bin Abi Murthid Al-Ghanawi volunteered to guard. [Abu Da'ud]

On their way to Hunain they saw a great green *Nabk* plant that was called *Dhat-Anwat* (the one with suspenders). That was because the Arabs used to hang their weapons on it, slay beasts under it and keep to it. So some of army members asked the Messenger of Allâh to make them a *Nabk* with suspenders as the one they had. "Allâh is the Greatest of all!"

He said, "I swear by the One in Whose Hand is Muhammad's soul that you have just said what the people of Moses said to him. They said 'Make us a god as the one they have.' Surely you are ignorant people. These are *Sunnah,* but you will follow and comply with the modes of life of those who preceded you." [At-Tirmidhi]

Seeing how great in number the army was, some of them said: "We shall not be defeated." Their statement sounded hard upon the Messenger of Allâh.

THE ISLAMIC ARMY STUNNED THE ARCHERS AND THE ATTACKERS

On Wednesday night the tenth of Shawwal, the Muslim army arrived at Hunain. Malik bin 'Awf, who had previously entered the valley by night, gave orders to his army to hide inside the valley and lurk for the Muslims on roads, entrances, and narrow hiding places. His orders to his men were to hurl stones at Muslims whenever they caught sight of them and then to make a one-man attack against them. At early dawn the Messenger of Allâh started mobilizing his army and distributing posts and flags to people.

In the dark and just before dawn the Muslims moved towards Hunain Valley. They started descending into it unaware of the presence of an enemy lurking for them inside the valley. So at the moment they were camping, arrows began showering intensively at them, whereas the enemy's battalions started a fierce attack against the Muslims, who had to retreat in disorder and utter confusion. It was such a shatteringly defeat that Abu Sufyan bin Harb, who had recently embraced Islam, said that their retreat would not stop till they got to the Red Sea. Jablah or Kildah bin Al-Junaid commented on that by saying: "Surely magic has grown inactive today."

The Messenger of Allâh turned to the right and said: "Come on, people! I am the Messenger of Allâh. I am Muhammad, the son of Abdullah." Those who stoodfast by him were only few Emigrants and some of his kinsmen. The matchless bravery of the Prophet [R] was then brought to light. He went on and on in his attempts to make his mule standfast in the face of the disbelievers while saying loudly:

"Truly saying, I am the Prophet
I am the (grand) son of Abdul Muttalib."

However, Abu Sufyan, who was then holding the rein of the Prophet's mule and Al-'Abbas, who was holding its stirrup; were endeavouring to make it halt. The Messenger of Allâh dismounted and asked his Lord to render him help.

"O, Allâh, send down Your Help!"

MULSIMS' RETURN TO THE BATTLEFIELD AND THE FIERCENESS OF THE FIGHT

The Messenger of Allâh ordered his uncle Al-'Abbas-who was a sonorous voiced man-to call out on the followers. As loudly as he could, Al-'Abbas shouted: "Where are the lancers?" "By Allâh," Al-'Abbas said, "Upon hearing my voice calling them back, they turned round to the battlefield as if they had been oryxes (wild cows) tending towards their calves."

"Here we are, at your service. Here we are." [Sahih Muslim 2/100] They said. There you see them trying to stop their camels and reverse to the battle. He who was unable to force his camel to turn back, would take his armour, fling it round his neck, and hastily dismount his camel with his weapon in his hand letting his camel move freely and run towards the voice source. Voices would grow louder and louder till a hundred of them gathered round the Prophet and resumed the fight. Those who were called out upon next were Al-Ansar, the Helpers, "O, folks of Al-Ansar! Folks of Al-Ansar!"

The last group to be called out upon was Bani Al-Harith bin Al-Khazraj. Muslims battalions poured successively into the battlefield in the same manner that they had left it. The stamina of both parties was superb. Both of them stoodfast and fought fiercely. The Messenger of Allâh was so eagerly and furiously watching the battle that he said:

"Now the fight has grown fierce."

Picking up a handful of earth, he hurled it at their faces while saying:

"May your faces be shameful?"

Their eyes were thick with dust and the enemy began to retreat in utter confusion.

REVERSE OF FORTUNES AND THE ENEMY'S UTTER DEFEAT

Few hours had elapsed since the earth-handful was hurled at the enemy's faces, when they were shatteringly defeated. About seventy men of Thaqif alone were killed, and the Muslims plundered all their riding camels, weapons and cattle. Allâh, Glory is to Him, alluded to this sudden change in the *Quran* when He said:

> "...and on the Day of Hunain (battle) when you rejoiced at your great number but it availed you naught and the earth, vast as it is, was straitened for you, then you turned back in flight. Then Allâh did send down His *Sakinah* (calmness, tranquillity, and reassurance, etc.) on the Messenger (Muhammad) and on the believers, and sent down forces (angels) which you saw not, and punished the disbelievers. Such is the recompense of disbelievers." [Al-Qur'an 9:25]

HOT PURSUIT OF THE ENEMY

After their defeat, some enemy troops headed for Ta'if, others to Nakhlah and Awtas. A group of Muslims headed by Abu 'Amir Al-Ash'ari, were despatched to chase the enemy, some skirmishes took place during which Abu 'Amir was killed. A similar battalion of horsemen pursued the idolaters who threaded the track to Nakhlah and caught up with Duraid bin As-Simmah, who was killed by Rabi'a bin Rafi'. After collecting the booty, the Messenger of Allâh left for Ta'if to face the greatest number of the defeated idolaters.

The booty was six thousand captives, twenty four thousand camels; over forty thousand sheep and four thousand silver ounces. The Messenger of Allâh gave orders that booty should be confined at Al-J'iranah and ordained Mas'ud bin 'Amr Al-Ghifari to be in charge of it. It was only when he was entirely free from Ta'if Campaign, that one of the captives As-Shaimâ', the daughter of Al-Harith As-Sa'diya, the Messenger's foster sister was brought to the Messenger of Allâh, she introduced herself to him. Upon recognizing her by a certain mark, he honoured her, spread for her his garment and seated her on it. He was graceful and released her and made her turn back to her people.

TA'IF CAMPAIGN

Ta'if Campaign is in fact an extension of Hunain *Ghazwah;* that is because the majority of the defeated troops of Hawazin and Thaqif went into Ta'if with the general commander-Malik bin 'Awf An-Nasri-and fortified themselves within it. So upon finishing with Hunain Invasion, he gathered the booty at Al-Ji'ranah in the very month (i.e. Shawwal) and in the eighth year A.H. A vanguard battalion of a thousand men led by Khalid bin Al-Waleed marched towards At-Ta'if.

Whereas the Messenger of Allâh proceeded passing through Nakhlah Al-Yamaniyah, Qarn Al-Manazil and through Laiyah. At Laiyah there was a castle that belonged to Malik bin 'Awf, so the Messenger of Allâh gave orders to have it destroyed. He resumed his march till he got to Ta'if.

There he dismounted, camped near its castle and laid siege to the castle inhabitants; but not for long.

How long the siege continued, is still a matter of disagreement. It however stands between 10-20 days. [Sahih Muslim, narrated by Anas [AWS]; Fath Al-Bari 8/45]

A lot of arrow-shooting and rock-hurling occurred during the siege. For as soon as the Muslims laid siege round the castle, its people started shooting arrows against them. The arrows were so intense and fierce that they looked as if they had been locusts on the move. A number of Muslims were wounded and twelve were killed.

To be far from the arrow-range, the Muslims had to ascend to a higher location and camped on-i.e. to what is now called At-Ta'if Mosque. The Prophet set up a mangonel and shelled the castle. Eventually a gap was made in the castle wall, through which a number of Muslims managed to pass into the castle, sheltered by a wooden tank, with the purpose of setting fire into it. Anyway, the enemy poured down molten hot iron on them. Affected by this the Muslims stepped out of the tank and were again exposed to arrow shooting and consequently some of them were killed.

To force the enemy to surrender, the Prophet tended to a war policy of burning and cutting the enemy's crops. His order was to cut their vineyards and burn them. Seeing that the Muslims started rapidly cutting and burning their vines, they implored the Prophet to stop and have mercy on them for the sake of Allâh and out of kinship motives. So the Prophet agreed. When the caller of the Messenger of Allâh called out unto people saying "He whosoever descends and steps out of the castle is free." Twenty-three men came out. [Sahih Al-Bukhari 2/620] One of them was Abu Bakrah who tied himself to a wall and let himself down by means of a small wheel that would normally be used for drawing up water from a well.

The way he let himself down made the Prophet nickname him "Abu Bakrah", i.e. the man with the wheel. The Messenger of Allâh set them all free and entrusted each one of them to a Muslim to care about their living affairs, which was too hard for the castle folkspeople to bear.

Seeing that the siege lasted too long and that the castle was immune and could stand any siege (for they had already stored a supply that suffices for over a year) and that the Muslims were suffering-day by day-from arrow-shots and heated iron hooks, the Messenger of Allâh consulted Nawfal bin Mu'âwiyah Ad-Daili about that. He said: "They are like a fox hiding inside its burrow. If you stoodfast at it you would catch it, but if you parted with it, no harm would afflict you."

The Messenger of Allâh decided to lift the siege and depart. 'Umar bin Al-Khattab, who was ordered by the Prophet to notify people, said to them "If Allâh will, we are leaving the castle and going back tomorrow." As it was too hard for the Muslims to go back and leave the castle un-conquered they complained saying, "Should we go away while the castle is still unopened?" His reply was: "Then, start fighting in the morning." In the morning they fought and were wounded. So when he repeated this statement: "If Allâh will, we are leaving the castle and going back tomorrow", they were pleased and carried out the order submissively and started moving, which made the Messenger of Allâh laugh.

As soon as they mounted and started moving the Messenger said:

> "Say! Here we are returning, repenting, worshipping (Allâh) and to our Lord we offer praise."

When the Messenger of Allâh was asked to invoke Allâh against Thaqif, he said:

> "O Allâh, guide Thaqif and bring them to us as Muslims."

DISTRIBUTION OF THE BOOTY AT AL-JI'RANAH

Upon returning and lifting the siege in Ta'if, the Messenger of Allâh had stayed over ten nights at Al-Ji'ranah before starting to distribute the booty. Distribution delay was due to the Prophet's hope that Hawazin's delegation might arrive and announce their repentance and consequently reclaim their loss. Seeing that none of them arrived, he started dividing the booty so as to calm down the tribes' chiefs and the celebrities of Makkah. The first to receive booty and the ones who obtained the greatest number of shares were the people who had recently embraced Islam.

Abu Sufyan bin Harb was given a hundred camels and forty (gold) ounces and yet he said, "What about my son, Yazeed's Share?" So he was given the same quantity for his son as well. But yet he exclaimed: "And what about the share of Mu'âwiyah, my second son?" So the Prophet gave Mu'âwiyah as much as he gave his father and brother. Hakeem bin Hizam was given a hundred camels, but he was given a hundred more when he demanded. Safwan bin Omaiyah was given three hundred camels - a hundred camels at each time. It is thus mentioned in Shifâ' [Ash-Shifa 1/86], Book by Qadi Iyadh. The Prophet gave Al-Harith bin Harith bin Kilda a hundred camels. He also gave some chiefs of Quraish and other clans a hundred camels; he gave others fifty and some others had forty.

Eventually it was spread among people that "Muhammad grants generously and fears not to grow poor." This made bedouins gather around him expecting to be given some wealth. They were so many that they forced the Prophet to seek refuge against a tree and they even took away his garment, "O people!" He said, "Give me back my garment! For I swear by the One in Whose Hand is Muhammad's soul, that if I had as many numerous camels as the number of Tihama trees, I would distribute them among you. You know quite well that I am neither mean nor coward or a liar." Standing by his camel he plucked out a hair of his camel's hump and held it between his two fingers, lifted it up and said: "O people, I swear by Allâh that I get nothing but one-fifth of your booty, and this very fifth goes back to you."

As soon as he had given the new converts, the Messenger of Allâh ordered Zaid bin Thabit to fetch the booty and summon people. Then he ordained shares to people. A footman's share was four camels and forty sheep, and a horseman would take twelve camels and a hundred and twenty sheep. This distribution of booty was based on a wise policy. In this world there are lots of people who know the truth only when it comes through their stomachs and they do not recognize it if it comes through their brains. The similitude of such people is as the guidance of an animal to its herd by means of a bunch of clover held at a constant distance off its mouth. The animal would try all the time to catch it, so it would eventually go into the herd safely. In the same way you have to do various kinds of temptations to make certain kind of people familiarize Islam and be pleased with. [Fiqh As-Seerah p.298, 299]

THE HELPERS (*AL-ANSAR*) ARE FURIOUS AT THE MESSENGER OF ALLÂH

At first the Prophet's policy of distribution was uncomprehended by many a man. Therefore sharp-tongued people started expressing their objections. The Helpers were among those who were afflicted by this policy. They were deprived of Hunain gifts though they had been the ones who were summoned at Hunain hard times and they were the first to rush to fight with the Messenger of Allâh and standfast till the defeat turned into victory. Now here they are watching those who escaped fill their hands with booty while they are given nothing.

On the authority of Ibn Ishaq: "When the Messenger of Allâh had given Quraish and Arab tribes those gifts and allotted nothing to the Helpers, a group of the Helpers felt so uneasy about it that a lot of ill-statements against the Prophet were spread among them to an extent that one of them said: "By Allâh, the Messenger of Allâh was ill-spoken of by his folksmen!" And those ill-statements went on spreading till Sa'd bin 'Ubadah met the Messenger of Allâh, who in his turn faced his people after a while.

Sa'd bin 'Ubadah said: "O Messenger of Allâh, this group of the Helpers are furious at you about the distribution of the booty that you had won. You have allotted shares to your own kinsmen and forwarded lots of gifts to the Arab tribes.

But this group has obtained nothing." The Prophet asked Sa'd exclaiming: "Sa'd, what do you think of all that?" Sa'd replied: "O Messenger of Allâh. You know that I am nothing but a member of this group." "Call out on your people and bring them forth to me into this shed." Said the Prophet.

So Sa'd went out and summoned them. When some Emigrants came, he let them in but forbade others. When they were all gathered together, he informed the Prophet saying: "these groups of the Helpers have just arrived to meet you in compliance with your orders." As soon as the Messenger faced them he thanked Allâh and praised Him, then said to them inquiring, "I have been told that you are angry with me. Didn't I come to you when you were astray and Allâh guided you? You were poor and Allâh gave you wealth. Weren't you foes and Allâh made you love one another?" "Yes," they said, "Allâh and His Messenger are better and more gracious." Then he said: "What prevents you from replying to the Messenger of Allâh, O tribe of Helpers?" They said, "What should be the reply, O Messenger of Allâh, while to the Lord and to his Messenger belong all benevolence and grace."

The Prophet again said:

> "But by Allâh, you might have answered and answered truly, for I would have testified to its truth myself: 'You came to us belied and rejected and we accepted you; you came to us as helpless and we helped you; a fugitive, and we took you in; poor and we comforted you'. You Helpers, do you feel anxious for the things of this world, wherewith I have sought to incline these people unto the Faith in which you are already established?
>
> Are you not satisfied, O group of Helpers that the people go with ewes and camels while you go along with the Messenger of Allâh () to your dwellings. By Him in Whose Hand is my life, had there been no migration, I would have been one of the Helpers. If the people would go through a valley and passage, and the Helpers go through another valley and passage, I would go through

the valley and passage of the Helpers. Allâh! Have mercy on the Helpers, their children and their children's children."

The audience wept until tears rolled down their beards as they said:

"Yes, we are satisfied, O Prophet of Allâh ( )! with our lot and share."

Then the Prophet left the gathering and the people also dispersed. [Ibn Hisham 2/499,500; and like this quoted by Bukhari 2/620, 621]

ARRIVAL OF THE HAWAZIN DELEGATION

Hawazin's delegation arrived a Muslims just after the distribution of spoils. They were fourteen men headed by Zuhair bin Sard. The Messenger's foster uncle was one of them. They asked him to bestow upon them some of the wealth and spoils. They uttered so touching words that the Messenger of Allâh said to them: "You surely see who are with me. The most desirable speech to me is the most truthful. Which is dearer to you, your wealth or your women and children?" They replied: "Nothing whatsoever compares with kinship." Then when I perform the noon prayer, stand up and say: "We intercede with the Messenger of Allâh to exhort the believers, and we intercede with the believers to exhort the Messenger of Allâh to forego the captives of our people fallen to their lot." So when the Messenger of Allâh performed the noon prayer, they stood up and said what they had been told to say.

The Messenger, then, said: "As for what belongs to me and to the children of Abdul Muttalib, you may consider them, from now on, yours. And I will ask my folksmen to give back theirs." Upon hearing that the Emigrants and the Helpers said: "What belongs to us is, from now on, offered to the Messenger of Allâh." But Al-Aqra'bin Habis said, "We will grant none of what belongs to me and to Bani Tamim," so did 'Uyaina bin Hisn, who said: "As for me and Bani Fazarah, I say 'No'." Al-'Abbas bin Mirdas also refused and said: "No" for Bani Saleem and him. His people, however, said otherwise: "Whatever spoils belong to us we offer to the Messenger of Allâh (.)" "You have undermined my position." Said Al-'Abbas bin Mirdas spontaneously.

Then the Messenger of Allâh said: "These people have come to you as Muslims. For this I have already carried the distribution of the booty. Besides, I have granted them a fair option but they refused to have anything other than their women and children. Therefore he, who has some of theirs and will prefer willingly to give them back, let them do. But those who favours to keep what he owns to himself, let them grant them back too, and he will be given as recompense six times as much from the first booty that Allâh may provide us." People then said, "We will willingly offer them all for the sake of the Messenger of Allâh."

The Messenger of Allâh said: "But in this way we are not able to find out who is content and who is not. So go back and we will be waiting for your chiefs to convey to us your decisions." All of them gave back the women and children. The only one who refused to comply with the Messenger's desire was 'Uyaina bin Hisn. He refused to let an old woman of theirs go back at first. Later on he let her go back. The Messenger of Allâh gave every captive a garment as a gift.

LESSER PILGRIMAGE (AL-'UMRAH) TO MAKKAH AND LEAVING FOR MADINAH

Having accomplished the distribution of the spoils at Al-Ji'ranah he left it while wearing *Al-'Umrah* clothes and proceeded to Makkah to perform *Al-'Umrah.* The Messenger of Allâh turned back from there to Madinah after appointing 'Itab bin Usaid on Makkah as governor. His arrival to Madinah was by the last six nights of Dhul-Qa'dah, in the year 8 A.H. On this occasion Muhammad Al-Ghazali said:

"What a great change it is between the victorious period of Muhammad at present which Allâh has towered with a manifest conquest, and that period of the past during which Muhammad first arrived at this town, eight years ago."

When he first came to Madinah, he was pursued and wanted. He was seeking a secure shelter. He was a lonely stranger who sought companionship and comfort. The people of Madinah welcomed him, gave him residence and aided him and embraced the light of Islam, which had been sent down upon him. They, for his sake, did not care about the enmity of other peoples. Here he is entering Madinah again, after the lapse of eight years of that first visit. Madinah, the town that had received him once, when he was a frightened Emigrant; it receives him once again when Makkah has become in his hands and at his disposal. It is Makkah that has got rid of its pride and *Jahiliyah* (i.e. pre-Islamic period and traditions). It is now proud again and mighty in Islam.

The Messenger of Allâh forgave all the errors and wrongs of its people. "Verily, he who fears Allâh with obedience to Him (by abstaining from sins and evil deeds, and by performing righteous good deeds), and is patient, then surely, Allâh makes not the reward of the good-doers to be lost." [Al-Qur'an 12:90] [Fiqh-us-Seerah 303; Za'd Al-Ma'ad 2/160-201; Ibn Hisham 2/389-501; Sahih Bukhari: Chapter Fath Ghazwal, Hunian, Awtas and At-Ta'if 2/612-622. Fath Al-Bari 8/3-58]

MISSIONS AND PLATOONS

AFTER THE CONQUEST

Upon returning from this long successful travel, the Messenger of Allâh stayed in Madinah where he received delegates and dispatched agents and appointed preachers and callers to Islam everywhere. Those whose hearts were still full of prejudice against Islam and therefore were too proud to embrace Allâh's religion, were decisively muffled on their non-acquiescence in the *status quo* prevalent then in Arabia. Here is a mini-image about the believed ones. We have already stated that the Messenger's arrival in Madinah was by the last days of the eighth year of Al-Hijra. No sooner the crescent of Muharram of the ninth year turned up than the Messenger of Allâh dispatched the believed ones, to the tribes as shown in the list below:

1. 'Uyaina bin Hisn to Bani Tamim.
2. Yazeed bin Husain to Aslam and Ghifar.
3. 'Abbad bin Bishr Al-Ashhali to Sulaim and Muzainah.
4. Rafi'bin Mukaith to Juhainah.
5. 'Amr bin Al-'As to Bani Fazarah.
6. Ad-Dahhak bin Sufyan to Bani Kilab.
7. Basheer bin Sufyan to Bani Ka'b.
8. Ibn Al-Lutabiyah Al-Azdi to Bani Dhubyan.
9. Al-Muhajir bin Abi Omaiyah to Sana'a' (Al-Aswad Al-'Ansi called him when he was in it).
10. Ziyad bin Labid to Hadramout.
11. 'Adi bin Hatim to Tai' and Bani Asad.
12. Malik bin Nuwairah to Bani Hanzalah.
13. Az-Zabraqan bin Badr to Bani Sa'd (a portion of them).
14. Qais bin 'Asim to Bani Sa'd (a portion of them).
15. Al-'Alâ' bin Al-Hadrami to Al-Bahrain.
16. 'Ali bin Abi Talib to Najran (to collect *Sadaqa* & *Jizya*).

Some of these agents were despatched in Muharram, 7 A.H., others were sent later until the tribes they were heading for had completely converted into Islam. Such a move clearly demonstrates the great success that the Islamic *Da'wah* (Call) enjoyed after Al-Hudaibiyah Treaty. However, shortly after the conquest of Makkah, people began to embrace Islam in large hosts.

THE PLATOONS

In the same way that the believed ones were dispatched to the tribes, we understand that dispatching some more platoons to all regions of Arabia is a necessity for the prevalence and domination of security on all lands of Arabia.

Here is a list of those platoons:

1. 'Uyaina bin Hisn Al-Fazari's platoon in Al-Muharram, the ninth year of Al-Hijra to Bani Tamim. It consisted of fifty horsemen; none of them was an Emigrant or a Helper.

This expedition was dispatched due to the fact that Bani Tamim had already urged other tribes not to pay tribute (*Al-Jizya*) and eventually stopped them from paying it. Therefore, 'Uyaina bin Hisn set out to fight them. All the way long he marched by night and lurked by day. He went on that way till he overtook them and attacked them in the desert. They fled back for their lives. Eleven men, twenty-one women and thirty boys were captured then. He drove them back to Madinah and was housed in Ramlah bint Al-Harith's residence. Ten of their leaders, who came to the Prophet's door, called out unto him saying: "O Muhammad come out and face us." When he went out they held him and started talking.

He exchanged talk with them for a while then left them and went to perform the noon-prayer. After prayer he sat in the mosque-patio. They proclaimed a desire to show boasting and self-pride. For this purpose they introduced their orator 'Utarid bin Hajib who delivered his speech. The Messenger of Allâh asked Thabit bin Qais bin Shammas-the Muslim orator-to respond. He did that. In return, they brought forth their poet Az-Zabraqan bin Badr who recited some boastful poetry. Hassan bin Thabit, the poet of Islam, promptly replied back. When talks and poetry came to an end, Al-Aqra'bin Habis said: "Their orator is more eloquent than ours, and their poet is more poetically learned than ours. Their voices and sayings excel ours, as well." Eventually they announced their embracing Islam. Consequently, the Messenger of Allâh acknowledged their Islamization, awarded them well, and rendered them back their women and children.

2. A platoon headed by Qutbah bin 'Amir to a spot called Khath'am in Tabalah, a plot of land not far from Turbah. That was in Safar, 9 A.H. Accompanied by twenty men and only ten camels to mount alternatively on, Qutbah raided them and fought so fiercely that a great number of both parties were wounded and some others were killed. The Muslims drove back with them camels, women and sheep to Madinah.
3. The mission of Dahhak bin Sufyan Al-Kilabi to Bani Kilab in Rabi' Al-Awwal in the year 9 A.H. This mission was

sent to Bani Kilab to call them to embrace Islam. Refusing to embrace Islam, they started to fight against the Muslims, but were defeated and sustained one man killed.

4. The three hundred men expedition of 'Alqamah bin Mujazziz Al-Mudlaji to Jeddah shores in Rabi'Al-Akhir. This expedition was dispatched to fight against some men from (Al-Habasha) Abyssinia (Ethiopia), who gathered together near the shores of Jeddah and exercised acts of piracy against the Makkans. Therefore he crossed the sea till he got to an island. But as soon as the pirates had learned of Muslims' arrival, they fled. [Fath Al-Bari 8/59]
5. The task of the platoon of 'Ali bin Abi Talib was to demolish Al-Qullus, which was an idol that belonged to Tai' tribe. That was in Rabi'Al-Awwal in the year 9 A.H. 'Ali was dispatched by the Messenger of Allâh with one hundred fifty men. A hundred of them were on camels. The other fifty were on horseback. He held a black flag and a white banner.

At dawn they raided *Mahallat* Hatim, demolished the idol and filled their hands with spoils, camels and sheep booties, whereas 'Adi fled to Ash-Sham. The sister of 'Adi bin Hatim was one of the captives. Inside Al-Qullus safe, Muslims found three swords and three armours. On the way they distributed the spoils and put aside the best things to the Messenger of Allâh. They did not share the Hatims.

Upon arrival in Madinah, the sister of 'Adi bin Hatim begged the Messenger of Allâh to have mercy on her and said: "O Messenger of Allâh, my brother is absent and father is dead, and I am too old to render any service. Be beneficent to me so that Allâh may be bountiful to you." He said: "Who is your brother?" She said: "It is 'Adi bin Hatim." "Is he not the one who fled from Allâh and his Messenger?" Said the Prophet then went away from her. Next day she reiterated the same thing as the day before and received the same answer. A day later she uttered similar words, this time he made benefaction to her. The man who was beside the Prophet, and whom she thought to be 'Ali, said to her: "Ask for an animal from him to ride on." And she was granted her request.

She returned to Ash-Sham where she met her brother and said to him: "The Messenger of Allâh has done me such noble deed that your father would never have done it. Therefore, willy-nilly, frightened or secure, you should go and see him." Unsecure neither protected by some one, not even recommended by a letter as a means of protection, 'Adi came and met the Prophet. The Messenger of Allâh took him home with him. As soon as he sat before him, the Messenger of Allâh thanked Allâh and praised him, then said: "What makes you flee? Do you flee lest you should say there is no god but Allâh? Do you know any other god but Allâh?" "No" he said, then talked for a while.

The Messenger of Allâh went on saying: "Certainly you flee so that you may not hear the statement saying 'Allâh is the Greatest.' Do you know anyone who is greater than Allâh?" "No" he said. "The Jews are those whose portion is wrath, and the Christians are those who have gone astray," the Prophet retorted. "I am a Muslim and I believe in one God (Allâh)." 'Adi finally proclaimed with a joyous face. The Prophet ordered him a residence with one of the Helpers. From that time he started calling at the Prophet in the mornings and in the evenings.

On the authority of Ibn Ishaq, when the Prophet made him sit down in front of him in his house, the Prophet said, "O 'Adi, were you not cast in disbelief?" "Yes". 'Adi said. "Did you not share one quarter of your people's gains?" "Yes". Said 'Adi. The Messenger of Allâh said: "It is sinful in your religion to do such a thing, and you should not allow yourself to do it." "Yes, by Allâh, that is true", said 'Adi. "Thus I worked out that he was a Prophet inspired by Allâh, and sent to people. He knows what is unknown."

In another version, the Prophet said: "'Adi, embrace Islam and you shall be secure." "But I am a man of religion." Said 'Adi. "I know your religion better than you." Said the Prophet. "Do you know my religion better than me?" 'Adi asked. The Prophet replied, "Yes". He said: "Are you not cast in disbelief because you appropriate to yourself the fourth of your people's gains?" "Yes". Said 'Adi. "It is unlawful in your religion to do such a thing." The Prophet said, and "Adi added: "He did not need to say it again for I immediately acquiesced it." [Musnad Imam Ahmad]

Al-Bukhari narrates that 'Adi said: While we were with the Prophet, a man came in and complained to him about poverty. Then another man came in and complained about highway robbery. The Messenger of Allâh then said: "O 'Adi, have you ever been to Al-Hirah? If you were doomed to live long life, you would be able to see a riding camel woman travel from Hirah till it circumambulates Al-Ka'bah fearing none but Allâh; and if you were to live long enough you would open the treasures of Kisra.

And if you were to live long you would be able to see man offering a handful of gold or silver to others but none accepts to take it."

At the end of this *Hadith* 'Adi later on says: "I have seen a riding camel woman travel from Al-Hirah till it circumambulates the Ka'bah fearing none but Allâh, I have also been one of those who opened the treasures of Kisra bin Hurmuz. If you were to live long life you would witness what the Prophet, Abul Qasim, had already said about 'offering a handful of ...' i.e. the Prophet's prophecies did really come true." [Sahih Al-Bukhari; Mishkat Al-Masabih 2/524]

INVASION OF TABUK IN RAJAB, IN THE YEAR 9 A.H.

The invasion and the conquest of Makkah was considered a decisive one between the truth and the error. As a result of which, the Arabs had no more doubt in Muhammad's mission. Thus we see that things went contrary to the pagans' expectations. People started to embrace Islam, the religion of Allâh, in great numbers.

This is manifested clearly in the chapter-The delegations, of this book. It can also be deduced out of the enormous number of people who shared in the *Hajjatul-Wadâ'*(Farewell Pilgrimage). All domestic troubles came to an end. Muslims, eventually felt at ease and started setting up the teachings of Allâh's Laws and intensifying the Call to Islam.

THE UNDERLYING REASONS

The Byzantine power, which was considered the greatest military force on earth at that time, showed an unjustifiable opposition towards Muslims. As we have already mentioned, their opposition started at killing the ambassador of the Messenger of Allâh, Al-Harith bin 'Umair Al-Azdi, by Sharhabeel bin 'Amr Al-Ghassani. The ambassador was then carrying a message from the Prophet to the ruler of Busra. We have also stated that the Prophet consequently dispatched a brigade under the command of Zaid bin Haritha, who had a fierce fight against the Byzantines at Mu'tah. Although Muslim forces could not have revenge on those haughty over-proud tyrants, the confrontation itself had a great impression on the Arabs, all over Arabia.

Caesar-who could neither ignore the great benefit that Mu'tah Battle had brought to Muslims, nor could he disregard the Arab tribes' expectations of independence, and their hopes of getting free from his influence and reign, nor he could ignore their alliance to the Muslims-realizing all that, Caesar was aware of the progressive danger threatening his borders, especially Ash-Sham-fronts which were neighbouring Arab lands. So he concluded that demolition of the Muslims power had grown an urgent necessity. This decision of his should, in his opinion, be achieved before the Muslims become too powerful to conquer, and raise troubles and unrest in the adjacent Arab territories. To meet these exigencies, Caesar mustered a huge army of the Byzantines and pro-Roman Ghassanide tribes to launch a decisive bloody battle against the Muslims.

GENERAL NEWS ABOUT THE BYZANTINES AND GHASSANIDE PREPARATIONS FOR WAR

No sooner news about the Byzantine's preparations for a decisive invasion against Muslims reached Madinah than fear spread among them. They started to envisage the Byzantine invasion in the least sound they could hear. This could be clearly worked out of what had happened to 'Umar bin Al-Khattab one day. The Prophet had taken an oath to stay off his wives for a month in the ninth year of Al-Hijra. Therefore, he deserted them and kept off in a private place. At the beginning, the Companions of the Messenger of Allâh were puzzled and could not work out the reason for such behaviour. They thought the Prophet had divorced them and that was why he was grieved, disturbed and upset.

In 'Umar's version of the very story he says: "I used to have a Helper friend who often informed me about what happened if I weren't present, and in return I always informed him of what had taken place during his absence. They both lived in the high part of Madinah. Both of them used to call at the Prophet alternatively during that time of suspense. Then one day I heard my friend, knock at the door saying: "Open up! Open up!" I asked wondering, "What's the matter? Has the Ghassanide come?" "No it is more serious than that. The Messenger of Allâh has deserted his wives."

In another version, 'Umar said, "We talked about Ghassanide preparations to invade us. When it was his turn to convey the news to me, he went down and returned in the evening. He knocked at the door violently and said 'Is he sleeping?' I was terrified but I went out to meet him. 'Something serious had taken place.' He said. 'Has the Ghassaindes arrived?' Said I. 'No,' he said, 'it is greater and more serious. The Messenger of Allâh has divorced his wives.'" This state of too much alertness manifests clearly the seriousness of the situation that Muslims began to experience. The seriousness of the situation was confirmed to a large degree by the hypocrites behaviour, when news about the Byzantines' preparations reached Madinah.

The fact that the Messenger of Allâh won all the battles he fought, and that no power on earth could make him terrified, and that he had always proved to be able to overcome all the obstacles that stood in his way - did not prevent the hypocrites, who concealed evil in their hearts, from expecting an affliction to fall upon the Muslims and Islam. They used to harbour evil and ill-intentions against the whole process of Islam and the Muslims.

On grounds of illusory hopes of destroying this great religious edifice, they erected a hotbed of conspiracy and intrigue in the form of a mosque-*Masjid-e-Darar* (the mosque of harm). They approached the Prophet with the request that he should come and consecrate the place by praying in it himself. As he was at the moment about to start for Tabuk, he deferred compliance with their request till his return. Meanwhile he came to know through Divine Revelation that it was not a Mosque for devotion and prayer but a meeting place for the anti-Islamic elements. On his return, therefore, the Prophet sent a party to demolish the new structure.

PARTICULAR NEWS ABOUT THE BYZANTINE AND GHASSANIDE PREPARATIONS FOR WAR

A magnified image of the prominent danger threatening the Muslims life was carried to them by the Nabateans who brought oil from Ash-Sham to Madinah. They carried news about Heraclius' preparations and equipment of an enormous army counting over forty thousand fighters besides Lukham, Judham and other tribes allied to the Byzantines. They said that its vanguard had already reached Al-Balqâ'. Thus was the grave situation standing in ambush for the Muslims? The general situation was aggravated seriously by other adverse factors of too much hot weather, drought and the rough and rugged distance they had to cover in case they decided to encounter the imminent danger.

The Messenger of Allâh's concept and estimation of the situation and its development was more precise and accurate than all others. He thought that if he tarried or dealt passively with the situation in such a way that might enable the Byzantines to paddle through the Islamic controlled provinces or to go as far as Madinah, this would-amid these circumstances-leave the most awful impression on Islam as well as on the Muslims' military credibility. The pre-Islamic beliefs and traditions (*Al-Jahiliyah*) which were at that time dying because of the strong decisive blow that they had already had at Hunain, could have had a way to come back to life once again in such an environment.

The hypocrites who were conspiring against the Muslims so they might stab them in the back whereas Byzantines would attack them from the front. If such a thing came to light and they succeeded in their evil attempts, the Prophet and his Companions' efforts to spread Islam would collapse and their profits which were the consequences of successive and constant fights and invasions would be invalidated. The Messenger of Allâh realised all that very well. So-in spite of the hardships and drought that Muslims were suffering from-the Prophet was determined that the Muslims should invade the Byzantines and fight a decisive battle at their own borders. He was determined not to tarry at all in order to thwart any Roman attempt to approach the land of Islam.

When the Messenger of Allâh had made up his mind and took his final decision, he ordered his Companions to get ready for war and sent for the Makkans and the other Arab tribes asking for their assistance. Contrary to his habit of concealing his real intention of the invasion by means of declaring a false one, he announced openly his intention of meeting the Byzantines and fighting them. He cleared the situation to his people so that they would get ready, and urged them to fight in the way of Allâh. On this occasion a part of *Surat Bara'a* was sent down by Allâh, urging them to steadfastness and stamina.

On the other hand, the Messenger of Allâh cherished them to pay charities and to spend the best of their fortunes in the way of Allâh. No sooner had the Muslims heard the voice of the Messenger of Allâh calling them to fight the Byzantines than they rushed to comply with his orders. With great speed they started getting ready for war. Tribes and phratries from here and there began pouring in Madinah. Almost all the Muslims responded positively. Only those who had weakness at their hearts favoured to stay behind. They were only three people. Even the needy and the poor who could not afford a ride came to the Messenger of Allâh asking for one so that they would be able to share in the fight against the Byzantines. But when he said:

> "...'I can find no mounts for you' they turned back while their eyes overflowing with tears of grief that they could not find anything to spend (for *Jihad*)." [Al-Qur'an 9:92]

The Muslims raced to spend out money and to pay charities to provide this invasion. 'Uthman, for instance, who had already rigged two hundred, saddled camels to travel to Ash-Sham, presented them all with two hundred ounces (of gold) as charity. He also fetched a thousand dinars and cast them all into the lap of the Messenger of Allâh, who turned them over and said: "From this day on nothing will harm 'Uthman regardless of what he does." Again and again 'Uthman gave till his charity toped to nine hundred camels and a hundred horses, besides the money he paid.

Abdur Rahman bin 'Awf, on his side, paid two hundred silver ounces, whereas Abu Bakr paid the whole money he had and left nothing but Allâh and His Messenger as a fortune for his family. 'Umar paid half his fortune. Al-'Abbas gifted a lot of money. Talhah, Sa'd bin 'Ubadah and Muhammad bin Maslamah, gave money for the welfare of the invasion. 'Asim bin 'Adi, on his turn, offered ninety camel-burdens of dates. People raced to pay little and much charities alike. One of them gave the only half bushel (or the only bushel) he owned. Women shared in this competition by giving the things they owned; such as musk, armlets, anklets, ear-rings and rings. No one abstained from spending out money, or was too mean to grant money or anything except the hypocrites:

> "Those who defame such of the believers who give charity (in Allâh's cause) voluntarily and those who could not find to give charity (in Allâh's cause) except what is available to them so they mock at them (believers)."

THE MUSLIM ARMY IS LEAVING FOR TABUK

Upon accomplishing the equipment of the army, the Messenger of Allâh ordained that Muhammad bin Maslamah Al-Ansari should be appointed over Madinah-in another version Siba'bin 'Arftah. To 'Ali bin Abu Talib he entrusted his family's safety and affairs and ordered him to stay with them. This move made the hypocrites undervalue 'Ali, so he followed the Messenger of Allâh and caught up with him. But the Prophet made 'Ali turn back to Madinah after saying: "Would it not suffice you to be my successor in the way that Aaron (Harun) was to Moses'?" Then he preceded saying: "But no Prophet succeeds me."

On Thursday, the Messenger of Allâh marched northwards to Tabuk. The army that numbered thirty thousand fighters was a great one, when compared with the previous armies of Islam. Muslims had never marched with such a great number before. Despite all the gifts of wealth and mounts the army was not perfectly equipped. The shortage of provisions and mounts was so serious that eighteen men mounted one camel alternatively. As for provisions, members of the army at times had to eat the leaves of trees till their lips got swollen. Some others had to slaughter camels-though they were so dear-so that they could drink the water of their stomach; that is why that army was called "The army of distress".

On their way to Tabuk, the army of Islam passed by Al-Hijr-which was the native land of Thamud who cut out (huge) rocks in the valley; that is "Al-Qura Valley" of today. They watered from its well but later the Messenger of Allâh told them not to drink of that water, nor perform the ablution with it. The dough they made, he asked them to feed their camels with. He forbade them to eat anything whatsoever of it. As an alternative he told them to water from that well which Prophet Salih's she-camel used to water from.

On the authority of Ibn 'Umar: "Upon passing by Al-Hijr the Prophet said:

> "Do not enter the houses of those who erred themselves lest what had happened to them would afflict you, but if you had to do such things let it be associated with weeping."

Then he raised his head up and accelerated his strides till he passed the valley out." [Sahih Al-Bukhari 2/637]

Shortage of water and the army's need to it made them complain to the Messenger of Allâh about that. So he supplicated Allâh, who sent a rainful cloud. It rained and so all people drank and supplied themselves with their need of water. When they drew near Tabuk, the Prophet said: "If Allâh will, tomorrow you will arrive at Tabuk spring. You will not get there before daytime. So whoever reaches it should not touch its water; but wait till I come." Mu'adh said: "When we reached the spring it used to gush forth some water. We found that two men had already preceded us to it.

The Messenger of Allâh asked them: 'Have you touched its water?' They replied: 'Yes'. He said what Allâh inspired him to say, then he scooped up little water of that spring, thin stream which gathered together, he washed his face and hand with it and poured it back into it; consequently plenty of water spouted out of it so people watered. 'Mu'adh', said the Messenger of Allâh, 'if you were doomed to live long life you will see in here fields full of vegetation.'" On the way to Tabuk, or as soon as they reached Tabuk, the Messenger of Allâh said: 'Severe wind will blow tonight, so none of you should stand up. Whoever has a camel should tie it up.' Later on when the strong wind blew, one of the men stood up and the wind carried him away to Tai' Mountain.

All the way long the Messenger of Allâh was intent on the performance of the combined prayer of noon and the afternoon; and so did he with sunset and evening prayers. His prayers for both were either pre-time or post-time prayers.

THE ARMY OF ISLAM AT TABUK

Arriving at Tabuk and camping there, the Muslim army was ready to face the enemy. There, the Messenger of Allâh delivered an eloquent speech that included the most inclusive words. In that speech he urged the Muslims to seek the welfare of this world and the world to come. He warned and cherished them and gave them good tidings. By doing that he cherished those who were broken in spirits, and blocked up the gap of shortage and mess they were suffering from due to lack of supplies, food and other substances. Upon learning of the Muslims' march, the Byzantines and their allies were so terrified that none of them dared set out to fight.

On the contrary they scattered inside their territory. It brought, in itself, a good credit to the Muslim forces. That had gained military reputation in the mid and remote lands of Arabian Peninsula. The great and serious political profits that the Muslim forces had obtained were far better than the ones they could have acquired if the two armies had been engaged in military confrontation. The Head of Ailah, Yahna bin Rawbah came to the Messenger of Allâh, made peace with him and paid him the tribute (*Al-Jizya*). Both of Jarba' and Adhruh peoples paid him tribute, as well. So the Messenger of Allâh gave each a guarantee letter, similar to Yahna's, in which he says:

"In the Name of Allâh, the Most Beneficent, the Most Merciful.

This is a guarantee of protection from Allâh and Muhammad the Prophet, the Messenger of Allâh, to Yahna bin Rawbah and the people of Ailah; their ships, their caravans on land and sea shall have the custody of Allâh and the Prophet Muhammad, he and whosoever are with him of Ash-Sham people and those of the sea. Whosoever contravenes this treaty, his wealth shall not save him; it shall be the fair prize of him that takes it. Now it should not be lawful to hinder the men from any springs which they have been in the habit of frequenting, nor from any journeys they desire to make, whether by sea or by land."

The Messenger of Allâh dispatched Khalid bin Al-Waleed at the head of four hundred and fifty horsemen to 'Ukaidir Dumat Al-Jandal and said to him: "You will see him hunting oryxes." So when Khalid drew near his castle and was as far as an eye-sight range, he saw the oryxes coming out rubbing their horns against the castle gate. As it was a moony night Khalid could see Ukaidir come out to hunt them, so he captured him-though he was surrounded by his men-and brought him back to the Messenger of Allâh, who spared his life and made peace with him for the payment of two thousand camels, eight hundred heads of cattle, four hundred armours and four hundred lances. He obliged him to recognize the duty of paying tribute and charged him with collecting it from Dumat, Tabuk, Ailah and Taima'.

The tribes, who used to ally the Byzantines, became quite certain that their dependence oinn their former masters came to an end. Therefore they turned into being pro-Muslims. The Islamic state had therefore enlarged its borders to an extent that it, touched the Byzantines' and their agents' borders.

RETURNING TO MADINAH

The Muslim army returned from Tabuk victoriously, undeceived or wronged. That was because Allâh had sufficed them the evils of fight. On the way back and at a mountain road, twelve hypocrites sought the Prophet's life and that was while he was passing along that mountain road with only Ammar holding the rein of his she-camel and Hudhaifa bin Al-Yaman driving it, at the time that people had already gone down into the bottom of the valley. The hypocrites seized that opportunity to seek the Prophet's life. As the Messenger of Allâh and his two companions were moving along, they heard thrusts of people coming towards him from behind with their faces veiled. Hudhaifa, who was sent by the Prophet to see what, was going on, saw them and stroke their mounts' faces with a crook in his hand and Allâh cast fear into their hearts. They fled away and overtook their people.

However, Hudhaifa named them to the Messenger of Allâh and informed him of their intentions. So that was why Hudhaifa was called the "confidant" of the Messenger of Allâh. About this event Allâh, the Exalted says:

> "And they resolved that (plot to murder Prophet Muhammad) which they were unable to carry out." [Al-Qur'an 9:74]

When his headquarters, Madinah, began to loom at the horizon, the Prophet said: "This is a cheerful sight. This is Uhud, which is a mountain, we like it and it likes us." When the

Madinese learnt of their arrival they set out to meet the army. Women, youths, youngsters and small children went out of town to celebrate their home-return wholeheartedly singing:

> "The full moon shone down upon us, through the traits of Al-Wada'Mountain. Thanks is due to us, as long as a supplicator invokes to Allâh."

The Messenger of Allâh's march to Tabuk was in Rajab and his return in Ramadan. So we see that this *Ghazwah* took fifty days, twenty days of which were spent in Tabuk and the others on the way to and fro. Tabuk Invasion was the last one made by the Prophet.

THE PEOPLE WHO LAGGED BEHIND

Due to its particular circumstances, this invasion was a peculiar severe trial provided by Allâh only to try the believers'Faith and sort them out of others. This is Allâh's permanent Will in such circumstances. In this respect He says:

> "Allâh will not leave the believers in the state in which you are now, until He distinguishes the wicked from the good." [Al-Qur'an 3:179]

Lagging and hanging back from full participation in that invasion amounted to the degree of hypocrisy. Whenever the Messenger of Allâh was informed of a man's lingering, he would say: "Leave him alone! If Allâh knows him to be good He will enable him to follow you; but if he were not so, Allâh would relieve us of him."

Nobody stayed behind except those who were either hindered by a serious excuse or the hypocrites who told lies to Allâh and His Messenger. Some of those hypocrites' lingering was due to an excuse based on forgery and delusion. Some others tarried but didn't ask for an instant permission. But there were three believers who unjustifiably lingered. They were the ones whom Allâh tried their Faith, but later on He turned to them in mercy and accepted their repentance.

As soon as the Messenger of Allâh had entered Madinah, he prayed two *Rak'a* then he sat to receive his people. The hypocrites who were over eighty men [Fath Al-Bari 8/119] came and offered various kinds of excuses and started swearing. The Prophet acknowledged their excuses and invoked Allâh's forgiveness for them but he entrusted their inner thoughts and Faith to Allâh.

As for the three faithful believers-Ka'b bin Malik, Murara bin Ar-Rabi', and Hilal bin Omaiyah-who favoured telling the truth, the Messenger of Allâh bade his Companions not to talk to them.

Consequently they were subject to a severe boycott and were excluded from the life of the community. Everybody turned them their back. So they felt as if the whole land had become constrained to them in spite of its spaciousness and they felt awkward and uneasy. The hard times they lived and which lasted for over forty days were towered by an order to them to forsake their wives. After fifty days' boycott Allâh turned to them and revealed that in *Quran*:

> "And (He did forgive also) the three (whom the Prophet left (i.e. he did not give his judgement in their case, and their case was suspended for Allâh's Decision) till for them the earth, vast as it is, was straitened and their ownselves were straitened to them, and they perceived that there is no fleeing from Allâh, and no refuge but with Him. Then, He accepted their repentance that they might repent (unto Him). Verily, Allâh is the One Who accepts repentance, Most Merciful." [Al-Qur'an 9:118]

Allâh's turning to them was a great joy for both Muslims and the three concerned. The joy of the stayers behind was unaccountable in aim and degree. It was the happiest day in their lives. The good tiding cherished them and filled their hearts with delight. As for those who lingered due to disability or sickness or any other serious excuse, Allâh, the Exalted said about them:

> "There is no blame on those who are weak or ill or who find no resources to spend [in holy warfare (*Jihad*)], if they are sincere (in duty) to Allâh and His Messenger." [Al-Qur'an 9:91]

When he approached Madinah, the Messenger of Allâh said:

"Inside Madinah, there are certain men, who though being left back due to serious excuses, they have, all the time, been with you. Lingerers as they are, they have been while you were passing valleys or walking along roads." "Do you mean that they have done that while they are still in Madinah?" They wondered. "Yes though they are in Madinah." The Prophet said.

THE INVASION OF TABUK AND ITS FAR-REACHING RAMIFICATIONS

The effect of this invasion is great as regards extending and confirming the Muslims' influence and domination on the Arabian Peninsula. It was quite obvious to everybody that no power but Islam's would live long among the Arabs. The remainders of *Jahiliyin* and hypocrites - who used to conspire steadily against the Muslims and who perpetually relied on Byzantine power when they were in need of support or help - these people lost their expectations and desires of ever reclaiming their ex-influence. Realizing that there was no way out and that they were to submit to the *fait accompli*, they gave up their attempts.

From that time on, hypocrites were no longer treated leniently or even gently by the Muslims. Allâh not only bade Muslims to treat them severely but He also forbade them to take their gift charities or perform prayer on their dead, or ask Allâh's forgiveness for them or even visit their tombs. Allâh bade the Muslims to demolish the mosque, which they verily appointed and used as a hiding place where they might practise their plots, conspiracy and deceit. Some Quranic verses were sent down disclosing them publicly and utterly so that everybody in Madinah got to know their reality.

The great impact that this invasion produced could be perceived in of the great number of delegations who came successively to meet the Messenger of Allâh. Naturally, deputations used to come to meet him at the end of an invasion particularly after Makkah Conquest [Ibn Hisham 2/515-537;

Za'd Al-Ma'ad 3/2-13; Sahih Al-Bukhari 2/633,635-637, 1/252, 414; Fath Al-Bari 8/110-126; Mukhtasar Seerat Ar-Rasool p.391-407] but they were not as many as these nor were they as frequent as they were then in the wake of Tabuk event. It was certainly the greatest.

QUR'ANIC VERSES RELATING TO THIS INVASION

Many a verse of *Bara'a* (*Tauba*) Chapter handling the event of Tabuk was revealed. Some verses were revealed before the march, while others after setting out for Tabuk, i.e. in the context of the battle. Some other verses were also revealed on the Prophet's arrival in Madinah. All of which covered the incidents that featured this invasion: the immanent circumstances of the battle, exposure of the hypocrites, the prerogatives and special rank earmarked for the strivers in the cause of Allâh, acceptance of the repentance of the truthful believers who slackened and those who hung back, etc.

SOME IMPORTANT EVENTS THAT FEATURED THAT YEAR

During this year many events of great significance took place. They were:

1. After the Messenger's return from Tabuk, the sworn allegation of infidelity [In case of an infidelity accusation that lacks evidence, both husband and wife swear by Allah that they are innocent and did not commit infidelity. The Husband invokes Allah's curses on himself if he is lying and the women invokes Allah's wrath on her if she is lying] between 'Uwaimir Al-'Ajlani and his wife took place.
2. Pelting with stones the Ghamidiyah woman who confessed committing adultery. She was pelted with stones only after weaning her child off her breast milk.
3. Negus Ashama; the king of Abyssinia (Ethiopia), died so the Prophet performed prayer in absentia for him.
4. The death of Umm Kulthum, the daughter of the Prophet, the Prophet felt extremely sad at her death. "Had I got

a third daughter, I would let you marry her." He said to 'Uthman.

5. The death of 'Abdullah bin Abi Salool, the head of hypocrites, after the Prophet's return from Tabuk. The Messenger of Allâh asked Allâh's forgiveness for him. He also prayed for him in spite of 'Umar's disapproval and his attempt to prevent him from doing that. Later on a *Quran*ic verse was revealed attesting to 'Umar's right viewpoint.

ABU BAKR PERFORMS THE PILGRIMAGE

In the month Dhul-Qa'dah or in Dhul-Hijjah of the very year (the ninth of Al-Hijra), the Messenger of Allâh dispatched Abu Bakr [R], the truthful, as a deputy prince of *Al-Hajj* (pilgrimage), so that he would lead the Muslims in performing of the pilgrimage rituals. Soon after the departure of the Muslims, there came a Revelation from Allâh: the opening passages of the Chapter 9 entitled 'Repentance' (*Surah Tauba* or *Bara'a*) in which 'freedom from obligation' is proclaimed from Allâh in regard to those idolatrous tribes who had shown no respect for the treaties which they had entered into with the *Prophet.* Communication of this news went in line with the Arabian traditions of making public any change relating to declining conventions of blood and fortunes.

'Ali bin Abi Talib was deputed to make this declaration. He overtook Abu Bakr at Al-'Arj or Dajnan. Abu Bakr inquired whether the Prophet had put him in command or he had just been commissioned to make the announcement. "I have been deputed to make the proclamation only" replied 'Ali. The two Companions then proceeded with the pilgrimage process. Towards the close of the rituals, on the day of the ritual sacrifice, 'Ali stood at *Al-Jamrah* (a spot at which stones are pelted) and read aloud to the multitudes that thronged around him and declared quittance from covenants with idolaters and giving them four months' respite to reconsider their position. As for the other idolaters with whom the believers had a treaty and had abated nothing of the Muslims' rights nor had supported anyone against them, then the terms of the treaty would run valid until the duration of which expired.

Abu Bakr then sent some Muslims to declare publicly that no disbeliever would after that year do not perform pilgrimage, nor would anyone be allowed to make the *Tawaf* (going round) of the Sacred House unclothed. That proclamation in fact vetoed all aspects of paganism out of Arabia and stated quite unequivocally that those pre-Islam practices were no longer in operation.[Sahih Al-Bukhari 1/220, 415, 2/626,671; Za'd Al-Ma'ad 3/25,26; Ibn Hisham 2/543-546]

A MEDITATION ON THE GHAZAWAT

Meditation on the Prophet's *Ghazawat*, missions, and the battalions he formed and dispatched, will certainly give us and everybody a true and clear impression that the Prophet was the greatest military leader in the whole world as well as the most righteous, the most insightful and the most alert one. He was not a man of superior genius for this concern but he was also the Master and the greatest of all Messengers as far as Prophethood and Heavenly Message are concerned. Besides, all the battles that he had fought were standard in their application to the requirements of strictness, bravery, and good arrangements that fitted the terms and conditions of war.

None of the battles he fought was lost as a consequence of shortage of wisdom or due to any other technical error in army mobilization or a location in a wrong strategical position. The loss of any of his battle was not due to misjudgement about occupying the best and the most appropriate sites of battles, nor was it due to a mischoice of leaders of the fight, for he had proved himself to be a peculiar sort of leader that differs from any of those leaders that our world had known and experienced. As regards Uhud and Hunain events, there were consequences of weakness in some military elements in Hunain; and disobedience to orders in Uhud.

Their non-compliance with wisdom and the plan of the battle played a passive role in the course of those two invasions.

His genius was clearly shown in these two battles when the Muslims were defeated; for he stoodfast facing the enemy and managed, by his super wisdom, to thwart the enemy's aim as was the case in Uhud. Similarly he managed to change the Muslims' defeat in Hunain into a victory. Nothwithstanding the fact that serious grave developments in military operations usually leave the worst impression on the military leaders and entice them to flee for their lives.

We have, so far, discussed the mere aspects of military leadership of the invasions. On the other hand, through these invasions he was able to impose security, institute peace, diffuse dissension and destroy the military might of the enemies through relentless struggle between Islam and paganism. The Prophet had also profound insight and could differentiate the faithful from the hypocrites and plotters. Great was the group of military leaders who fought and excelled the Persians and the Byzantines in the battlefields of Ash-Sham and Iraq with respect to war strategy and leading the fight procedures. The very leaders, who succeeded Muhammad, managed to drive off the enemies of Islam, from their lands and countries, their gardens and springs, and their farms. They drove them off their honourable residence and from the grace and provisions they owned and enjoyed. Those Muslim leaders were all Muhammad's men. They were imbued with the spirit of Islam at the hand of the Prophet.

Thanks to these battles, the Messenger of Allâh managed accommodation, secured land and provided chances of work for all Muslims. He, even, made a lot of inquiries about the refugee problems who (then) had no houses or fortunes. He equipped the army with weapons, horses and expenditures. He had all that realized without exercising a particle weight of injustice. The Prophet has altered the standards and aims of pre-Islamic wars. Their war was no more than robbing, killing, plundering, tyranny and aggression-oriented wars. Those wars focused on winning victory, oppressing the weakling and demolishing their houses and constructions. For them, war was a means by which they can rape or unveil women, practise cruelty against the weakling, the babies and small children, spoil tillage and race, and spread corruption on the earth. Islamic wars are different from pre-Islamic wars.

A "war" in Islam is a *Jihad*. That is to say it is a noble sacred fight in the way of Allâh for the verification of a Muslim society that seeks to free man from oppression, tyranny and aggression. It is a society that everyone everywhere and at all times should be proud of. Pre-Islamic thoughts and traditions of *Al-Jahiliyah* period have been turned upside down by Islam. These were so hard upon the weakling that they had to invoke Allâh to enable them to get away from that pre-Islamic environment by saying:

> "Our Lord, rescue us from this town whose people are oppressors, and rise for us from You one who will protect, and rise for us from You one who will help."

The war of corruption, slaying and robbing that used to prevail has now turned into a sacred one, *Al-Jihad*. One of the greatest aims of *Al-Jihad* is to free man from the aggression, the oppression and the tyranny of men of power. A man of power, in Islam, is a weakling till after the right of the poor is taken from him. War, in Islam, is a *Jihad* for the purification of the land of Allâh from deception, treachery, sinful deeds and aggression. It is a sacred war that aims at spreading security, safety, mercy and compassion as well as observing the rights and magnanimity.

The Messenger of Allâh had issued honourable strict rules about war and bade his soldiers and leaders to comply with them. They were forbidden to break those rules under any circumstances. In reference to Sulaiman bin Buraidah's version, who said that his father had told him that whenever the Messenger of Allâh appointed a leader on an army or on a battalion, he used to recommend him to fear Allâh, the Great and All-Mighty, when dealing with those who were closest to him and to be good with all Muslims. Then the Prophet would say to him:

> "Let your invasion be in the Name of Allâh and for His sake. Fight those who disbelieve in Allâh. Invade but do not exaggerate nor commit treachery. Never deform the corpse of a dead person or kill an infant child."

The Messenger of Allâh asked people to facilitate but he forbade them to bear down hard on others or constrain. "Pacify", he said, "and do not disincline". [Sahih Muslim 2/ 82,83] When it happened that he arrived at the battlefield by night, he would never invade the enemy till it was morning. He utterly forbade burning (i.e. torturing people) in fire, killing children and women or even beating them. He also forbade theft and robbery and proceeded so far as to say gains acquired through plundering are not less forbidden than the flesh of a corpse. Corruption of tillage and race and cutting down of trees were all forbidden unless they were badly needed and there was no other substitute:

> "Do not kill a wounded person nor run after a fleeing one or kill a captive."

He decreed that envoys cannot be killed. He also stressed on not killing those who made covenants. He even said:

> "He whoever kills one who is under pledge to a covenant shall not smell Paradise, though its smell could be experienced at a forty-year distance from it."

There were some other noble rules which purified wars from their *Al-Jahiliyah* (pre-Islamic) filthiness and turned them into sacred wars. [Za'd Al-Ma'ad 2/64-68; and for details Jihad in Islam p.216-262]

PEOPLE EMBRACE THE RELIGION OF ALLÂH IN LARGE CROWDS

The invasion and the conquest of Makkah were - as we have already stated - a decisive battle that destroyed paganism utterly. The Arabs as a result of that battle were able to differentiate the truth from the error. Delusion no longer existed in their life. So they raced to embrace Islam. 'Amr bin Salamah said: "We were at water (spring) where the passage of people was. So when camel riders passed by us we used to ask them: 'What is the matter with people? What is this man (i.e. the Prophet) like?' They would say, 'He claims that Allâh has revealed so and so.' I used to memorize those words as if they had been recited within my chest. The Arabs used to ascribe their Islamization to the conquest.

They would say: 'Leave him alone to face his people. If he were a truthful Prophet he would overcome them.' So when the conquest took place, peoples hastened to declare their Islam. My father was the quickest of all my people to embrace Islam. Arriving at his people he said: 'By Allâh I have just verily been to the Prophet. And he said: 'Perform so a prayer at such a time, and so and so prayers at such and such time.

When the prayer time is due let one of you call for the prayer and appoint the most learned of the *Quran* among you to be an *Imam* (leader) of yours. [Sahih Al-Bukhari 2/615,616]" This Prophetic tradition manifests the great effect of the conquest of Makkah on the phase of events. It certainly shows the influence of the conquest of Makkah upon the consolidation of Islam as well as on the Arabs' stand and their surrender to Islam. That influence was absolutely confirmed and deeply rooted after the invasion of Tabuk.

A clear and an obvious evidence of that influence could be deduced from the great number of delegations arriving in Madinah successively in the ninth and tenth years of Al-Hijra. The immense crowds of people who raced to embrace the religion of Allâh and the great army which included ten thousand fighters in the invasion of the conquest of Makkah had grown big enough to include thirty thousand fighters sharing in Tabuk invasion. It was only in less than a year after the conquest of Makkah that this growth in Islamic army had taken place. A hundred thousand or a hundred and forty four thousand Muslim pilgrims shared in *Hajjatul -Wada'*(i.e. Farewell Pilgrimage); it was such an enormous number of Muslims surging-as an ocean of men-round the Messenger of Allâh, that the horizon echoed their voices and the expanses of land shook whereby while saying *Labbaik* (i.e. Lord, here we are worshipping), glorifying and magnifying Allâh, and thanking Him.

THE DELEGATIONS

The number of delegations listed in *Ahl Al-Maghazi* was over seventy. Investigating such a large number is not an accessible thing; besides stating them in detail is not of a great benefit. Therefore, I am going to reveal an expose about what is historically wonderful or highly significant. Anyway a reader should always keep in mind that whilst the majority of tribes arrived in Madinah after the conquest, there were also pre-conquest delegations.

1. **The delegation of 'Abdul Qais**: This tribe had two arrivals. The first was in the fifth year of Al-Hijra or before that date. Munqidh bin Haiyan, a member of that tribe, used to trade in Madinah. So, as soon as he heard of Islam when he had arrived in it for trading-that was after the migration-he embraced Islam and carried a pledge from the Prophet to his people who eventually became Muslims too. Thirteen or fourteen of them came to the Prophet in one of the *Hurum* Months. It was then that they asked the Prophet's advice about the Faith and drinks. Their chief was Al-Ashaj Al-Usri, to whom the Messenger of Allâh said: "You have two qualities that Allâh likes: They are deliberatenessandclemency."

Their second arrival was in the Year of Delegations. They were forty men. Al-Jarud bin Al-'Alâ' Al-'Abdi, who was Christian but turned to be a good Muslim, was one of that groups. [Explanation of Sahih Muslim by An-Nawawi 1/33; Fath Al-Bari 8/85, 86]

2. **Daws Delegation**: The arrival of this tribe was in the early times of the seventh year and that was when the Messenger of Allâh was in Khaibar. At-Tufail bin 'Amr Ad-Dawsi, that we have already talked about and explained how he became a Muslim at the time the Messenger of Allâh was in Makkah. He went back home to his people where he kept calling people to Islam but they tarried till he despaired of them and returned to the Messenger of Allâh and asked him to invoke Allâh against Daws but the Messenger of Allâh invoked Allâh to guide

Daws. Later on, Daws embraced Islam. So At-Tufail arrived in Madinah accompanied by seventy or eighty families of his people in the early times of the seventh year of Al-Hijra, at the time that the Messenger of Allâh was at Khaibar, so he overtook him there.

3. **Farwah Bani 'Amr Al-Judhami's Messenger**: Farwah was an Arab leader in the Byzantine army. He was a Byzantine agent ruler by proxy on the Arabs allied to the Byzantines. His home was at Mu'an and the surrounding area of Ash-Sham lands. Seeing the stamina and courage of the Muslims he became a Muslim. The battle of Mu'tah - which took place in the eighth year of Al-Hijra-compelled his admiration. He sent a white mule gift with a messenger of his to the Messenger of Allâh to inform him of his conversion into Islam. When the Byzantines learnt of his embracing Islam, they sent him to prison. At first they gave him an opportunity to choose one of the two - "either he defects from Islam or death shall be his punishment." Refusing to defect they crucified him and cut his neck at a water (fountain) called 'Afra' in Palestine. [Za'd Al-Ma'ad 3/45; Tafheem-ul-Qur'an 2/169]
4. **Sudâ' Delegation**: The arrival of this delegation was after the departure of the Messenger of Allâh from Al-Ji'ranah in the eighth year of Al-Hijra. It was because the Messenger of Allâh had already dispatched a mission that comprised four hundred Muslims and asked them to go to where Sudâ' was. Sudâ' was (a fresh-water fountain) in Yemen. While the mission was camping there at the starting point of a canal. Ziyad bin Al-Harith As-Sudâ'i learned of their stay, so he came to the Messenger of Allâh and said: "I have come to you as a deputy of my people, so tell your army to go back and I guarantee of my people." The army were sent away off the canal. In his turn As-Sudâ'i went back, cherished and urged his people to come and meet the Messenger of Allâh. Eventually fifteen of them came and pledged allegiance to him as true Muslims. Returning home, they in their turn urged the rest to be Muslims. Thus Islam spread

among them. Later on, a hundred men joined the Messenger of Allâh in *Hajjatul-Wada'*(Farewell Pilgrimage.)

5. **The arrival of Ka'b bin Zuhair bin Abi Sulma**: Ka'b who was a member of a family of poets, was considered one of the most poetic Arab poets. He used to satirize the Prophet when he wasn't a Muslim. In the eighth year of Al-Hijra and at the time that the Messenger of Allâh had already gone back from At-Ta'if invasion, Bujair bin Zuhair wrote a letter to his brother Ka'b warning and advising him: "The Messenger of Allâh had killed some men in Makkah who used to satirize and harm him, and that the other poets who had survived fled in all directions for their lives. So if you want to save your skin, hasten to the Messenger of Allâh. He never kills those who resort to him as repentant. If you refuse to do as I tell, it is up to you to try to save your skin by any means." The two brothers corresponded with one another for a long time till Ka'b was awkward and felt as if the earth had constrained on him. Arriving in Madinah, he stayed at a man's house from Juhainah as a guest. They performed the dawn prayer together; but when he was about to leave, the man suggested that he go to the Messenger of Allâh. He went there; sat by him, put his hand in his. The Messenger of Allâh who had never seen Ka'b before, did not recognize him. Ka'b then said: "O, Messenger of Allâh! Ka'b bin Zuhair has come to you as a repentant Muslim; will he be secure and forgiven if I fetch him?" The Messenger of Allâh said, "Yes." "I am Ka'b bin Zuhair," said he. Upon hearing that one of the Helpers rose to his feet and asked the Messenger's allowance to cut his throat. "Leave him alone!" Said the Prophet, "He has become a repentant Muslim after his disposal of the past." Ka'b then recited his well-known poem "*Su'ad appeared...*" in which he praised the Prophet, thanked him and apologized for the wrongs he had done. He acknowledged Muhammad's mission. Both Emigrants and Helpers were spoken of in this poem but differently. He praised the Emigrants but criticized the Helpers, for one of them demanded a Prophet's permission to kill him.

Later on Ka'b tried to compensate for that by praising the Helpers too but that was in another poem.

6. **'Udharah Delegation**: This delegation which consisted of twelve men had arrived in Madinah in Safar, the ninth year of Al-Hijra. They spent three days there. One of them was Hamza bin An-Nu'man. When they were asked who they were, they said "We are Bani 'Udharah, the foster brothers of Qusai to his mother. We are the ones who supported Qusai, and removed Khuza'a and Bani Bakr from the bosom of Makkah. We have relatives and kinspeople." So the Messenger of Allâh welcomed them and gave good tidings to them, which was Ash-Sham Conquest; but he, on the other hand, forbade them from consulting a soothsayer and from eating the slain animals they slaughtered. Eventually they became Muslims, stayed there for several days then went back.
7. **Bali Delegation**: Their arrival was in Rabi' Al-Awwal, the ninth year of Al-Hijra. They embraced Islam, stayed in Madinah for three days. Their chief Abu Ad-Dabeeb wondered whether hospitality was rewarded by Allâh. The Messenger of Allâh said:

   "Yes, and so is any charity you offer to poor or rich people that is *Sadaqah*."

He also inquired about the time allotted to hospitality. "Three days," said he. "What about the stray ewe?" The Prophet said: "It is either yours or your brother's; otherwise it goes to the wolf." He inquired about the stray camel. "It is not of your business. Leave it alone! Its owner will try to find it."

8. **Thaqif Delegation**: Their arrival was in Ramadan, the ninth year of Al-Hijra, after the return of the Messenger of Allâh from Tabuk. As to how they became Muslims, this could be deduced from the following:

Their chief 'Urwah bin Mas'ud Ath-Thaqafi came to see the Messenger of Allâh after the latter's return from At-Ta'if in Dhul-Qa'dah in the year 8 A.H. 'Urwah became a Muslim. He thought that when he will tell his people and call them to embrace Islam, they would obey him, because he had always been an obeyed Master. He was even more beloved to them than their own firstborn. But contrary to that, when he called them to Islam they shot arrows at him from everywhere and killed him. They remained as they were for months before they started discussing the situation again among themselves. Upon realizing that they were incapable of fighting the neighbouring Arabs who had paid allegiance to the Prophet and converted to Islam, they made up their mind to dispatch a man to the Messenger of Allâh. They concluded that 'Abd Yalail bin 'Amr would be the right messenger.

'Abd refused to do such a thing lest they should kill him as they had killed 'Urwah. "I will not do such a thing till you send some other men with me," said 'Abd. So they sent two men of their allies and three others from Bani Malik. The six of them including 'Uthman bin Abi Al-'As Ath-Thaqafi who was the youngest among them all. When they entered into the Prophet's audience, a tent was pitched up in a corner of the mosque so that they might listen to the *Quran* and see people at prayer.

During their stay they came again and again to the Prophet who kept on calling them to embrace Islam, till their chief asked the Messenger of Allâh to enter into a peace treaty between him and Thaqif by means of which he allows them to commit fornication, drink wine and deal with usury. They also asked him not to injure their tyrant idol "Al-Lat" or to oblige them to perform the prayer. Finally they insisted that they would not knock down the idols themselves. But the Messenger of Allâh turned down all their requests. They went aside to council. Realizing that there were no other alternatives they yielded and professed Islam. The only condition that they insisted on was that the demolition of Al-Lat should be dealt with and handled by the Messenger of Allâh whereas Thaqif should in no way knock it down them. The Messenger of Allâh agreed and took a pledge with them.

Being the most attentive and the keenest to study jurisprudence and learn *Quran*, 'Uthman bin Abi Al-'As was appointed by the Messenger of Allâh a prince on his people. His keenness and carefulness to learn the *Quran* and study jurisprudence were clearly discernible through his behaviour during their stay. Everyday morning, the group of delegates used to go and see the Messenger of Allâh. Being the youngest one, 'Uthman bin Abi Al-'As was left behind with their camels and things to keep an eye on. At noon when they came back and slept, 'Uthman used to go to the Messenger of Allâh in order to learn the *Quran* and inquire about religious matters. If it happened that the Messenger of Allâh was asleep, he would then go to Abu Bakr for the same purpose.

With the passage of time, he turned out to be a source of blessing to his people. For at the Apostasy Times (*Ar-Riddah*) when Thaqif were determined to apostatize, he addressed them saying: "O, folkmen of Thaqif! You have been the latest at embracing Islam, so do not be the first to apostatize." Consequently they gave up apostasy and clung fast to Islam. The group of delegates returned home but they were determined to conceal the truth for a while. They told their people to expect fight at any moment. They pretended to be grieved and depressed. They claimed that the Messenger of Allâh demanded that they should embrace Islam and abandon adultery, drinking wine and dealing with usury and some other things, or else he would fight them.

Seized by the arrogance and zeal of *Al-Jahiliyah* (pre-Islamic traditions), Thaqif remained for days intent on fighting. Then Allâh cast terror and dismay in their hearts in such a way that they gave up fighting and thought that the delegation should go back to him and announce their approval. It was until then that the group of delegates told them the truth and revealed the items of their peace-talk with the Prophet, consequently Thaqif embraced Islam. The Messenger of Allâh sent some men to demolish the idol called "Al-Lat" under the command of Khalid bin Al-Waleed. Al-Mugheerah bin Shu'bah, stood to his feet, held the hoe and the axe and said: "By Allâh, I will make you laugh at Thaqif." He struck with them, and pretended to fall down while running.

The people of Thaqif trembled at that sight and said: "May Allâh dismay Al-Mugheerah off. The goddess has killed him." Hearing that Al-Mugheerah leapt up to his feet and said: "May Allâh bring shame on you. Al-Lat is nothing but a mass of dirt and stones." Then he struck the door and broke it. He mounted its highest wall, and so did the other men. They knocked Al-Lat down till they levelled it with the ground. Then they dug up its foundation and brought out its jewels and garments; to the great astonishment of Thaqif. Khalid bin Al-Waleed and his group came back to the Messenger of Allâh carrying Al-Lat's jewels and garments. The Messenger of Allâh distributed them and thanked Allâh for helping his Prophet and solidifying his religion. [Za'd Al-Ma'ad 3/26-28; Ibn Hisham 3/537-542]

9. **The message of the Yemeni kings**: After the return of the Messenger of Allâh from Tabuk, a message came to him from the kings of Himyar, Al-Harith bin 'Abd Kilal, Na'eem bin 'Abd Kilal, An-Nu'man bin Qeel Dhi Ra'in, Hamdan and Mu'afir. Their messenger was Malik bin Murrah Ar-Rahawi. They sent him in order to inform the Prophet about their embracing Islam and their parting with polytheism. In reply to their message, the Messenger of Allâh gave them the pledge of Allâh and the pledge of His Messenger provided they paid the tribute, which was still overdue. He sent to them some of his Companions under the command of Mu'adh bin Jabal [R].
10. **Hamdan Delegation**: The arrival of this delegation was in the ninth year of Al-Hijra after the Messenger's return from Tabuk. So the Messenger of Allâh gave them a pledge to guarantee the fulfillment of their demands. He sent to them Malik bin An-Namt as their chief, and appointed him as an agent on those of his people who embraced Islam. Khalid bin Al-Waleed was appointed for them all with a purpose of calling them to Islam. He stayed with them for six months calling them to Islam but no one responded to his call. Later on 'Ali bin Abi Talib was dispatched there and Khalid was ordered to come back. Upon arriving at Hamdan, 'Ali communicated

to them a message from the Messenger of Allâh and called them to Islam. They responded to the call and became Muslims. 'Ali wrote to the Messenger of Allâh informing him of the good tidings. The Messenger of Allâh was briefed on the content of that letter, so he prostrated, then raised his head up and said: "Peace be upon Hamdan. Peace be upon Hamdan."

11. **The Delegation of Bani Fazarah**: Upon the Messenger's return from Tabuk, the delegation of Bani Fazarah came to see him. That was in the ninth year of Al-Hijra. The group of delegates were over ten men. They came in order to profess Islam and complain about the drought of their region. The Messenger of Allâh ascended the pulpit, lifted his hands up and implored Allâh to send rain forth onto them and said:

    "O Allâh let rain fall down, and waters. Your country and animals, and spread Your mercy and bring to life the dead lands. O Allâh send rain that would be saving, comforting, and sprouting grass, and overwhelming vast areas sooner and later. Let it be useful rain and not harmful. O Allâh let it be rain of mercy and not rain of torture and chastisement. Let that rain not be destructive or floody. O Allâh send us down water and help to fight the enemies." [Za'd Al-Ma'ad 3/48]

12. Najran's Delegation: Najran is rather a big area of land. It was at a distance of seven trip stages southwards of Makkah towards Yemen. It included seventy three villages. It took a fast-rider one day ride to get there. [Fath Al-Bari 8/94] Its military forces consisted of a hundred thousand fighters.

Their arrival was in the year 9 A.H. The delegation comprised sixty men. Twenty-four of them were of noble families. Three out of twenty-four were at one time leaders of Najran. *Al-'Aqib*, i.e. who was in charge of princehood and government affairs. His name was 'Abdul Maseeh. The second was *As-Saiyid* (the Master) under whose supervision was the educational and political affairs; his name was Al-Aiham or Sharhabeel. Abu Haritha bin 'Alqamah was the third. He was a bishop to whom all religious presidency and spiritual leadership belonged and were his charge.

When that group of delegates arrived in Madinah, they met the Prophet, exchanged inquiries with him; but when he called them to Islam and recited the *Quran* to them, they refused. They asked him what he thought about 'Isa (i.e. Jesus), [AWS], he tarried a whole day till the following *Quran*ic reply was revealed to him:

> "Verily, the likeness of Jesus before Allâh is the likeness of Adam. He created him from dust, then (He) said to him: 'Be!'-and he was. (This is) the truth from your Lord, so be not of those who doubt. Then whoever disputes with you concerning him (Jesus) after (all this) knowledge that has come to you, (i.e. Jesus being a slave of Allâh, and having no share in Divinity) say: (O Muhammad) 'Come, let us call our sons and your sons, our women and your women, ourselves and yourselves-then we pray and invoke (sincerely) the Curse of Allâh upon those who lie." [Al-Qur'an 3:59-61]

When it was morning, the Messenger of Allâh told them what 'Iesa (Jesus) was in the light of the recently revealed verses. He left them a whole day to consult and think it over. So when it was next morning and they still showed disapproval to admit Allâh's Words about 'Isa or to embrace Islam, the Prophet suggested *Al-Mubahala* that is each party should supplicate and implore Allâh to send His Curse upon him or them if they were telling lies. After that suggestion of his, the Prophet came forward wrapping Al-Hasan and Al-Husain under his garment whereas Fatimah was walking at his back. Seeing that the Prophet was serious and prepared to face them firmly, they went aside and started consulting. *Al-'Aqib* and *As-Saiyid* (i.e. the Master) said to each other: "We shall not supplicate. For, I swear by Allâh, if he is really a Prophet and exchanges curses with us, we will never prosper nor will the descendants of ours. Consequently neither us nor our animals will survive it."

Finally they made their mind to resort to the Messenger of Allâh's judgement about their cause. They came to him and said: "We grant you what you have demanded." The Messenger of Allâh then admitted that agreement and ordered them to pay *Al-Jizya* (i.e. tribute) and he made peace with them for the provision of two thousand garments, one thousand of them to be delivered in Rajab, the other thousand ones in Safar. With every garment they had to pay an ounce (of gold). In return they will have the covenant of Allâh and His Messenger. He gave them a covenant that provides for practicing their religious affairs freely. They asked the Prophet to appoint a trustworthy man to receive the money agreed on for peace, so he sent them the trustworthy man of this nation Abu 'Ubaidah bin Al-Jarrah to receive the amounts of money agreed on in the peace treaty.

By the time Islam started to spread in Najran, naturally, they did not have to pay *Al-Jizya* that usually non-Muslims paid. Whatever the case was, it was said that *Al-Aqib* and *As-Saiyid* embraced Islam as soon as they reached Najran on their journey back home. It is also said that the Prophet sent to them 'Ali too, for the collection of charities and tribute. [Fath Al-Bari 8/94, 95; Za'd Al-Ma'ad 3/38-40]

13. **Bani Haneefa Delegation**: They arrived in Madinah in the ninth year of Al-Hijra. They were 17 in number and included the Master of Liars, Musailima [Fath Al-Bari 8/87] bin Thumamah bin Kabeer bin Habeeb bin Al-Harith of Bani Haneefa The group of delegates were housed in a Helper's house. They came to the Prophet and declared their Islamization. As for Musailima the liar, versions vary concerning his embracing Islam. Contemplation of all these versions shows clearly that Musailima expressed disapproval and revealed haughtiness, boastful spirit and expectations to be a prince.

At first the Prophet attempted going on well with him. He dealt with him nicely and charitably but that did not do with him. The Messenger of Allâh perceived evil in his soul and recognized that he was one of those three evils he dreamt of while asleep. The Prophet had already dreamt that he had been granted the treasures of earth. His hand fell upon two golden bracelets, which distressed and worried him a lot. He was taught by inspiration to blow them off, so he did that and they were gone off. They were interpreted to be two liars who would turn up after the death of Muhammad. So when Musailima acted that way and showed disapproval, he realized that he would be one of the two liars.

However Musailima used to say, "If Muhammad appointed me a successor of his, I would be a Muslim. Later on the Messenger of Allâh came to him, with a piece of palm leaf in his hand, and in the company of his orator, Thabit bin Qais bin Shammas. He was among some of his friends. The Prophet talked to him but Musailima addressed him saying: "If you agree to transfer the whole thing to me after your death, I will not stand in your way." The Messenger of Allâh replied: "If you asked me to give you this (i.e. a piece of a palm leaf), I would not grant it to you. You are doomed. Even if you repented and stopped what you were doing, Allâh appointed that you would be slain. By Allâh, I swear, that I see you now in the very state that has been revealed to me. Here is Thabit! You will hear my answer (from him)." Then he went away. [Sahih Al-Bukhari 2/627, 628; Fath Al-Bari 8/87-93]

Finally, the Prophet's predictions of Musailima came true; for when Musailima returned to Yamama, he kept on thinking about the Prophet and how he would be his partner. His dreams and thoughts went so far as to claim that he himself was a prophet. To confirm his prophecy he started uttering rhymed statements. He said that it was lawful to drink wine and commit adultery.

He, however, bore witness that the Messenger of Allâh was a real Prophet. His people, who were fascinated by what he allowed them to do, followed him and made bargains with him. He grew so prominent among them that they called him the beneficent of Al-Yamama. He wrote to the Messenger of Allâh saying: "I have been appointed an associate with you, so I will have a half and Quraish will have the other half of the people's affairs." The Messenger of Allâh's reply was a letter saying that:

> "Verily, the earth is Allâh's. He gives it as a heritage to which He will of His slaves, and the (blessed) end is

for the *Muttaqûn* (pious)." [Al-Qur'an 7:128] [Za'd Al-Ma'ad 3/31, 32]

On the authority of Ibn Mas'ud, he says: When the two messengers of Musailima-Ibn An - Nawaha and Ibn Athal-came to the Messenger of Allâh, he asked them: "Do you bear witness that I am the Messenger of Allâh?" Their reply was "We testify that Musailima is the Messenger of Allâh." "I believe in Allâh and in His Messenger," said the Prophet, "If I had ever thought of killing a messenger I would have killed you both." [Mishkat Al-Masabeeh 2/347]

Musailima's pretence to prophethood was in the tenth year of Al-Hijra. But he was killed in Al-Yamama war during Abu Bakr As-Siddeeq era, in Rabi'Al-Awwal, in the twelfth year of Al-Hijra. He was killed by Wahshi, the killer of Hamzah. The second person who claimed to be a prophet was Al-Aswad Al-'Ansi who was in Yemen. He was killed by Fairuz. His head was cut off a day and a night before the Prophet's death. So when the delegates came he told them the news that reached him through Divine Revelation. News about his death reached Abu Bakr [R] from Yemen. [Fath Al-Bari 8/93]

14. **The Delegation of Bani 'Amir bin Sa'sa'a**: Among the group of delegates were 'Amir bin At-Tufail-the enemy of Allâh, Arbad bin Qais-Labid's maternal brother, Khalid bin Ja'far, and Jabbar bin Aslam. All of them were the leaders and satans of their people. 'Amir was the one who double-crossed the group of Ma'una well. When this delegation made their mind to come to Madinah, 'Amir and Arbad conspired to kill the *Prophet.* So when the group of delegates arrived, 'Amir kept on talking to the Prophet whereas Arbad turned aside trying to draw his sword. He managed to draw a span of hand long but Allâh stilled his hand so that he was unable to proceed with its withdrawal. Allâh protected the *Prophet.* The Prophet invoked Allâh against them. So when they returned, Allâh sent down a thunderbolt unto Arbad and his camel and he was burnt. As for 'Amir he called at a house of a woman who was from Bani Salul and had a gland sore. He eventually died while he was saying:

"What am I like? I have a gland similar to a camel's. And here I am dying in the house of the woman from Bani Salul."

In *Sahih Al-Bukhari* it is narrated that 'Amir came to the Prophet and said: "I grant you an opportunity to choose one of two: you will have the flat land people and I will have towns people; or I will succeed you. Otherwise, I will invade your people with a thousand he-camels and a thousand she-camels." But, later on he got plague-stricken in a woman's house. So he said: "What! I have a gland similar to a camel's, and here I am in a woman's house of Bani so and so people. Fetch me my mare!" He mounted it but died on its back.

15. **Tujeeb Delegation**: They came to Madinah carrying the surplus of charities (*Sadaqat)* of their people. That is to say the extra charities they had after they had distributed the poor-due. They were thirteen men. They asked about the *Quran* and *Sunnah* (the Prophet's saying, deeds and sanctions) so that they might learn them. They demanded things from the Messenger of Allâh to which he gave them pledges. They did not stay long; so when the Messenger of Allâh acknowledged their demands and allowed them to depart, they sent him a boy whom they had already left at their property. The young man said to the Prophet : "By Allâh, I swear, I have left my home (for Madinah) with a purpose that you invoke Allâh, the Great and All-Mighty for me to forgive me and have mercy on me and to make my heart a source of content and sufficiency." The Messenger of Allâh supplicated Allâh to grant him what he demanded.

From that time on, he was the most contented person. In *Ar-Riddah* (i.e. the Apostasy Times), he stoodfast as a Muslim and warned his people and reminded them of Allâh and went on preaching them till they stoodfast and did not apostatize. The group of delegates met the Prophet again in the Farewell Pilgrimage in the tenth year of Al-Hijra.

16. **Tai' Delegation**: One of those groups of delegates who came to meet the Prophet was Zaid Al-Khail. They talked

to the Prophet who urged them to embrace Islam. They agreed and grew good Muslims. About Zaid, the Messenger of Allâh said: "The Arabs are never exact at estimating people. They have never told me about the virtues of a man correctly; for when I see the man concerned I realize that they have overestimated him except Zaid Al-Khail, when I met him I knew that they had underestimated him." Then he named him 'Zaid Al-Khair' (i.e. Zaid, the bounteous).

The delegations arrived successively in Madinah during the ninth and tenth of Al-Hijra. Biographers and invasion-writers have written down about some of Yemen delegations. They were Al-Azd; Bani Sa'd Hadheem from Quda'ah, Bani 'Amir bin Qais; Bani Asad, Bahra', Khaulan, Muharib, Bani Al-Harith bin Ka'b, Ghamid, Bani Al-Muntafiq, Salaman, Bani 'Abs, Muzainah, Murad, Zabid, Kinda, Dhi Murrah, Ghassan, Bani 'Aish, and Nakh'which were the last group of delegates. Nakh'Delegation comprised two hundred men and they arrived in the middle of Muharram in the eleventh year of Al-Hijra. The majority of these groups of delegates arrived during the ninth and tenth years of Al-Hijra. The arrival of some of them tarried till the eleventh year of Al-Hijra.

The succession of these delegations indicated the great degree of the entire acceptance which the Islamic Call reached. It manifested its influence and domination on vast areas of Arabia. The Arabs observed Al-Madinah with such a great respect and estimation that they could do nothing but surrender and submit to it. Al-Madinah had become the headquarters of all Arabia; so it was impossible to avoid it. We dare not say that all the Arabians were possessed and enchanted by this religion. There were lots of hard-hearted bedouins - among the Arabs - who surrendered (i.e. became Muslims) only because their master did so. Their souls were not sanctified yet. Their tendency to raids had been deeply rooted in their souls. The teachings of Islam had not crystallized their souls well yet. Accounting some of them the *Quran* says:

"The bedouins are the worst in disbelief and hypocrisy, and more likely to be in ignorance of the limits (Allâh's Commandments and His legal laws, etc.) which Allâh has revealed to His Messenger. And Allâh is All-Knower, All-Wise. And of the bedouins there are some who look upon what they spend (in Allâh's cause) as a fine and watch for calamities for you, on them be the calamity of evil. And Allâh is All-Hearer, All-Knower." [Al-Qur'an 9:97, 98]

The *Quran* praised others saying:

"And of the bedouins there are some who believe in Allâh and the Last Day, and look upon what they spend in Allâh's cause as approaches to Allâh, and a cause of receiving the Messenger's invocations. Indeed these are an approach for them. Allâh will admit them to His Mercy. Certainly Allâh is Oft-Forgiving, Most Merciful." [Al-Qur'an 9:99]

Those of them who were present at Makkah, Madinah and Thaqif and in many other areas of Al-Yemen and Al-Bahrain were different because Islam had been firmly rooted in their souls. Some of them were great Companions and Masters of Muslims. [Muhadarat Tareekh Al-Umam Al-Islamiyah 1/44; Sahih Al-Bukhari 1/13, 2/626-630; Ibn Hisham 2/501-503, 510-514, 537-542, 560-601; Za'd Al-Ma'ad 3/26-60; Fath Al-Bari 8/83-103; Rahmat-ul-lil'alameen 1/184-217]

THE SUCCESS AND IMPACT OF THE CALL

Before we move one more step and meditate on the last days of the Messenger of Allâh's life, we ought to cast a quick glance at the great work that was a peculiarity of his. That very peculiarity that made him excels all other Prophets and Messengers and made him so superb that Allâh made him atop the formers and the latters. It was him that was addressed by:

"O you wrapped in garments (i.e. Prophet Muhammad)! Stand (to pray) all night, except a little." [Al-Qur'an 73:1, 2]

And said:

"O you (Muhammad) enveloped (in garments). Arise and warn!" [Al-Qur'an 74:1,2]

So he arose and kept on like that for over twenty years. During those years he undertook to carry the burdens of the great expectations on his shoulders for the sake of the whole mankind and humanity, the Faith and *Jihad* in various fields.

The Messenger of Allâh undertook the burdens of struggle and *Al-Jihad* in the conscience of mankind which was then drowning in the illusions of *Al-Jahiliyah* and its images that were loaded with the ground weights and gravitations. He took upon his shoulder to free man's conscience which was chained with desires and lusts. As soon as he had freed the conscience of his Companions from the burdens and heaps of *Al-Jahiliyah* and earthly life, he started another battle in another field or rather successive battle against the enemy of Allâh's Call, and against those who conspired against it. It was a battle against those who conspired against the believers and against those who were so careful to tend that pure plant in its implantation before it grew up and stretched its roots in soil and extended its branches up into the air and thus dawned upon other areas. No sooner had he finished the battles in the Arabian Peninsula than the Byzantines began preparations to destroy this new nation on the northern borders.

The first battle - i.e. the battle of conscience - was not over yet. It was in fact a perpetual one. Satan, who was its leader, did not spare a moment without exercising his activity in the depth of human conscience. Muhammad, on the other hand was attending on calling to Allâh's religion there and he was keen on fighting that perpetual battle in all fields in spite of their hard circumstances and the world's conspiracy against him. He went on calling effectively and actively surrounded by the believers who were seeking security through ceaseless toil and great patience.

The Companions acted perpetually and patiently by day and they spent the night worshipping their Lord, reciting and memorizing the *Quran* glorifying and magnifying Allâh and imploring Him by night; all that at the behest of their

Lord, the All-Mighty. [Fi Zilal Al-Qur'an 29/168,169]

For over twenty years the Messenger of Allâh had been leading that progressive steady battle, disregarding any other affairs that kept him off that noble goal. He went on that way till the Islamic Call proved to be successful on a large scale that puzzled all men possessed of good reason.

The Islamic Call eventually prevailed all over Arabia. It removed all traces of *Al-Jahiliyah* from the horizon of the peninsula. The sick minds of *Al-Jahiliyah* grew healthy in Islam. They did not only get rid of idol-worship, but they also knocked them down. The general atmosphere began to echo "there is no god but Allâh." The calls to prayers were heard five times a day penetrating space and breaking the silence of the dead desert and bringing back life through the new belief. Reciters and memorizers of the *Quran* set out northwards and southwards reciting verses of the *Quran* and carrying out Allâh's injunctions.

Scattered people and tribes were united and man moved from man's worship of man to man's worship of Allâh. There were no more oppressors nor oppressed; no masters nor slaves, nor people bound to other people, nor aggressors that would practise aggression. All people were slaves of Allâh. They were beloved brothers obeying Allâh's rules. Thanks to Allâh they disposed of arrogance and the boastful spirit:

> "An Arab is no better than a non-Arab. In return a non-Arab is no better than an Arab. A red raced man was not better than a black one except in piety. Mankind is all Adam's children and Adam was created from dust."

Thanks to the Islamic Call, the Arab unity had become a reality, and so was the case with human unity and social justice as far as their earthly and heavenly affairs were concerned. The time course of events had changed, the features on the earth's surface and the crooked line of history had grown straight and the mentality had been rectified.

The spirit and the corrupted conscience of people, the distorted values and measures of *Al-Jahiliyah* had overwhelmed the whole world during that period of *Al-Jahiliyah.* The prevalence of slavery, injustice, extravagant luxury, adultery, depression, deprivity, disbelief, stray from the straight path and darkness; all of those were *fait accomplis* in spite of the existence of the heavenly religions. The teachings of those religions had grown weak and lost all influence on men's souls and spirits and became mere lifeless ritual traditions.

When this Call had accomplished its role in human life, it freed mankind's spirit of superstitions, illusions, white slavery, corruption and man's worship of man. Islam had freed the human society of filth, dissolution, injustice and tyranny. There were no more social distinctions, nor clergymen's or governors' dictatorship. Islam had set up a world built on solid virtuous and clean foundations; it was based on positivity, righteous construction, freedom and renewal. Truth, faith, dignity active steady deeds, the development and improvement of means of living and reclaim of rights were all bases upon which the Islamic state was built. [Madha Khasira Al-'Alam bi-Inhitatil-Muslimeen p.14]

Thanks to these evolutions, Arabia witnessed such an unprecedented blessed resurrection, since construction and establishment found its way to it. Never had its history been so religious, pious and brilliant as it had been during those peculiar days of its life.

4

The Farewell Pilgrimage

After the accomplishment of the Call, the proclamation of the Message and the establishment of a new society on the basis of 'There is no god but Allâh,' and on Muhammad's mission, a secret call uprose in the heart of the Messenger of Allâh telling him that his stay in the Lower World was about to terminate. That was clear in his talk to Mu'adh whom he had dispatched to Yemen in the tenth year of Al-Hijra: "O, Mu'adh! You may not see me after this current year. You may even pass by this very Mosque of mine and my tomb." Upon hearing that Mu'adh cried for fear that he would part with the Messenger of Allâh.

Allâh's care was so bounteous as to let the Prophet see the fruits of his Call for the sake of which he suffered various sorts of trouble for over twenty years. Those twenty years had elapsed actively. He used to spend his last days meeting, at the outskirts of Makkah, members of tribes and their representatives who used to consult him and learn the laws and legislation of Islam from him, and in return he used to exact their testimony that he had delivered trust and communicated the Message and counselled the people. The Messenger of Allâh announced an intention to proceed with this blessed pilgrimage journey himself.

Enormous crowds of people came to Madinah, all of whom seek the guidance and *Imamate* of the Messenger of Allâh in the pilgrimage (*Al-Hajj*). [Sahih Muslim 1/394] On a

Saturday of the last four days of Dhul-Qa'dah, the Prophet started the departure preparations procedure. [Fath Al-Bari 8/104] He combed his hair, applied some perfume, wore his garment, saddled his camel and set off in the afternoon. He arrived at Dhul-Hulaifa before the afternoon prayer. He performed two *Rak'a* and spent the night there. When it was morning he said to his Companions:

> "A comer, sent by my Lord, has called on me tonight and said: 'Pray in this blessed valley and say: I intend *'Umrah* combined with pilgrimage (*'Umrah* into *Al-Hajj*).[Sahih Al-Bukhari 1/207]

Before performing the noon prayer, he bathed for *Ihram* (ritual consecration), and 'Aishah [R] perfumed him on both his body and head with her hand with a *Dharira* (a plant) and with a perfume containing musk. The thick sticky layer of perfume could be seen among his parts of hair and beard. He left it unwashed, wore his loincloth and garment. He performed the noon prayer shortened, two *Rak'a*. He proclaimed pilgrimage procedure associated with *'Umrah* at his prayer-place. He, then mounted his she-camel 'Al-Qaswa', and proclaimed: 'There is no god but Allâh'. When he moved into the desert, he acclaimed the Name of Allâh.

He proceeded with his journey till he approached Makkah. He spent the night at Dhi Tuwa and entered Makkah after performing the dawn prayer. He had a bath on Sunday morning, the fourth of Dhul-Hijjah the tenth year of Al-Hijra. He spent eight days on the way, which was an average period. As soon as he entered Al-Haram Mosque he circumambulated Al-Ka'bah and walked to and fro (*Sa'i*) between As-Safa and Al-Marwah. He did not finish the *Ihram* (ritual consecration) because he was *Qarin* (i.e. intending *'Umrah* and *Al-Hajj* associated). He then took *Al-Hadi* (i.e. the sacrificial animals) in order to slaughter them. He camped on a high place of Makkah-Al-Hajun. As for circumambulation, he performed only that of *Al-Hajj* (pilgrimage circumambulation).

Those of his Companions who had no *Hadi* with them to sacrifice, were ordered to observe *Ihram* (i.e. the state of ritual consecration) into *'Umrah* (i.e. lesser pilgrimage), and circumambulate Al-Ka'bah and stride ritually to and fro between As-Safa and Al-Marwah. After that they could relieve themselves from *Ihram*. They, however, showed reluctance to do what they had been told. Thereupon, the Messenger of Allâh said: "Had I known beforehand what I knew afterward, I would not bring *Hadi*, and if I did not have *Hadi*, I would break *Ihram*. On hearing these words, his Companions obeyed the orders to the latter.

On the eighth day of Dhul-Hijjah-that is the Day of *Tarwiyah*, he left for Mina where he performed the noon, the afternoon, the sunset, the evening and the dawn prayers. - i.e. five prayers. Then he stayed for a while till the sun rose up then he passed along till he reached 'Arafah, where there was a tent built for him at Namirah. He sat inside till the sun went down. He ordered that Al-Qaswa', his she-camel, should be prepared for him. They saddled it and had it ready, so he went down the valley where a hundred thousand and twenty-four or forty-four thousand people gathered round him. There he stood up and delivered the following speech:

> "O people! Listen to what I say. I do not know whether I will ever meet you at this place once again after this current year. [Ibn Hisham 2/603] It is unlawful for you to shed the blood of one another or take (unlawfully) the fortunes of one another. They are as unlawful, (*Haram*) as shedding blood on such a day as today and in such a month as this *Haram* month and in such a sanctified city as this sacred city (i.e. Makkah and the surrounding areas)."
>
> "Behold! All practices of paganism and ignorance are now under my feet. The blood-revenge of the Days of Ignorance (pre-Islamic time) are remitted. The first claim on blood I abolish is that of Ibn Rabi'a bin Harith who was nursed in the tribe of Sa'd and whom Hudhail killed. Usury is forbidden, and I make a beginning by remitting the amount of interest which 'Abbas bin 'Abdul Muttalib has to receive. Verily, it is remitted entirely."

"O people! Fear Allâh concerning women. Verily you have taken them on the security of Allâh and have made their persons lawful unto you by Words of Allâh! It is incumbent upon them to honour their conjugal rights and, not to commit acts of impropriety which, if they do, you have authority to chastise them, yet not severely. If your wives refrain from impropriety and are faithful to you, clothe and feed them suitably."

"Verily, I have left amongst you the Book of Allâh and the *Sunnah* (Traditions) of His Messenger which if you hold fast, you shall never go astray." [Sahih Muslim 1/397]

"O people, I am not succeeded by a Prophet and you are not succeeded by any nation. So I recommend you to worship your Lord, to pray the five prayers, to fast Ramadan and to offer the *Zakat* (poor-due) of your provision willingly. I recommend you to do the pilgrimage to the Sacred House of your Lord and to obey those who are in charge of you then you will be awarded to enter the Paradise of your Lord." [Rahmat-ul-lil'alameen 1/263]

"And if you were asked about me, what wanted you to say?"

They replied:

"We bear witness that you have conveyed the message and discharged your ministry."

He then raised his forefinger skywards and then moved it down towards people while saying:

"O Allâh, Bear witness."

He said that phrase thrice. [Sahih Muslim 1/397]

The one who repeated the Prophet's statements loudly at 'Arafat was Rabi'a bin Omaiyah bin Khalaf. [Ibn Hisham 2/605]

As soon as the Prophet had accomplished delivering the speech, the following *Quran*ic verse was revealed to him:

"This day I have perfected your religion for you, completed My Favour upon you, and have chosen for you Islam as your religion." [Al-Qur'an 5:3]

Upon hearing this verse 'Umar cried. "What makes you cry?" He was asked. His answer was: "Nothing succeeds perfection but imperfection." [Rahmat-ul-lil'alameen 1/265]

Bilal called for prayer after the speech, and then made the second call. The Prophet performed both of the noon and the afternoon prayers separately, with no prayers in between. He then mounted his she-camel Al-Qaswa', approached the location of the vigil, directed his face towards *Al-Qiblah,* kept on standing till sunset when the sky yellow colour vanished a bit and the disc of the sun disappeared. Osamah added that the Prophet moved onward to Muzdalifa where he observed the sunset and the evening prayers with one 'First call' and two 'second calls'. He did not entertain the Glory of Allâh between the two prayers. Then he lay down till it was dawn prayer time. He performed it with one first call and one second calls at almost daybreak time. Mounting on his Al-Qaswa', he moved towards *Al-Mash'ar Al-Haram.*

He faced *Al-Qiblah* and started supplicating: "Allâh is the Greatest. There is no god but Allâh." He remained there till it was clear morning and before the sun rose high, he made his way to Mina. He walked a little and threaded the mid-road leading to the big *Jamrah* where he stopped and pelted seven pebbles at it saying "Allâh is the Greatest" each time. They were like small pebbles hurled from the bottom of the valley. Then he set off to the sacrificial place, where he sacrificed sixty-three camels with his hands, and asked 'Ali to slaughter the others, a hundred and thirty-seven altogether. He made 'Ali shares him in *Al-Hadi.* A piece of meat from each slaughtered animal was ordered to be cooked in a pot and from which both men ate, and drank the soup.

Then the Messenger of Allâh mounted his she-camel and returned to the House where he observed the noon prayer at Makkah and there he came upon the children of 'Abdul

Muttalib was supplying drinking water to people at Zamzam Well. "Draw up water, children of 'Abdul Muttalib, I would draw up with you if I were not afraid that people would appropriate this honour after me." They handed him a pail of water and he drank to his fill. [Sahih Muslim 1/397-400]

At the daytime of the tenth of Dhul-Hijjah on the Slaughtering Day (*Yaum An-Nahr*) The Prophet delivered another speech. That was at high time morning, while he was mounting a grey mule. 'Ali conveyed his statements to the people, who were standing or sitting. [Abu Da'ud 1/270] He repeated some of the statements that he had previously said the day before. The two Sheikhs (Bukhâri and Muslim) reported a version narrated by Abi Bakrah who said:

The Prophet made a speech on *Yaum An-Nahr* (day of slaughtering) and said:

> "Time has grown similar in form and state to the time when Allâh created the heavens and the earth. A year is twelve months. Four of which are Sacred Months (*Hurum*). Three of the four months are successive. They are Dhul-Qa'dah, Dhul-Hijjah, and Al-Muharram. The fourth Month is Rajab Mudar, which comes between Jumada and Sha'ban."

"What month is this month?" He asked. We said: "Allâh and His Messenger know best of all." He kept silent for a while till we thought he would attach to it a different appellation. "Is it not Dhul-Hijjah?" He wondered. "Yes. It is." We said. Then he asked, "What is this town called?" We said: "Allâh and His Messenger know best of all." He was silent for a while till we thought he would give it a different name. "Is it not *Al-Baldah?* (i.e. the town)" asked he. "Yes. It is." We replied. Then he asked again, "What day is it today?" We replied: "Allâh and His Messenger know best of all." Then he kept silent for a while and said wondering: "Is it not '*An-Nahr*' (i.e. slaughtering) Day?" "Yes. It is." Said we. Then he said:

> "(Shedding) the blood of one another and eating or taking one another's provisions (unwillingly) and your

honour are all inviolable (*Haram*). It is unlawful to violate their holiness. They must be as sacred to one another as this sacred day, in this sacred month, in this sacred town."

"You will go back to be resurrected (after death) to your Lord. There you will be accounted for your deeds. So do not turn into people who go astray and kill one another."

"Have I not delivered the Message (of my Lord)?" "Yes you have." Said they. "O Allâh! Bear witness! Let him that is present convey it unto him who is absent. For haply, many people to whom the Message is conveyed may be more mindful of it than the audience," said he. [Sahih Al-Bukhari 1/234]

In another version it is said that the Prophet had said in that very speech:

"He whoever plunges into misfortune will certainly aggrieve himself. So let no one of you inflict an evil upon his parents. Verily Satan has utterly despaired being worshipped in this country of yours; but he will be obeyed at your committing trivial things you disdain. Satan will be contented with such things." [At-Tirmidhi 2/38, 135; Mishkat Al-Masabih 1/234]

The Messenger of Allâh spent *At-Tashreeq* Days (11th, 12th and 13th of Dhul-Hijjah) in Mina performing the ritual teachings of Islam, remembering Allâh (praying), following the ways of guidance of Ibrahim, wiping out all traces and features or polytheism. On some days of *At-Tashreeq* he delivered some speeches as well. In a version to Abu Da'ûd with good reference to Sira,' the daughter of Nabhan; she said: "The Messenger of Allâh made us a speech at the *Ru'us* (Heads) Day in which he said: "Is it not this the middle day of *At-Tashreeq* Days." [Abu Da'ud 1/269]

His speech that day was similar to that of *An-Nahr* Day's. It was made after the revelation of *Surat An-Nasr*.

On the second day of *An-Nafr* (i.e. Departure)-on the thirteenth of Dhul-Hijjah, the Prophet proceeded with *An-*

Nafr to Mina and stayed at a high place of a mountain side at Bani Kinanah from Al-Abtah. He spent the rest of that day and night there - where he performed the noon, the afternoon, the sunset and the evening prayers.

Then he slept for a short while and mounted leaving for the Ka'bah. He performed the Farewell Circumambulation (*Tawaf Al-Wada'*), after ordering his Companions to do the same thing. Upon the accomplishment of his religious rituals he quickened his move to the purified Madinah. He went there not to seek rest but to resume the strife and struggle in the way of Allâh. [Sahih Al-Bukhari 1/631, 2/631; Ibn Hisham 2/601-605; Za'd Al-Ma'ad 1/196, 218-220]

THE LAST EXPEDITIONS

The pride of the Byzantine State made it deny Muslims their right to live. The Byzantine arrogance made them even kill those agents of theirs, who embraced Islam. Killing Farwah bin 'Amr Al-Judhami, who was their agent on Mu'an, was an evidence of their arrogance. Due to that arrogance and presumptuousness of the Byzantines, the Messenger of Allâh started to mobilize a great army in Safar in the eleventh year of Al-Hijra and made it under the command of Osamah bin Zaid bin Haritha with orders to have the horses of Muslims tread on the lands bordering Al-Balqa' and Ad-Darum of Palestine. His aim was to terrorize Byzantines and to implant confidence into the hearts of Arabs who were settled at the borders of the Byzantines. His other purpose was to deliver a message to everybody there, so that no one may dare say that the Church brutality can't go with impunity; and that Islamization is not synonymous with fear and vulnerability.

The leadership of Osamah was subject to criticism. Because he was still too young, people tarried at joining his expedition. The Messenger of Allâh addressed people saying:

> "No wonder now you contest his leadership, for you have already contested the ex-leadership of his father. Yes, by Allâh, his father, who was one of the most beloved people to me, was quite efficient for leadership;

and this son of his is one of the most beloved individuals to me after his father." [Sahih Al-Bukhari 2/612]

So people started tending towards Osamah and joined his army. The number of volunteers in his army was so enormous that they formed such a long queue that they had to descend the escarpment-which was a parasang off Madinah. The anxiety-provoking news about the Messenger of Allâh's sickness, however, made the expedition tarry again in order to know what Allâh had willed as regards His Messenger.

It was Allâh's Will that Osamah's expedition would be the first one dispatched during the caliphate of the veracious Abu Bakr. [Ibn Hisham 2/560, 606; Sahih Al-Bukhari 2/612]

THE JOURNEY TO ALLÂH, THE SUBLIME

SYMPTOMS OF FAREWELL

When the Call to Islam grew complete and the new faith dominated the whole situation. The Messenger of Allâh started to develop certain symptoms that bespoke of leave-taking. They could be perceived through his statements and deeds:

In Ramadan in the tenth year of Al-Hijra he secluded himself for twenty days in contrast to ten, previously.

The archangel Gabriel reviewed the *Quran* twice with him.

His words in the Farewell Pilgrimage (i.e. *Al-Wida'*):

"I do not know whether I will ever meet you at this place once again after this current year."

The revelation of *An-Nasr* Chapter amid *At-Tashreeq* Days. So when it was sent down on him, he realized that it was the parting time and that *Surah* was an announcement of his approaching death.

On the early days of Safar in the eleventh year of Al-Hijra, the Prophet went out to Uhud and observed a farewell prayer to the martyrs. It looked like saying goodbye to both the dead and the living alike. He then ascended the pulpit and addressed the people saying:

"I am to precede you and I have been made witness

upon you. By Allâh, you will meet me at the 'Fountain' very soon. I have been given the keys of worldly treasures. By Allâh, I do not fear for you that you will turn polytheists after me. But I do fear that acquisition of worldly riches should entice you to strike one another's neck." [Sahih Al-Bukhari 2/585]

One day, at midnight he went to Al-Baqee'cemetry, and implored Allâh to forgive the martyrs of Islam. He said: "Peace be upon you tomb-dwellers! May that morning that dawns upon you be more relieving than that which dawn upon the living. Afflictions are approaching them like cloudy lumps of a dark night-the last of which follows the first. The last one is bearing more evil than the first." He comforted them saying: "We will follow you."

THE START OF THE DISEASE

On Monday the twenty-ninth of Safar in the eleventh year of Al-Hijra, he participated in funeral rites in Al-Baqee'. On the way back he had a headache, his temperature rose so high that the heat effect could be felt over his headband. He led the Muslims in prayer for eleven days though he was sick. The total number of his sick days was either thirteen or fourteen.

THE LAST WEEK

When his sickness grew severe he asked his wives: "Where shall I stay tomorrow?" "Where shall I stay?" They understood what he wanted. So they allowed him to stay wherever he wished. He moved to 'Aishah's room leaning-while he was walking-on Al-Fadl bin Al-'Abbas and 'Ali bin Abi Talib. Head banded as he was, he dragged his feet till he came into her abode. It was there that he spent the last week of his life. During that period, 'Aishah used to recite *Al-Mu'awwidhat* (Chapters 113 and 114 of the *Quran*) and other supplications which he had already taught her.

FIVE DAYS BEFORE DEATH

On Wednesday, five days before he died the Prophet's

temperature rose so high signalling the severeness of his disease. He fainted and suffered from pain. "Pour out on me seven *Qirab* (water skin pots) of various water wells so that I may go out to meet people and talk to them." So they seated him in a container (usually used for washing) and poured out water on him till he said: "That is enough. That is enough." Then he felt well enough to enter the Mosque. He entered it band-headed, sat on the pulpit and made a speech to the people who were gathering together around him. He said:

> "The curse of Allâh falls upon the Jews and Christians for they have made their Prophets' tombs places of worship." [Sahih Al-Bukhari 1/62; Mustta' Imam Malik p.360]

Then he said:

> "Do not make my tomb a worshipped idol." [Muatta' Imam Malik p.65]

Then he offered himself and invited the people to repay any injuries he might have inflicted on them, saying:

> "He whom I have ever lashed his back, I offer him my back so that he may avenge himself on me. He whom I have ever blasphemed his honour, here I am offering my honour so that he may avenge himself."

Then he descended, and performed the noon prayer. Again he returned to the pulpit and sat on it. He resumed his first speech about enmity and some other things.

A man then said: "You owe me three Dirhams." The Prophet said: "Fadl, pay him the money." He went on saying:

> "I admonish you to be good to *Al-Ansar* (the Helpers). They are my family and with them I found shelter. They have acquitted themselves credibly of the responsibility that fell upon them and now there remains what you have to do. You should fully acknowledge and appreciate the favour that they have shown, and should overlook their faults."

In another version:

> "The number of believers would increase, but the

number of Helpers would decrease to the extent that they would be among men as salt in the food. So he who from among you occupies a position of responsibility and is powerful enough to do harm or good to the people, he should fully acknowledge and appreciate the favour that these benefactors have shown and overlook their faults." [Sahih Al-Bukhari 1/536]

And said:

"Allâh, the Great, has given a slave of His the opportunity to make a choice between whatever he desires of Allâh's provisions in this world, and what He keeps for him in the world, but he has opted for the latter."

Abu Sa'îd Al-Khudri said: "Upon hearing that, Abu Bakr cried and said: 'We sacrifice our fathers and mothers for your sake.' We wondered why Abu Bakr said such a thing. People said: 'Look at that old man! The Messenger of Allâh says about a slave of Allâh who was granted the right between the best fortunes of this world and the bounty of Allâh in the Hereafter, but he says: We sacrifice our fathers and mothers for your sake!' It was later on that we realized what he had aimed at. The Messenger of Allâh was the slave informed to choose. We also acknowledged that Abu Bakr was the most learned among us." [Mishkat Al-Masabih 2/546]

Then the Messenger of Allâh said:

"The fellow I feel most secure in his company is Abu Bakr. If I were to make friendship with any other one than Allâh, I would have Abu Bakr a bosom friend of mine. For him I feel affection and brotherhood of Islam. No gate shall be kept open in the Mosque except that of Abu Bakr's." [Sahih Al-Bukhari 1/22, 429, 449, 2/638; Mishkat Al-Masabih 2/548]

FOUR DAYS BEFORE HIS DEATH

On Thursday, four days before the death of the Messenger of Allâh, he said to people-though he was suffering from a severe pain: "Come here. I will cause you to write something so that you will never fall into error." Upon this

'Umar bin Al-Khattab said: "The Prophet of Allâh is suffering from acute pain and you have the *Quran* with you; the Book of Allâh is sufficient unto you." Others however wanted the writing to be made. When Muhammad heard them debating over it, he ordered them to go away and leave him alone. [Sahih Al-Bukhari 2/637]

That day he recommended three things:

1. Jews, Christians and polytheists should be expelled out of Arabia.
2. He recommended that delegations should be honoured and entertained, in a way similar to the one he used to do.
3. As for the third - the narrator said that he had forgotten it. It could have been adherence to the Holy Book and the *Sunnah.* It was likely to be the accomplishment and the mobilization of Osamah's army, or it could have been performance of prayers and being attentive to slaves.

In spite of the strain of disease and suffering from pain, the Prophet used to lead all the prayers till that Thursday - four days before he died. On that day he led the sunset prayer and recited:

> "By the winds (or angels or the Messengers of Allâh) sent forth one after another." [Al-Qur'an 77:1] [Mishkat Al-Masabih 1/102]

In the evening he grew so sick that he could not overcome the strain of disease or go out to enter the Mosque. 'Aishah said: The Prophet asked: "Have the people performed the prayer?" "No. They haven't. They are waiting for you." "Put some water in the washing pot." Said he. We did what he ordered. So he washed and wanted to stand up, but he fainted. When he came round he asked again "Have the people prayed?" Then the same sequence of events took place again and again for the second and the third times from the time he washed to the time he fainted after his attempts to stand up. Therefore he sent to Abu Bakr to lead the prayer himself. Abu Bakr then led the prayer during those days. [Sahih Al-

Bukhari 1/99] They were seventeen prayers in the lifetime of Muhammad.

Three or four times 'Aishah talked to the Prophet to exempt Abu Bakr from leadership in prayer lest people should despair of him, but he refused and said:

> "You (women) are like the women who tried to entice Joseph (Yusuf) into immorality. Convey my request to Abu Bakr to lead the prayer."

A DAY OR TWO PRIOR TO DEATH

On Saturday or on Sunday, the Prophet felt that he was well enough to perform the prayer; so he went out leaning on two men in order to perform the noon prayer. Abu Bakr, who was then about to lead the prayer withdrew when he saw him coming; but the Prophet made him a gesture to stay where he was and said: "Seat me next to him." They seated him on the left hand side of Abu Bakr. The Prophet led the prayer, and Abu Bakr followed him and raised his voice at every '*Allâhu Akbar*' (i.e. Allâh is the Greatest) the Prophet said, so that the people may hear clearly. [Sahih Al-Bukhari 1/98, 99]

A DAY BEFORE HIS DEATH

On Sunday, a day before he died, the Prophet set his slaves free, paid as a charity the seven Dinars he owned and gave his weapons as a present to the Muslims. So when night fell 'Aishah had to borrow some oil from her neighbour to light her oil-lantern. Even his armour was mortgaged as a security with a Jew for thirty *Sa'*(a cubic measure) of barley.

THE LAST DAY ALIVE

In a narration by Anas bin Malik, he said: "While the Muslims were performing the dawn prayer on Monday-led by Abu Bakr, they were surprised to see the Messenger of Allâh raising the curtain of 'Aishah's room. He looked at them while they were praying aligned properly and smiled cheerfully. Seeing him, Abu Bakr withdrew to join the lines and give way to him to lead the prayer. For he thought that the Prophet wanted to go out and pray." Anas said: "The Muslims, who were praying, were so delighted that they were almost too enraptured at their prayers. The Messenger of Allâh made them a gesture to continue their prayer, went into the room and drew down the curtain." [ibid 2/640]

The Messenger of Allâh did not live for the next prayer time. When it was daytime, the Prophet called Fatimah and told her something in a secret voice that made her cry. Then he whispered to her something else which made her laugh. 'Aishah enquired from her after the Prophet's death, as to this weeping and laughing to which Fatimah replied: "The first time he disclosed to me that he would not recover from his illness and I wept. Then he told me that I would be the first of his family to join him, so I laughed." [Sahih Al-Bukhari 2/638]

He gave Fatimah glad tidings that she would become the lady of all women of the world. [Rahmat-ul-lil'alameen 1/282]

Fatimah witnessed the great pain that afflicted her father. So she said: "What great pain my father is in!". To these words, the Prophet remarked:

"He will not suffer any more when today is over." [Sahih Al-Bukhari 2/641]

He asked that Al-Hasan and Al-Husain be brought to him. He kissed them and recommended that they be looked after. He asked to see his wives. They were brought to him. He preached them and told them to remember Allâh. Pain grew so much severe that the trace of poison he had at Khaibar came to light. It was so sore that he said to 'Aishah: "I still feel the painful effect of that food I tasted at Khaibar. I feel as if death is approaching." [ibid 2/637] He ordered the people to perform the prayers and be attentive to slaves. He repeated it several times. [ibid 2/637]

THE PROPHET BREATHES HIS LAST

When the pangs of death started, 'Aishah leant him

against her. She used to say: One of Allâh's bounties upon me is that the Messenger of Allâh died in my house, while I am still alive. He died between my chest and neck while he was leaning against me. Allâh has mixed his saliva with mine at his death. For 'Abdur Rahman-the son of Abu Bakr-came in with a *Siwak* (i.e. the root of a desert plant used for brushing teeth) in his hand, while I was leaning the Messenger of Allâh against me.

I noticed that he was looking at the *Siwak*, so I asked him - for I knew that he wanted it - "Would you like me to take it for you?" He nodded in agreement. I took it and gave it to him. As it was too hard for him, I asked him "Shall I soften it for you?" He nodded in agreement. So I softened it with my saliva and he passed it (on his teeth).

In another version it is said: "So he brushed (*Istanna*) his teeth as nice as he could." There was a water container (*Rakwa*) available at his hand with some water in. He put his hand in it and wiped his face with it and said:

> "There is no god but Allâh. Death is full of agonies." [Sahih Al-Bukhari 2/640]

As soon as he had finished his *Siwak* brushing, he raised his hand or his finger up, looked upwards to the ceiling and moved his lips. So 'Aishah listened to him. She heard him say: "With those on whom You have bestowed Your Grace with the Prophets and the Truthful ones (*As-Siddeeqeen*), the martyrs and the good doers.

O Allâh, forgive me and have mercy upon me and join me to the Companionship on high." [ibid 2/638-641] Then at intervals he uttered these words: "The most exalted Companionship on high. To Allâh we turn and to Him we turn back for help and last abode." This event took place at high morning time on Monday, the twelfth of Rabi'Al-Awwal, in the eleventh year of Al-Hijrah. He was sixty-three years and four days old when he died.

THE COMPANIONS' CONCERN OVER THE PROPHET'S DEATH

The great (loss) news was soon known by everybody in

Madinah. Dark grief spread on all areas and horizons of Madinah. Anas said:

> "I have never witnessed a day better or brighter than that day on which the Messenger of Allâh came to us; and I have never witnessed a more awful or darker day than that one on which the Messenger of Allâh died on." [Mishkat-ul-Masabih 2/547]

When he died, Fatimah said: "O Father, whom his Lord responded to his supplication! O Father, whose abode is Paradise, O Father, whom I announce his death to Gabriel." [Sahih Al-Bukhari 2/641]

'UMAR'S ATTITUDE

'Umar, who was so stunned that he almost lost consciousness and stood before people addressing them: "Some of the hypocrites claim that the Messenger of Allâh died. The Messenger of Allâh did not die, but went to his Lord in the same way as Moses bin 'Imran did. He stayed away for forty nights, but finally came back though they said he had been dead. By Allâh, the Messenger of Allâh will come back and he will cut off the hands and legs of those who claim his death." [Ibn Hisham 2/655]

ABU BAKR'S ATTITUDE

Abu Bakr left his house at As-Sunh and came forth to the Mosque on a mare-back. At the Mosque, he dismounted and entered. He talked to nobody but went on till he entered 'Aishah's abode, and went directly to where the Messenger of Allâh was. The Prophet was covered with a Yemeni mantle. He uncovered his face and tended down, kissed him and cried. Then he said: "I sacrifice my father and mother for your sake. Allâh, verily, will not cause you to die twice. You have just experienced the death that Allâh had ordained."

Then he went out and found 'Umar talking to people. He said: "'Umar, be seated." 'Umar refused to do so. People parted 'Umar and came towards Abu Bakr, who started a speech saying:

"And now, he who worships Muhammad is dead now. But he who worships Allâh, He is Ever Living and He never dies. Allâh says:
'Muhammad is no more than a Messenger, and indeed (many) Messengers have passed away before him. If he dies or is killed, will you then turn back on your heels (as disbelievers)? And he who turns back on his heels, not the least harm will he do to Allâh, and Allâh will give reward to those who are grateful.'" [Al-Qur'an 3:144]

Ibn 'Abbas said: "By Allâh, it sounded as if people had never heard such a *Quran*ic verse till Abu Bakr recited it as a reminder so people started reciting it till there was no man who did not recite it."

Ibn Al-Musaiyab said that 'Umar had said: "By Allâh, as soon as I heard Abu Bakr say it, I fell down to the ground. I felt as if my legs had been unable to carry me so I collapsed when I heard him say it. Only then did I realize that Muhammad had really died." [Sahih Al-Bukhari 2/640,641]

BURIAL AND FAREWELL PREPARATIONS TO HIS HONOURABLE BODY

Dispute about who would succeed him broke out even before having the Messenger of Allâh's body prepared for burial. Lots of arguments, discussions, dialogues took place between the Helpers and Emigrants in the roofed passage (portico) of Bani Sa'ida. Finally they acknowledged Abu Bakr as a caliph. They spent the whole Monday there till it was night. People were so busy with their arguments that it was late night-just about dawn of Tuesday-yet his blessed body was still lying on his bed covered with an inked-garment. He was locked in the room. On Tuesday, his body was washed with his clothes on. He was washed by Al-'Abbas, 'Ali, Al-Fadl and Qathm-the two sons of Al-'Abbas, as well as Shaqran-the Messenger's freed slave, Osamah bin Zaid and Aws bin Khauli. Al-'Abbas, Al-Fadl and Qathm turned his body round, whereas Osamah and Shaqran poured out water. 'Ali washed him and Aws leant him against his chest.

They shrouded him in three white Sahooli cotton cloths which had neither a headcloth [Sahih Al-Bukhari 1/169; Sahih Muslim 1/306] nor a casing and inserted him in. A sort of disagreement arose with regard to a burial place. Abu Bakr said: "I heard the Messenger of Allâh say: 'A dead Prophet is buried where he dies.' So Abu Talhah lifted the bed on which he died, dug underneath and cut the ground to make the tomb. People entered the room ten by ten. They prayed for the *Prophet*. The first to pray for him were people of his clan. Women prayed for him after men. The young were the last to pray.

This process took Tuesday long and Wednesday night (i.e. the night which proceeds Wednesday morning). 'Aishah said: "We did not know that the Prophet was being buried till we heard the sound of tools digging the ground at the depth of Wednesday night." [Mukhtasar Seerat Ar-Rasool p.471; Ibn Hisham 2/649-665; Talqeeh Fuhoom Ahl Al-Athar p.38, 39; Rahmat-ul-lil'alameen 1/277-286]

THE PROPHETIC HOUSEHOLD

1. **Khadijah Bint Khuwailid**: In Makkah-prior to Hijra-the Prophet's household comprised him and his wife Khadijah bint Khuwailid. He was twenty-five and she was forty when they got married. She was the first woman he married. She was the only wife he had till she died. He had sons and daughters with her. None of their sons lived long. They all died. Their daughters were Zainab, Ruqaiya, Umm Kulthum and Fatimah.

Zainab was married to her maternal cousin Abu Al-'As bin Al-Rabi'and that was before Al-Hijra. Ruqaiya and Umm Kulthum were both married to 'Uthman bin' successively (i.e. he married one after the death of her sister). Fatimah was married to 'Ali bin Abi Talib; and that was in the period between Badr and Uhud battles. The sons and daughters that Fatimah and 'Ali had were Al-Hasan, Al-Husain, Zainab and Umm Kulthum.

It is well-known that the Prophet was exceptionally authorized to have more than four wives for various reasons. The wives he married were thirteen. Nine of them outlived him. Two died in his lifetime: Khadijah and the Mother of the poor (*Umm Al-Masakeen*)-Zainab bint Khuzaima, besides two others with whom he did not consummate his marriage.

2. **Sawdah bint Zam'a**: He married her in Shawwal, in the tenth year of Prophethood, a few days after the death of Khadijah. Prior to that, she was married to a paternal cousin of hers called As-Sakran bin 'Amr.
3. **'Aishah bint Abu Bakr**: He married her in the eleventh year of Prophethood, a year after his marriage to Sawdah, and two years and five months before Al-Hijra. She was six years old when he married her. However, he did not consummate the marriage with her till Shawwal seven months after Al-Hijra, and that was in Madinah. She was nine then. She was the only virgin he married, and the most beloved creature to him. As a woman she was the most learnèd woman in jurisprudence.
4. **Hafsah bint 'Umar bin Al-Khattab**: She was *Aiyim* (i.e. husbandless). Her ex-husband was Khunais bin Hudhafa As-Sahmi in the period between Badr and Uhud battles. The Messenger of Allâh married her in the third year of Al-Hijra.
5. **Zainab bint Khuzaimah**: She was from Bani Hilal bin 'Amir bin Sa'sa'a. Was nicknamed *Umm Al-Masakeen*, because of her kindness and care towards them. She used to be the wife of 'Abdullah bin Jahsh, who was martyred at Uhud, was married to the Prophet in the fourth year of Al-Hijra, but she died two or three months after her marriage to the Messenger of Allâh.
6. **Umm Salamah Hind bint Abi Omaiyah**: She used to be the wife of Abu Salamah, who died in Jumada Al-Akhir, in the fourth year of Al-Hijra. The Messenger of Allâh married her in Shawwal of the same year.
7. **Zainab bint Jahsh bin Riyab**: She was from Bani Asad bin

Khuzaimah and was the Messenger's paternal cousin. She was married to Zaid bin Haritha-who was then considered son of the *Prophet*. However, Zaid divorced her. Allâh sent down some *Quran*ic verses with this respect:

"So when Zaid had accomplished his desire from her (i.e. divorced her), We gave her to you in marriage." [Al-Qur'an 33:37]

About her, Allâh has sent down some verses of *Al-Ahzab* Chapter that discussed the adoption of children in detail-anyway we will discuss this later. The Messenger of Allâh married her in Dhul-Qa'dah, the fifth year of Al-Hijra.

8. **Juwairiyah bint Al-Harith**: Al-Harith was the head of Bani Al-Mustaliq of Khuza'ah. Juwairiyah was among the booty that fell to the Muslims from Bani Al-Mustaliq. She was a portion of Thabit bin Qais bin Shammas' share. He made her a covenant to set her free at a certain time. The Messenger of Allâh accomplished the covenant and married her in Sha'ban in the sixth year of Al-Hijra.
9. **Umm Habibah**: Ramlah, the daughter of Abu Sufyan. She was married to 'Ubaidullah bin Jahsh. She migrated with him to Abyssinia (Ethiopia). When 'Ubaidullah apostatized and became a Christian, she stoodfast to her religion and refused to convert. However 'Ubaidullah died there in Abyssinia (Ethiopia). The Messenger of Allâh dispatched 'Amr bin Omaiyah Ad-Damri with a letter to Negus, the king, asking him for Umm Habibah's hand-that was in Muharram, in the seventh year of Al-Hijra. Negus agreed and sent her to the Prophet in the company of Sharhabeel bin Hasnah.
10. **Safiyah bint Huyai bin Akhtab**: From the Children of Israel, she was among the booty taken at Khaibar battle. The Messenger of Allâh took her for himself. He set her free and married her after that conquest in the seventh year of Al-Hijra.
11. **Maimunah bint Al-Harith**: The daughter of Al-Harith, and the sister of Umm Al-Fadl Lubabah bint Al-Harith. The Prophet married her after the Compensatory *'Umrah*

(Lesser Pilgrimage). That was in Dhul-Qa'dah in the seventh year of Al-Hijra.

Those were the eleven women that the Messenger of Allâh had married and consummated marriage with them. He outlived two of them-Khadijah and Zainab, the *Umm Al-Masakeen* whereas the other nine wives outlived him. The two wives that he did not consummate marriage with were, one from Bani Kilab and the other from Kindah and this was the one called Al-Jauniyah. Besides these, he had two concubines. The first was Mariyah, the Coptic (an Egyptian Christian), a present gift from Al-Muqauqis, vicegerent of Egypt-she gave birth to his son Ibrâhim, who died in Madinah while still a little child, on the 28th or 29th of Shawwal in the year 10 A.H., i.e. 27th January, 632 A.D.

The second one was Raihanah bint Zaid An-Nadriyah or Quraziyah, a captive from Bani Quraiza. Some people say she was one of his wives. However, Ibn Al-Qaiyim gives more weight to the first version. Abu 'Ubaidah spoke of two more concubines, Jameelah, a captive and another one, a bond-woman granted to him by Zainab bint Jahsh. [Za'd Al-Ma'ad 1/29]

Whosoever meditates on the life of the Messenger of Allâh, will conceive that his marriage to this great number of women in the late years of his lifetime, after he had almost spent thirty years of his best days of youth sufficing himself to one old wife - Khadijah and later on to Sawdah, was in no way an overwhelming lustful desire to be satisfied through such a number of wives. These marriages were in fact motivated by aims and purposes much more glorious and greater than what normal marriages usually aim at.

The tendency of the Messenger of Allâh towards establishing a relationship by marriage with both Abu Bakr and 'Umar and his marriage to 'Aishah and Hafsah-and getting his daughter Fatimah married to 'Ali bin Abi Talib, and the marriage of his two daughters, Ruqaiyah and Umm Kulthum to 'Uthman-indicate clearly that he aimed at confirming the relationship among the four men - whose sacrifices and great achievements in the cause of Islam are well-known. Besides this, there was that tradition of the Arabs to honour the in-law relations. For them a son or a daughter-in-law was a means by which they sought the consolidation of relationship and affection with various phratries. Hostility and fights against alliances and affinities would bring an unforgettable shame, disgrace and degradation to them.

By marrying the Mothers of believers, the Prophet wanted to demolish or break down the Arab tribes' enmity to Islam and extinguish their intense hatred. Umm Salamah was from Bani Makhzum - the clan of Abu Jahl and Khalid bin Al - Waleed. Her marriage to the Messenger of Allâh produced good results. Khalid's deliberately undecisive attitude at Uhud - for instance - was due to the Messenger's marriage to Umm Salamah. Khalid went even further than that, in a short time he willingly became a keen obedient Muslim.

After the Messenger of Allâh's marriage to Umm Habibah, Abu Sufyan, her father, did not encounter him with any sort of hostility. Similarly his marriage to Juwairiyah and Safiyah made the two tribes stop all sorts of provocation, aggression or hostility against Islam. Better still, Juwairiyah, herself, was one of the greatest sources of blessing to her own people. On the occasion of her marriage to the Prophet, his Companions set a hundred families of her people free. They said: "It is for their affinity with the Messenger of Allâh." No need to say what great good impression this gratitude had on everybody's soul. One of the greatest motives of all is Allâh's bidding his Prophet to educate and purify the souls of people who had known nothing whatsoever about courtesy, education and culture. He had to teach them to comply with the necessities of civilization and to contribute to the solidification and the establishment of a new Islamic society.

An essential fundamental rule of the Muslim society is to prohibit mixing of men and women. Providing direct education for women, though highly compelling, is impossible in the light of this Islamic norm. Therefore, the Prophet had to select some women of different ages and talents, and indoctrinate them systematically in order to educate she-bedouins and townswomen, old and young, and thus furnish them with the instruments of propagating the true faith. The Mothers of believers (i.e. wives of the Prophet) were in such a convenient position that they could convey the state of the Prophet and his affairs to people (men and women). Being educated and taught the teachings and rules of Islam, his wives, especially those who outlived him, played a very important role in conveying Prophetic traditions *Ahadith* to the Muslims. 'Aishah, for instance, related a large number of the Prophet's deeds and statements.

His marriage to his paternal cousin Zainab bint Jahsh was a peculiar case which aimed at eradicating a deeply rooted pre-Islamic tradition - i.e. the adoption of children. In *Al-Jahiliyah* the Arabs used to consider an adopted person exactly like a real son or daughter as far as rights and sanctities are concerned. That *Jahiliyah* tradition had been so deeply rooted in their hearts that it was not easy to remove or uproot it. This tradition in fact affronts the basic principles of Islam; especially those concerned with marriage, divorce and inheritance and some other cases, and brought about lots of corruptions and indecencies. Naturally Islam stands against such deeds, and attempts to remove them from the Islamic society.

For the eradication of this tradition, Allâh, the Exalted, bid His Messenger to marry his cousin Zainab bint Jahsh, who was an ex-wife to Zaid. She was at variance with Zaid to an extent that he intended to divorce her - that was at the time when the Confederates (*Al-Ahzab*) were making an evil alliance against the Messenger of Allâh and against the Muslims. The Messenger of Allâh feared that the hypocrites, the idolaters, and the Jews would make propaganda out of it and try to influence some Muslims of weak hearts. That was why he urged Zaid not to divorce her, in order not to get involved into that trial. Undoubtedly this hesitation and partiality were alien to the character of the Prophet.

They did not apply to the power of determination and will with which he had been sent. Allâh, the Exalted, blamed him for that by saying:

> "And (remember) when you said to him on whom Allâh has bestowed grace (by guiding him to Islam) and you (O Muhammad too) have done favour (by manumitting him), 'Keep your wife to yourself, and fear Allâh.' But you did hide in yourself (i.e. what Allâh has already made known to you that He will give her to you in marriage) that which Allâh will make manifest, you did fear the people (i.e. Muhammad married the divorced wife of his manumitted slave) whereas Allâh had a better right that you should fear him." [Al-Qur'an 33:37]

Finally Zaid divorced Zainab and the Messenger of Allâh married her at the time he laid siege to Bani Quraiza. That was after she had finished her *Iddat* (i.e. period during which a widow or a divorcee may not remarry). Allâh Himself had already ordained it, and so gave him no other alternative. Allâh had even started the marriage Himself by saying:

> "So when Zaid had accomplished his desire from her (i.e. divorced her), We gave her to you in marriage, so that (in future) there may be no difficulty to the believers in respect of (the marriage of) the wives of their adopted sons when the latter have no desire to keep them (i.e. they have divorced them)." [Al-Qur'an 33:37]

And that was in order to break down the tradition of child adoption in practice after He had done it in words:

> "Call them (adopted sons) by (the names of) their fathers, that is more just near Allâh." [Al-Qur'an 33:5]

> "Muhammad () is not the father of any man among you, but he is the Messenger of Allâh, and the last (end) of the Prophets." [Al-Qur'an 33:40]

Lots of deeply-rooted traditions cannot be uprooted or demolished or even adjusted by mere words. They must be matched and associated with the action of the advocate of the Message himself. This could be perceived through the deeds practised by the Muslims at Al-Hudaibiyah *'Umrah* (Lesser Pilgrimage) during which 'Urwah bin Mas'ud Al-Thaqafi saw certain Muslims tend to pick up any expectoration that fell down from the Prophet. He also saw them race to the water of his ablution and they almost quarrelled for it. There were others who competed to pledge allegiance to death and some others pledged not to flee from (the battlefield).

Among those people, were eminent Companions like 'Umar and Abu Bakr, who although dedicated all their lives to the Prophet and to the cause of Islam, but refused to carry out the Messenger's ordres with respect to slaughtering sacrificial animals after the ratification of Al-Hudaibiyah Peace Treaty, the thing that perturbed and caused the Prophet to feel anxious. However, when Umm Salamah [R] advised that he take the initiative and sacrifice his animals, his followers raced to follow his example; a clear evidence in support of the saying: Actions speak louder than words, in the process of exterminating a deeply-established tradition.

Hypocrites aroused a lot of suspicions and made a broad false propaganda against that marriage. Their acts and talks about that marriage had ill-effects on those Muslims whose Faith was still weak, particularly that Zainab was the fifth wife-and the Noble *Quran* limited the number up to four only; Zaid was traditionally his son, and so a father marrying his son's divorcee was a heinous sin in the eyes of the Arabians. *Al-Ahzab Surah* was revealed to shed full light on the two issues, i.e. Islam does not recognize adoption of children, and the Prophet is given (by Allâh) more freedom as regards the number of wives he can hold than other Muslims in order to achieve noble and honourable purposes.

However, the treatment of the Messenger of Allâh to his wives was of honourable, noble, and superb nature. His wives were on tops in respect of honour, satisfaction, patience, modesty, and service (that is to say the performance of housework and marriage duties). Although the Messenger's house-life was hard and unbearable, none of his wives complained. Anas said about the Prophet's life: "According to my knowledge, the Messenger of Allâh has never tasted a thin flattened loaf in all his lifetime, nor has he ever seen with his own eyes roasted mutton." [Sahih Al-Bukhari 2/956]

'Aishah said: "Over two months have elapsed - during which we have seen three crescents - and yet no fire has been kindled in the houses of the Messenger of Allâh (i.e. they did not cook food)." "What did you eat to sustain yourselves?" 'Urwah asked. She said "The two blacks: dates and water" [ibid 2/956]. Lots of information about the hard life of the Prophet was told. In spite of these hardships, straits and adversity of life in the house of the Prophet, none of his wives uttered a word of complaint worthy of reproach - but once. This exception was required by human instinctive inclinations.

However, it was not so important and consequently it did not require the decree of a legislative rule. Allâh has given them an opportunity to choose between two things, as clearly stated in the following verses:

> "O Prophet (Muhammad)! Say to your wives: 'If you desire the life of this world, and its glitter,-then come! I will make a provision for you and set you free in a handsome manner (divorce). But if you desire Allâh and His Messenger, and the Home of the Hereafter, then verily, Allâh has prepared for *Al-Muhsinat* (good doers) amongst you an enormous reward.'" [Al-Qur'an 33:28, 29]

They were so noble and honest that none of them preferred 'the life of this world and its glitter' to the abode in the Hereafter. Although they were many in number, nothing of the dispute occurrences that normally happen among co-wives, took place in their houses. Very few cases could be the only exception; but they were quite normal. Allâh reproached them for that, so they ceased to do such a thing. This incident is mentioned in *At-Tahreem* Chapter:

> "O Prophet! Why do you ban (for yourself) that which Allâh has made lawful to you ..." [Al-Qur'an 66:1] (to the end of the fifth verse).

Discussing polygamy - in my opinion - is not a necessity; since a person who is familiar with the Europeans, and indecent practices, sufferings, wickedness, their sorrows and distresses, the horrible crimes they commit in this respect as well as the trials, the disasters that they are involved in, and which emanate directly from their disregard of the principle of polygamy form a good reason (to justify the soundness of polygamy). The distorted picture of life in Europe with the ill-practices featuring it, could truthfully justify the existence and practice of polygamy. In this, there are Divine signs for all people possessed of lucid mind.

THE PROPHET, ATTRIBUTES AND MANNERS

The Prophet combined both perfection of creation and perfection of manners. This impression on people can be deduced by the bliss that overwhelmed their hearts and filled them with dignity. Men's dignity, devotion and estimation of the Messenger of Allâh were unique and matchless. No other man in the whole world has been so honoured and beloved.

Those who knew him well were fascinated and enchanted by him. They were ready to sacrifice their lives for the sake of saving a nail of his from hurt or injury. Being privileged by lots of prerogatives of perfection that no one else had been endowed with, his Companions found that he was peerless and so they loved him. Here we list a brief summary of the versions about his beauty and perfection. To encompass all which is, addmittedly, beyond our power?

BEAUTY OF CREATION

Describing the Messenger of Allâh, who passed by her tent on his journey of migration, Umm Ma'bad Al-Khuza'iyah said to her husband:

"He was innocently bright and had broad countenance. His manners were fine. Neither was his belly bulging out nor was his head deprived of hair. He had black attractive eyes finely arched by continuous eyebrows. His hair glossy and black, inclined to curl, he wore long. His voice was extremely commanding. His head was large, well formed and set on a slender neck. His expression was pensive and contemplative, serene and sublime.

The stranger was fascinated from the distance, but no sooner he became intimate with him than this fascination was changed into attachment and respect. His expression was very sweet and distinct. His speech was well set and free from the use of superfluous words, as if it were a rosary of beads.

His stature was neither too high nor too small to look repulsive. He was a twig amongst the two, singularly bright and fresh. He was always surrounded by his Companions. Whenever he uttered something, the listeners would hear him with rapt attention and whenever he issued any command, they vied with each other in carrying it out. He was a master and a commander. His utterances were marked by truth and sincerity, free from all kinds of falsehoods and lies."[Za'd Al-Ma'ad 2/45]

'Ali bin Abi Talib describing him said: "The Messenger of Allâh was neither excessively tall nor extremely short. He was medium height among his friends. His hair was neither curly nor wavy. It was in between. It was not too curly nor was it plain straight. It was both curly and wavy combined. His face was not swollen or meaty-compact.

It was fairly rounded. His mouth was white. He had black and large eyes with long haired eyelids. His joints (limbs) and shoulder joints were rather big. He had a rod-like little hair extending from his chest down to his navel, but the rest of his body was almost hairless.

He had thick hand palms and thick fingers and toes. At walking, he lifted his feet off the ground as if he had been walking in a muddy remainder of water. When he turned, he turned all. The Prophethood Seal was between his shoulders. He is the Seal of Prophets, the most generous and the bravest of all. His speech was the most reliable. He was the keenest and the most attentive to people's trust and was very careful to pay people's due in full. The Prophet was the most tractable and the most yielding companion, seeing him unexpectedly you fear him and venerate him. He who has acquaintance with him will like him. He who describes him says:

'I have never seen such a person neither before nor after seeing him.' "[Ibn Hisham 1/401; Jami' At-Tirmidhi 4/303]

Jabir bin Samurah reported that Allâh's Messenger had a broad face with reddish (wide) eyes and lean heels. [Sahih Al-Muslim 2/258]

Abu At-Tufail said: "He was white, good-looking. He was neither fat nor thin; neither tall nor short."

Anas bin Malik said: "He had unfolded hands and was pink-coloured. He was neither white nor brown. He was rather whitish. In both his head and beard there were as many as twenty grey hairs, besides some grey hairs at his temples." In another version: "and some scattered white hairs in his head." [Sahih Al-Bukhari 1/502]

Abu Juhaifa said: "I have seen some grey colour under his lower lip." Al-Bara' said: "He was of medium height, broad-shouldered; his hair went up to his earlobes. I saw him dressed in a red garment and I (assure you) I have never seen someone more handsome. At first he used to let his hair loose so as to be in compliance with the people of the Book; but later on he used to part it." [ibid 1/503]

Al-Bara' also said: "He had the most handsome face and the best character." When he was asked: "Was the Messenger's face sword-like?" "No," he said: "it was moon-like." But in another version: he said, "His face was round." Ar-Rabi'bint Muawwidh said: "Had you seen him, you would have felt that the sun was shining." Jabir bin Samurah said, "I saw him at one full-moony night. I looked at him. He was dressed in a red garment. I compared him with the moon and found that - for me - he was better than the moon." [Mishkat Al-Masabeeh 2/518]

Abu Huraira said: "I have never seen a thing nicer than the Messenger of Allâh. It seems as if the sunlight were moving within his face. I have never seen one who is faster in pace than the Messenger of Allâh. It seemed as if the earth had folded itself up to shorten the distance for him and we used to wear ourselves out while he was at full ease."

Ka'b bin Malik said: "When he was pleased, his face would shine with so bright light that you would believe that it was a moon-piece." [Sahih Al-Bukhari 1/502] Once he sweated hot at 'Aishah's and the features of his face twinkled; so I recited a poem by Abu Kabeer Al-Hudhali:

"If you watch his face-features, you will see them twinkling like the lightning of an approaching rain." [Rahmat-ul-lil'alameen 2/72]

Whenever Abu Bakr saw him he would say:

"He is faithful, chosen (by Allâh), and calls for forgiveness. He shines like a full-moon light when it is far from dark (clouds)." [Khulasa As-Siyar p.20]

'Umar used to recite verses by Zuhair describing Haram bin Sinan:

"Were you other than a human being, you would be a lighted moon at a full-moon night."

Then he would add: "Thus was the Messenger of Allâh.

When he got angry his face would go so red that you would think it were "an inflected red skin-spot with pomegranate grains on both cheeks." [Mishkat Al-Masabeeh 1/22]

Jabir bin Samurah said: "His legs were gentle, delicate and in conformity. His laughter is no more than smiling. Looking at him will make you say 'He is black-eyed though he is not so.'" [Jami' At-Tirmidhi 4/306]

Ibn Al-'Abbas said: "His two front teeth were splitted so whenever he speaks, light goes through them. His neck was as pure and silvery as a neck of doll. His eyelids were long haired but his beard was thick. His forehead was broad; but his eyebrows were like the metal piece attached to a lance, but they were unhorned. His nose was high-tipped, middlecambered with narrow nostrils. His cheeks were plain, but he had (little hair) running down like a rod from his throat to his navel. He had hair neither on his abdomen nor on his chest except some on his arms and shoulders. His chest was broad and flatted.

He had long forearms with expansive palms of the hand. His legs were plain straight and stretching down. His other limbs were straight too.

The two hollows of his soles hardly touch the ground. When he walks away he vanishes soon; but he walks at ease (when he is not in a hurry). The way he walks seems similar to one who is leaning forwards and is about to fall down." [Khulasa As-Siyar p.19, 20]

Anas said: "I have never touched silk or a silky garment softer than the palm of the Prophet's; nor have I smelt a perfume or any scent nicer than his." In another version, "I have never smelt ambergris or musk or any other thing sweeter than the scent and the smell of the Messenger of Allâh."

Abu Juhaifa said: "I took his hand and put it on my head and I found that it was colder than ice and better scented than the musk perfume." [Sahih Al-Bukhari 1/503]

Jabir bin Samurah - who was a little child then - said: "When he wiped my cheek, I felt it was cold and scented as if it had been taken out of a shop of a perfume workshop." [Sahih Muslim 2/256]

Anas said, "His sweat was pearl-like." Umm Sulaim said: "His sweat smelt nicer than the nicest perfume."

Jabir said: "Whoever pursues a road that has been trodden by the Messenger of Allâh, will certainly scent his smell and will be quite sure that the Messenger of Allâh has already passed it."

The Seal of Prophethood, which was similar in size to a pigeon's egg, was between his shoulders on the left side having spots on it like moles. [ibid 2/259]

THE PERFECTION OF SOUL AND NOBILITY

The Prophet was noted for superb eloquence and fluency in Arabic. He was remarkable in position and rank. He was an accurate, unpretending straightforward speaker. He was well-versed in Arabic and quite familiar with the dialects and accents of every tribe. He spoke with his entertainers using their own accents and dialects. He mastered and was quite eloquent at both bedouin and town speech. So he had the strength and eloquence of bedouin language as well as the clarity and the decorated splendid speech of town.

Above all, there was the assistance of Allâh embodied in the revealed verses of the *Quran*. His stamina, endurance and forgiveness - out of a commanding position-his patience and standing what he detested - these were all talents, attributes and qualities Allâh Himself had brought him on. Even wise men have their flaws, but the Messenger of Allâh, unlike everybody, the more he was hurt or injured, the more clement and patient he became. The more insolence an ignorant anybody exercised against him the more enduring he became.

'Aishah said:

> "The Messenger of Allâh, whenever he is given the opportunity to choose between two affairs, he always chooses the easiest and the most convenient. But if he is certain that it is sinful, he will be as far as he could from it. He has never avenged himself; but when the sanctity of Allâh is violated he would. That would be for Allâh's not for himself. He is the last one to get angry and the first to be satisfied. His hospitality and generosity were matchless. His gifts and endowments manifest a man who does not fear poverty." [Sahih Al-Bukhari 1/503]

Ibn'Abbas said: "The Prophet was the most generous. He is usually most generous of all times in Ramadan, the times at which the angel Gabriel [AWS] comes to see him. Gabriel used to visit him every night of Ramadan and review the *Quran* with him. Verily the Messenger of Allâh is more generous at giving bounty or charity than the blowing wind."

Jabir said:

"The Prophet would never deny anything he was asked for."[Sahih Al-Bukhari 1/503]

His courage, his succour and his might are distinguishable. He was the most courageous. He witnessed awkward and difficult times and stoodfast at them. More than once brave men and daring ones fled away leaving him alone; yet he stood with full composure facing the enemy without turning his back.

All brave men must have experienced fleeing once or have been driven off the battlefield at a round at a time except the Prophet. 'Ali said: "Whenever the fight grew fierce and the eyes of fighters went red, we used to resort to the Prophet for succour. He was always the closest to the enemy." [As-Shifa 1/89]

Anas said: "One night the people of Madinah felt alarmed. People went out hurriedly towards the source of sound, but the Prophet had already gone ahead of them. He was on the horseback of Abu Talhah which had no saddle over it, and a sword was slung round his neck, and said to them: 'There was nothing to be afraid for.'" [Sahih Al-Bukhari 1/407; Sahih Muslim 2/252]

He was the most modest and the first one to cast his eyes down. Abu Sa'îd Al-Khudri said: "He was shier than a virgin in her boudoir. When he hates a thing we read it on his face. [Sahih Al-Bukhari 1/504] He does not stare at anybody's face. He always casts his eyes down. He looks at the ground more than he looks sky-wards. His utmost looks at people are glances. He is willingly and modestly obeyed by everybody. He would never name a person whom he had heard ill-news about - which he hated. Instead he would say: 'Why do certain people do so....'"

Al-Farazdaq verse of poem fits him very much and the best one to be said of:

"He casts his eyes modestly but the eyes of others are cast down due to his solemnity and words issue out of his mouth only while he is smiling."

The Prophet is the most just, the most decent, the most truthful at speech, and the honestest of all. Those who have exchanged speech with him, and even his enemies, acknowledge his noble qualities. Even before the Prophethood he was nicknamed *Al-Ameen* (i.e. the truthful, the truthworthy). Even then-in *Al-Jahiliyah*-they used to turn to him for judgement and consultation. In a version by At-Tirmidhi, he says that 'Ali had said that he had been told by Abu Jahl that he (Abu Jahl) said to the Messenger of Allâh : "We do not call you a liar; but we do not have faith in what you have brought." [Mishkat Al-Masabeeh 2/521] In His Book, Allâh, the Exalted, said about them:

"It is not you that they deny, but it is the Verses (the *Quran*) of Allâh that the *Zalimûn* (polytheists and wrong-doers) deny." [Al-Qur'an 6:33]

Even when Heraclius asked Abu Sufyan: "Have you ever accused him of lying before the ministry of Prophethood?" Abu Sufyan said: "No."

He was most modest and far from being arrogant or proud. He forbade people to stand up at his presence as other people usually do for their kings. Visiting the poor, the needy and entertaining them are some of his habits. If a slave invited him, he would accept the invitation. He always sat among his friends as if he were an ordinary person of them. 'Aishah said that he used to repair his shoes, sew or mend his dress and to do what ordinary men did in their houses. After all, he was a human being like others. He used to check his dress (lest it has some insects on).

Milking the she-sheep and catering for himself were some of his normal jobs. [ibid 2/520] The Prophet was the most truthful to his pledges, and it is one of his qualities to establish good and steady relationship with his relatives-'*Silat-Ar-Rahim*'. He is the most merciful, gentle and amiable to all people. His way of living is the simplest one. Ill-manners and indecency are two qualities completely alien to him. He was decent, and did not call anybody names. He was not the sort of person who cursed or made noise in the streets. He did not exchange offences with others. He pushed back an offence or an error by forgiveness and overlooking. Nobody was allowed to walk behind him (i.e. as a bodyguard). He did not feel himself superior to others not even to his slaves (men or women) as far as food or clothes were concerned.

Whoever served him should be served by him too. 'Ugh' (an utterance of complaint) is a word that had never been said by him to his servant; nor was his servant blamed for doing a thing or leaving it undone. Loving the poor and the needy and entertaining them or participating in their funerals was things the Prophet always observed. He never contempted or disgraced a poor man for his poverty. Once he was travelling with his Companions and when it was time to have food prepared, he asked them to slaughter a she-sheep. A man said: I will slaughter it, another one said: I will skin it out. A third said: I will cook it. So the Messenger of Allâh said: I will collect wood for fire. They said: "No. We will suffice you that work." "I know that you can do it for me, but I hate to be privileged. Allâh hates to see a slave of his privileged to others." So he went and collected fire-wood. [Khulasa As-Siyar p.22]

Let us have some of the description of Hind bin Abi Halah: "The Messenger of Allâh was continually sad, thinking perpetually. He had no rest (i.e. for long). He only spoke when it was necessary. He would remain silent for a long time and whenever he spoke, he would end his talk with his jawbone but not out of the corners of his mouth, i.e. (snobbishly). His speech was inclusive. He spoke inclusively and decisively. It was not excessive nor was it short of meaning. It was amiable. It was in no way hard discoroning. He glorified the bounty of Allâh; even if it were little. If he had no liking for someone's food, he would neither praise nor criticize.

He was always in full control of his temper and he would never get seemed angry unless it was necessary. He never got angry for himself nor did he avenge himself. It was for Allâh's sanctity and religion that he always seemed angry. When he pointed at a thing he would do so with his full hand-palm, and he would turn it round to show surprise. If he were angry he would turn both his body and face aside. When he was pleased, he cast his eyes down. His laughter was mostly smiling. It was then that his teeth which were like hail-stones were revealed.

He never spoke unless it was something closely relevant to him. He confirmed the brotherhood relationship among his Companions; and thus he made them intimate and did not separate them or implant enmity among them. Those who were honourable with their peoples, were honoured and respected by him and were assigned rulers over their own peoples. His cheerfulness was never withdrawn at anyone's face; even at those whom he warned his people from or those whom he himself was on the alert of. He visited friends and inquired about people's affairs. He confirmed what was right and criticized the awful and tried to undermine it. He was moderate in all affairs. He was equal to others and was not privileged. He would never act heedlessly, lest the others should get heedless. Each situation was dealt with in its proper due.

Righteousness was his target; so he was never short of it nor indifferent to it. People who sat next to him were the best of their people and the best of them all were-for him - those who provided common consultations. For him, the greatest ones and the highest in ranks were the best at providing comfort and co-ordination and succour. Remembrance (of Allâh) was a thing he aimed at and established whenever he sat down or stands up. No certain position was assigned for him to sit on. He sits at the end of the group, seated next to the last sitter in the place. He ordered people to do the same. He entertained his participiants in social gatherings alike so that the one addressed would think that there was no one honoured by the Prophet but himself.

He whoever sat next to him or interrupted him in order to ask for his advice about an affair of his, would be the first to start the talk and the one to end it. The Prophet would listen to him patiently till he ended his speech. He never denied a request to anyone, if unapproachable, and then few gratifying words would work, instead. His magnanimity, broad mindedness his tolerance could embrace all people and entitled him to be regarded as father for them all. In justice, all of them were almost equal. Nobody was better than another except on the criterion of Allâh fearing.

A favoured one, to him, did the most Allâh fear. His assembly was a meeting of clemency, timidness, patience and honesty. Voices were not raised in rows or riots. Inviolable things were never violable. Fearing Allâh and worship were their means to sympathy and compassion. They used to esteem the old and have mercy on the young. They assisted the needy and entertained strangers. The Messenger of Allâh was always cheerful, easy, pleasant-tempered and lenient. He was never rude or rough nor clamorous or indecent. He was neither a reproacher nor a praiser. He overlooked what he did not desire, yet you would never despair of him. Three qualities he disposed of: hypocrisy, excessiveness, and what was none of his concern. People did not fear him in three areas: - for they were not qualities or habits of his —: He never disparaged, or reproached nor did he seek the defects or shortages of others.

He only spoke things whose reward was divinely desirable. When he spoke, his listeners would attentively listen casting down their heads. They only spoke when he was silent. They did not have disputes or arguments about who was to talk. He who talked in his presence would be listened to by everybody till he finished his talk. Their talk would be about the topic discussed or delivered by their first speaker. The Messenger of Allâh used to laugh at what they laughed at and admired what they used to admire. He would always show patience with a stranger's harshness at talk. He used to say:

> "When you see a person seeking an object earnestly, assist him to get his need. And never ask for a reward except from the reward-Giver, i.e. Allâh." [Ash-Shifa 1/126]

Kharijah bin Zaid said: "The Prophet was the most

honoured among the people with whom he sat. His limbs could hardly be seen. He was often silent and rarely talked when speech was not a necessity. He turned away from those whose speech was rude or impolite. His laughter was no more than a smile. His speech, which was decisive, it was neither excessive nor incomplete. Out of reverence and esteem and following the example of their Prophet, the Companions' laughter at his presence-was smiling, as well." [As-Shifa 1/107]

On the whole the Prophet was ornamented with peerless attributes of perfection. No wonder to be like that for he was brought up, educated and taught (the *Quran*) by Allâh. He was even praised by Allâh:

> "And verily, you (O Muhammad) are on an exalted standard of character." [Al-Qur'an 68:4]

Those were the attributes and qualities that the Prophet enjoyed which made the hearts of souls of the people close to him, draw near to him and love him. Those traits made him so popular that the restraint and enmity of his people grew less and they started to embrace Islam in large crowds.

This description is in fact no more than rapid review or rather short brief lines of Muhammad's aspects of full perfection and trying to encompass the whole perfect picture of the Prophet.

No one can ever claim to be possessed of full knowledge or complete mastery of the great attributes of the greatest man in this universe. No one can ever give this man, the top of perfection, his due descrpition. He was a man who always sought Allâh's light, to such an extent that he was wholly imbued with the *Quran*ic approach.

O Allâh! Send your blessings (and the Holy Words of Yours) upon Muhammad and the family of Muhammad, as You have send blessings upon Ibrâhim and the family of Ibrâhim. You are worthy of all praise, All Glorious. O Allâh! Bless Muhammad and the family of Muhammad as You have already blessed Ibrâhim and the family of Ibrâhim. You are worthy of all praise, All Glorious.

5

The Ottoman Advent

The Ottomans dominated the money - rich areas of the Middle East, Asia, and were at one point, considered a major European power. From the 1300's up until the end of World War I, the Ottoman state was an impressive bureaucracy. It was the frequent updates and changes of the social structure which allowed the Ottoman State to live for so long. What of its geography? The Middle East (also known as the "Near East" by Europeans) is the area of Southwest Asia. The Balkan states (areas near Greece) were once considered to be part of the Ottoman Empire but have since been stripped of their "Middle East" association. The Ottoman Empire touches five major bodies of water, the Caspian, Black, Mediterranean, and Red Seas, as well as the Persian Gulf.

Most Middle Eastern empires, (the Ottomans were no exception) had the chief parts of their population within a few miles from river valleys. The major rivers in the Middle East are the Nile (in Egypt) and the Tigris-Euphrates Rivers (in present day Turkey, Syria, and Iraq). Most river transport in those times was "one-way". Rivers' currents were generally too strong to sail against. The Nile River was the one exception, which partially explains why the Egyptians were particularly powerful in ancient times.

The desert areas of the Middle Eastern peninsula were generally untouched by the Ottomans. Until the advent and importance of oil, these regions were fairly unimportant economically. Though, drought is a typical state for much of the Middle East, it is important to mention that there are areas (such as Yemen) that get significantly more rainfall than typical cities in the Northeastern United States. Areas by the coast of the Black Sea can get as much as four times the amount of rain as Binghamton, NY does in a year.

What of the Middle East's early history? It begins with the formation of city-states in 3500 B.C.E. in lower Iraq. The communities settled along the river-valleys between the Tigris and Euphrates rivers. These civilizations prospered and gained written alphabets and religious rituals as a by-product of their incredible resourcefulness. In 1400 B.C.E. political rivals began to emerge and regional empires began to form in place of the city-states. Many great dynasties conquered the Middle East region, including the Egyptians, the Acheminid Empire, and Alexander the Great's Greeks. The Middle East has been a very important region in terms of agricultural and mathematical development.

It was here in the Middle East that wheat and the concept of the number zero was invented. Turkey (which contained the capital of the Ottoman Empire) was the most populous and prosperous of the Holy Roman Empire's states. Anatolia (also known as Turkey and Asia Minor, depending on the source of the information) was also the influence for Hellenic ideas. There are still "Greek Ruins" in present day Turkey. The Byzantine Empire, the Holy Roman Empire's successor, controls the lion's share of the Middle East. It follows then that the Middle Eastern people are mostly Greek Orthodox Christian and Greek speaking.

There are still a few pagan religions or more correctly animist religions that play a role in society. The animists are famous for their practice of tying ribbons on to trees in an effort to receive favors from the spirits. Another religion that refused to be completely crushed was the religion of Zoroastrianism. Founded by Zarathushtra, the religion was Monotheistic, a true departure from the time when it was made. Its date of origin is suspect but is likely 600 B.C.E.

These are Persian (read Iranian) areas where Persian is spoken and the government is known as the Sasanian Empire. The religion had a profound effect on Judaism and Christianity and is still alive today, followed by some 140,000 people.

This religious sect put up a monumental fight with the Byzantine Empire. Some historians say that the Iranian Zoroastrians were a constant thorn in the side of the Byzantine Empire and may have been one of the chief causes of the Byzantine collapse. Where did Islam come from? Muslims believe that Mohammed received revelations from God (or more specifically the Angel Gabriel) from 610 to 632 C.E. His revelations are contained in the Islamic scripture; a tome called the Koran (also spelt Quran). Islam is considered a Semitic religion, like Judaism and Christianity. It is a monotheistic belief and Islam, in its purest, original form is considered an extension of Judaism, with Mohammed as the last prophet.

Two important Koranic tenets (that some may find interesting) are religious tolerance and the idea of women's rights. The Koran states that other "people of the book" believe in an incomplete faith but should be respected. It means that Jews and Christians should be as respected in Islamic society as a fellow coreligionist. The Islamic faith allowed women better rights than Judaism or Christianity. It allowed women the right to own property or money and it guaranteed them a percentage of her husband's property upon his death.

How did Islam spread? Mohammed convinced people in Medina, his hometown after being forced out of Mecca, to follow him in war and religion. His army was indeed powerful enough to conquer Mecca. From the 600's to the 700's C.E., there was much political turmoil as Mohammed and the succeeding caliphs, gathered forces in their sphere of influence. By 750 C.E. Muslim warriors have succeeded in taking over everything from Asia to France. After a brief peak of power, they are forced into Spain. Most Middle Eastern areas stay Arabic speaking and Islamic. Turkey remains Greek Orthodox and Greek speaking, the Europeans revert back to earlier religions and customs. In 1071, the Turks (in Asia Minor) change from animists to Muslims. Barbarians convert the local populace through limited force and persuasion.

The Barbarian/Turk mix then tries to conquer the Byzantine Empire and in 1453 they attempt and succeed in the conquest of Constantinople. Turkish speaking Muslims are now the chief people in Asia Minor. There are still limited pockets of Greeks speaking Christians and Kurds in Turkey left in Asia Minor at the end of the conquest. What of the origins of the Ottoman Empire? In fact, there was little study of the origins of the Ottoman Empire until the twentieth century. Herbert A. Gibbons, a historian, was the first person to utilize research and thought to make a guess on the origins; his work was published in 1916. He claimed that the Ottoman Empire was really an offshoot of the Byzantine Empire with an Islamic veneer.

The next group of historians to offer a different view was William Langer and Robert Blake in 1932. They argued that it was not Byzantine at all but a more indigenous empire of the Middle East. Pre-Ottoman Islamic states banded together to form the backbone of the empire. Their work put Ottoman study on a more academic level. In 1934, Fuat Koprulu disagreed in a Turkish historical journal. He claimed that the Ottoman state was purely Turkish. Turkish tribes moved from Asia to the Middle East and took over the areas. This was important as an argument for Turkish nationalism for the young nation. Also in 1934, Paul Wittek offered an explanation as to the start of the Empire. He claimed that the empire was a ghazi state. Ghazi means a holy, Islamic war. Ottoman persons in Anatolia fought for the faith and ended up in making an empire. This theory was particularly embraced by the West.

Colin Heywood- a student of Paul Wittek- penned in the 1980's that the intellectual climate while Wittek was growing up in Vienna influenced his writings. The Viennese appreciated the projection of the Ottoman State as warmongering. He suggested that Paul Wittek may have been in someway projecting a fallacy, despite his source from the

1400s, only a century after the founding of the Empire. Heath Lowry looked into Wittek's sources and found more reasons to question Wittek's version of events in 2003. Lowry proves that Ahmedi, the major source of information for Wittek's hypothesis, was a retainer of the court. His writing then is not that credible as it may have been influenced by important government officials. Ahmedi's text, Lowry conjectures, was a story and not meant to be taken literally. Lowry further proves that at the time ghaza did not mean holy war but instead, raiding and pillaging, therefore just typical warfare not religious or politically motivated warfare.

Piecing together the origins and the known history, the most likely origin is that a group of warrior-barbarians in Anatolia (present day Turkey) form a group to try and take over the civilization. They begin attacking the Byzantine Empire in an attempt to pillage the cities. Barbarians, at all points in time, attack civilization to attempt to pillage the civilization's belongings. Due to the attacks and the breakdown of the Byzantine Empire, there is a large amount of political instability in the relatively settled regions of Turkey. The once Greek and Christian settlements are converted to Turkish Muslims due to Turkish nomadic invaders that settle in the country. The Byzantine Empire manages to hold on to Constantinople and the Seljuk state begins to rise to power in the provinces.

The leaders of the Turkish nomads begin to form "tent communities" which house thousands of people. The communities war with each other often, as political instability strikes hold of the region. Osman, the leader of the Ottoman family, rises to the greatest power and wealth. His reign, as well as his territorial bounds gets notice from Bulgarian, Italian, and Byzantine chroniclers. Osman, it should be noted was Christian, meaning that the Ottoman Empire was by no means religiously founded. Christians frequently held positions of power in the beginning of Ottoman history. Nonetheless, it started to take on the role as an Islamic power soon after its rule began. What is the early history of the

Empire? In 1389, the battle of Kosovo destroyed the Serbian State. (It is interesting to note that in 1989 Milosevic, a historian, stands on the battlefield of Kosovo and creates a Serbian identity, saying that the Serbs were the victims of a brutal attack.)

The 1396 battle of Nicopolis, between the Ottomans and elements from France, Austria and Hungary ended with the Ottomans on top. The battle of Varna at the end of the 14th/ early 15th century ended the Bulgarian state. With the 1453 conquering of Constantinople over the Byzantines, the Ottoman Empire becomes a major force to be reckoned with. By 1500, the Ottomans had taken control of all of Turkey and much of the land from Europe to North Africa to Asia. Who runs the Empire? The Sultan of the Empire is the most important with the Grand Vizier being second in command. At times, the Grand Vizier becomes as or more important than the Sultan. One coup d'etat happens in 1453 after the conquest of Constantinople. Due to the increased popularity the Sultan has after the conquest, he feels safe in ordering his Grand Vizier killed.

Sultans were chosen from the sons of the previous Sultan. In the beginning, all the sons were given governing experience and any of them could be chosen to lead. Later in Ottoman history, the eldest son would become the next ruler. There were only two failed attempts to overthrow the ruling family, which suggests an extremely large amount of political stability. How do you make a living in society? Successful wars allowed pillage and new Timars (explained later) to be made. Also the transit trade (being the land bridge between Europe and the rest of Asia) and international trade made a large part of the economy of the Ottoman Empire. Domestic commerce, including the caravan system, was another common way for people to make a living in society. There were a few other ways to make a living including agriculture and fishing.

How do you pay for the soldiers? Pillage was a common answer in the Ottoman (and European) system. A small share (20%) of the plunder went to the Sultan. The Ottomans were particular in those cities that they would plunder. If the city surrendered, the Ottomans had to leave it alone. If they were met with resistance, then they received the affirmation to pillage the village. The Ottomans started the Timar system which broke up conquered areas into taxable units. These units were made specifically so that each Timar would be able to sustain a man and his horse. These Timars were given to members of the Sipahi Calvary, those servicemen of Muslim heritage. The taxes from the Timar would go directly into the Timar-holders pocket in exchange for loyalty and willingness to go to war when called upon.

This is not the same as the feudal system in Europe. Only the taxes from the land not the land itself was given to the Timar-holder. This system was popular from the 1400's until the late 1500's, when it starts to be replaced. (The system does continue with decreased popularity until the early seventeenth century.) As the Timar System begins to fall away, the idea of Tax Farms become more important. The Tax Farm system broke up land in much the same way as the Timar system and then the right to tax would be auctioned off. In other words, the government thought that it could get a certain amount of tax for this land. People would bid for the right to collect the tax and whatever amount of tax they collected, they could keep.

The amount of the tax was set by government but may have been cheated slightly by the tax collectors. The government then paid the soldiers from this income. It is interesting to note that money does not flow as cash in this society, so it is not cash that is being paid to the soldiers. What of law? There was an interest in the status quo of the empire. The primary law system was the Islamic courts but appointed Jews and Christians were allowed to have their own courts which ruled over their religious areas. Non-conflicting systems were by and large left alone. There were two main systems of law, the Sharia Law and the Kanun Law. There was Sharia Law which was evolved out of the Koran and from the word of Mohammed.

There was also Kanun Law which was the secular law of the Sultan. Both were taught at law schools, which existed in Bursa and Istanbul. The court was run by sultan-appointed kadi (read judges) and often included punishments including but not limited to fines, lashings, and capital punishment. Often Jews and Christians went to Islamic courts to get a more forceful ruling on an issue. Women almost always went to Islamic courts, as they tended to side more often with and gave fairer payments to women. In truth, the political judicial system was run for the betterment of the rulers. The Kanun overruled the Sharia Law, which show a level of respect for the Sultan over religion. What of the non-Muslim members of society? There are still significant pockets of Christianity in the empire. While the empire was not founded on religion, it has become increasingly important to be Muslim in the society.

Employ of Christians as Christians becomes decreasingly acceptable. To tap into the usefulness of the Christian members of society, the Ottomans create the Devshirme system. The Devshirme system collected boys from the Christian villages to be slaves in the army or the government. (This is not as evil as it sounds; in fact, there are records of mothers pleading for their boys to be taken into the system as it gave them a chance for social mobility.) The boys were sent to live with Turkish Muslims. Upon their conversion to Islam, they were sent to the army to be janissaries (soldiers) or sent to the Palace School to learn about government. These Devshirme boys were often promoted to high positions of power, generals in the army and grand viziers in the government.

The Janissaries do sometimes revolt after the year 1300. They usually demand more money (and they usually get it). Many Devshirme boys remained in contact with their hometowns. The boys, once in positions of power, had bridges, churches, schools, and hospitals built. This Devshirme system, despite some of its flaws, was an excellent brainchild of the Ottoman Empire. It allowed them to tap into the non-Muslim talent pool which would have been against policy if they had remained Christian. It also gave them a very well trained force running the state. The Devshirme boys' sons get help from their fathers navigating through the ranks. Due to this upsurge of interest in government and military by the sons of the Devshirme, there is no need to continue the system. Consequently, the Devshirme starts to break down in the late 1500's.

What of the rest of the Middle East? There are three "Gun Powder" Islamic States that peak around the same time. The Safevids were in the center of the Ottomans and the Mughals (who were an Islamic power in the East). The Safevids peaked in power between 1571 and 1722. The Mughal Empire (an extension of the Mongol empire) was powerful from 1483-1862 when it was taken over by the Europeans who took over all of India. The Southern tip of India started to fall to the Europeans as early as the 1500's. The Safevid Dynasty of Iran attempts to stop the influence of the Ottoman state through war. The Ottomans soundly defeat the Safevid Dynasty in the Battle of Chaldiran (1514) and push the Safevid people back into Iran. The Safevids convert to Shii Islam in an effort to maintain a national identity separate from the Ottomans.

The Mameluke Dynasty in Egypt who owned the land route to China was starting to crumble politically. To make sure the route was held in Muslim hands the Ottomans took over the area by soundly defeating the Mamelukes in 1516. The Ottoman territory expanded into Israel and Jordan and the Ottomans became the rulers of the holy cities of Mecca and Medina. The Mughal Empire is consolidated from indigenous Uzbekistani tribes. They practice very tolerant positions on religion. Akbar (1556-1605 C.E.) pushed for the acceptance of religious Hindu customs and also accepted the practices of Buddhism, Christianity, and Judaism.

There is much cultural difference and difference in the history of the three Islamic Empires and they refuse to reconcile their differences. There is communication between the three Islamic dynasties but it is infrequent. The Ottomans are de facto Caliphs (head of Islam) due to the conquering of the Mamelukes who were possibly descendants of the Caliphs. It is a somewhat vaguely substantiated claim and is not spoken of until significantly later times in the Empire's history. What of the Europeans? The Europeans saw the Ottoman Empire as a punishment from God. Ottomans were seen as the anti-Christ.

The Lutherans saw the Ottomans as proof that the papacy was corrupt and that the Ottomans were punishment for this abomination to Christianity. The Roman Catholics saw the Ottomans as punishment for allowing the Lutheran revolution. The Ottomans seemed an unstoppable force until the Ottomans attack Hapsburg Vienna in 1529. The Ottomans are defeated and begin a slow transition of power with limited territorial expansion and some contraction.

What of the languages? The Ottoman Empire remained Turkish speaking with a language creatively called Ottoman Turkish. The written language was Arabic with Turkish grammar. Though Ottoman Turkish was the official language of the empire, Persian and Arabic were common languages. The Safevid Empire was Turkish speaking but the court language was Persian. By keeping a different "official" language, the Safevids create a national identity. The Mughal Empire used Turkish and Persian in their courts. The conversion of the Safevids from Sunni to Shii also allowed the Safevids to claim themselves "Champions of the Shii", which further established their independence.

It is interesting to note that in early Islamic history there was a sharp division between the Arabic Muslims and the non-Arabic Muslims. The Arabic Muslims refused to treat the non-Arabs as worthwhile brethren. However, when three important Islamic empires are made, none of them have Arabic as an official spoken language. It is an interesting departure from the early history of the religion. This is wholly unimportant but interesting from a linguistic standpoint. Turkish is a Turkic language. Arabic is a Semitic language. Persian is a Kurdish/Indo-European Language.

These languages then are linguistically unrelated. Though these languages are pervasive in the same region and there have been hosts of conquests of these areas, the languages are essentially separate entities with no interrelation. What brought about the end of the Ottoman Empire? Long-term economic problems including decreased land travel from Europe to Asia, no access to the "New World", and slow moving bureaucracy allowed the Ottomans to slip from power. The Europeans were able to buy bigger and better weapons and were eventually able to significantly shrink and inhibit the Ottoman State until its ultimate collapse in 1922.

6

Colonialism Muslim Style

Political aspects of Islam are derived from the Quran, the Sunna, Muslim history and sometimes elements of political movements outside Islam. Traditional political concepts in Islam include leadership by successors to the Prophet known as Caliphs, (Imamate for Shia); the importance of following Islamic law or Sharia; the duty of rulers to seek Shura or consultation from their subjects; and the importance of rebuking unjust rulers but not encouraging rebellion against them. A sea change in the Islamic world was the abolition of the Ottoman caliphate in 1924, which some believed meant an end to the Islamic state both in "symbolic and practice terms".

In the 19th and 20th century a common theme has been resistance to Western imperialism, particularly the British Empire, and sometimes the perceived racist policies that discriminated against some Muslims. The defeat of Arab armies in the Six Day War, the collapse of the Soviet Union and the end of communism as a viable alternative with the end of the Soviet Union and the Cold War has increased the appeal of Islamism and Islamic fundamentalist movements, especially in the context of undemocratic and corrupt regimes all across the Muslim world.

THE POLITICAL CHARACTER OF ISLAM

Islam is a religion has existed for over fourteen centuries, (although Islamic teaching holds it has existed since the beginning of time), in many different countries. As such, diverse political movements in many different contexts have used the banner of Islam to lend legitimacy to their causes. Not surprisingly, practically every aspect of Islamic politics is subject to much disagreement and contention between different interpretions, particularly between conservative Islamists and liberal movements within Islam.

ISLAMISM

Islamist or Islamic parties exist in almost every democracy with a Muslim majority. This term has many different meanings which this chapter will explore, along with links to other political trends. The controversial term Islamofascism has also been coined by some non-Muslims to describe the political and religious philosophies of some militant Islamic groups. Both terms lump together a large variety of groups with varying histories and contexts. The articles on militant Islamic groups, Islamic parties and modern Islamic philosophy explain some of their actual views in detail.

MUHAMMAD, THE MEDINAN STATE AND ISLAMIC POLITICAL IDEALS

Islamists claim that the origins of Islam as a political movement are to be found in the life and times of Islam's prophet, Muhammad and his successors, (depending on the Islamist). In 622 CE, in recognition of his claims to prophethood, Muhammad was invited to rule the city of Medina. At the time the local Arab tribes of Aus and Khazraj dominated the city, and were in constant conflict. Medinans saw in Muhammad an impartial outsider who could resolve the conflict. Muhammad and his followers thus moved to Medina, where Muhammad drafted the Medina Charter.

This document made Muhammad the ruler, and recognized him as the Prophet of Allah. During his rule, Muhammad instituted the laws of the Qur'an, considered by Muslims to be divine revelation. Medina thus became a state based on Islamic law, which is still a basic demand of most Islamic movements. Muhammad gained a widespread following and an army, and his rule expanded first to the city of Mecca and then spread through the Arabian Peninsula through a combination of diplomacy and military conquest. This approach and thinking continued with the policies of succeeding Caliphs and by the jurists generally, until the advent of European colonialism and the demise of the Ottoman Caliphate.

THE EARLY CALIPHATE AND ISLAMIC POLITICAL IDEALS

After death of Muhammad, his community needed to appoint a new leader, giving rise to the title Caliph, meaning "successor". Thus the subsequent Islamic empires were known as Caliphates. Alongside the growth of the Umayyad empire, the major political development within Islam in this period was the sectarian split between Sunni and Shi'ite Muslims; this had its roots in a dispute over the succession of the Caliphate. Sunni Muslims believed the caliphate was elective, and any member of the Prophet's tribe, Quraysh, might serve as one. Shi'ites, on the other hand, believed the caliphate should be hereditary in the line of the Prophet, and thus all the caliphs, with the exception of Ali, were usurpers.

However, the Sunni sect emerged as triumphant in most of the Muslim world, and thus most modern Islamic political movements (with the exception of Iran) are founded in Sunni thought. Muhammad's closest companions, the four "rightly guided" Caliphs who succeeded him, continued to expand the state to encompass Jerusalem, Ctesiphon, and Damascus, and sending armies as far as the Sindh. The Islamic empire stretched from Al-Andalus (Muslim Spain) to Persia under the reign of the Umayyad dynasty. The conquering Arab armies took the system of Sharia laws and courts to their new military camps and cities, and built mosques for Friday jam'at (community prayers) as well as Madrasahs to educate local Muslim youth.

These institutions resulted in the development of a class

of ulema (classical Islamic scholars) who could serve as qadis (Sharia-court judges), imams of mosques and madrasah teachers. These classical scholars and jurists all owed their livelihood to the expansionary Islamic empire. Not surprisingly, these ulema gave legal and religious sanction to militarist interpretations of jihad. The political terminology of the Islamic state was all the product of this period. Thus, medieval legal terms such as khalifa, sharia, fiqh, maddhab, jizya, and dhimmi all remain part of modern Islamic vocabulary. Since the scholarly and legal traditions of the ulema were well-established by the time of the Abbasids, the later Middle Eastern empires and kingdoms (including the Ayyubid, Seljuk, Fatimid, Mamluk and Mongol) had little impact on modern Islamist political ideals.

One Islamic concept concerning the structure of ruling is shura, or consultation, which is the duty of rulers mentioned in two verses in the Quran, 3:153, and 42:36, and contrasted by Muslims with arbitrary personal rule. It is mentioned by Islamic traditionalists, commentators, and contemporary writers but is not commanded by Islamic law only recommended. One type of ruler not part of the Islamic ideal was the king, which was disparaged in Quran's mentions of the Pharaoh, "the prototye of the unjust and tyrannical ruler" (18:70, 79) and elsewhere. (28:34)

ELECTING OR APPOINTING A CALIPH

Fred Donner, in his book *The Early Islamic Conquests* (1981), argues that the standard Arabian practice during the early Caliphates was for the prominent men of a kinship group, or tribe, to gather after a leader's death and elect a leader from amongst them, although there was no specified procedure for this shura, or consultative assembly. Candidates were usually from the same lineage as the deceased leader, but they were not necessarily his sons.

Capable men who would lead well were preferred over an ineffectual direct heir, as there was no basis in the majority Sunni view that the head of state or governor should be chosen based on lineage alone. Al-Mawardi has written that the caliph should be Qurayshi. Abu Bakr Al-Baqillani has said that the leader of the Muslims simply should be from the majority. Abu Hanifa an-Nu'man also wrote that the leader must come from the majority.

MAJLIS ASH-SHURA

Traditional Sunni Islamic lawyers agree that *shura,* loosely translated as 'consultation of the people' is a function of the caliphate. The Majlis ash-Shura advises the caliph. The importance of this is premised by the following verses of the Qur'an:

> "...those who answer the call of their Lord and establish the prayer, and who conduct their affairs by Shura. [are loved by God]"
>
> "...consult them (the people) in their affairs. Then when you have taken a decision (from them), put your trust in Allah"

The majlis is also the means to elect a new caliph. Al-Mawardi has written that members of the majlis should satisfy three conditions: they must be just; they must have enough knowledge to distinguish a good caliph from a bad one, and must have sufficient wisdom and judgment to select the best caliph. Al-Mawardi also said in emergencies when there is no caliphate and no majlis, the people themselves should create a majlis, select a list of candidates for caliph, then the majlis should select from the list of candidates.

Some modern interpretations of the role of the Majlis ash-Shura include those by Islamist author Sayyid Qutb and by Taqiuddin al-Nabhani, the founder of a transnational political movement devoted to the revival of the Caliphate. In an analysis of the shura chapter of the Qur'an, Qutb argued Islam requires only that the ruler consult with at least some of the ruled (usually the elite), within the general context of God-made laws that the ruler must execute. Taqiuddin al-Nabhani, writes that Shura is important and part of the "the ruling structure" of the Islamic caliphate, "but not one of its pillars," and may be neglected without the Caliphate's rule becoming unIslamic. Non-Muslims may serve in the majlis, though they may not vote or serve as an official.

RULERS, ULAMA AND THE TRADITIONAL ISLAMIC STATE

One scholar argues that for hundreds of years until the twentieth century, Islamic states followed a system of government based on the coexistence of sultan and ulama following the rules of the sharia law. This system resembled to some extent some Western governments in possessing an unwritten constitution (like the United Kingdom), and possessing separate branches of government - two not three, the sultan and ulama - which provided Separation of powers in governance. A symbol of the success of this system is the current popularity of the Islamist movement which seeks to restore the Islamist state.

QURAN

According to scholar Bernard Lewis, the Qur'an has several points to make on governance. The Quran, for example, makes it clear that there is a duty of obedience: "Obey God, obey the Prophet, obey those who hold authority over you."

And this is elaborated in a number of sayings attributed to Muhammad. But there are also sayings that put strict limits on the duty of obedience. Two dicta attributed to the Prophet and universally accepted as authentic are indicative. One says, "there is no obedience in sin"; in other words, if the ruler orders something contrary to the divine law, not only is there no duty of obedience, but there is a duty of disobedience.

This is more than the right of revolution that appears in Western political thought. It is a duty of revolution, or at least of disobedience and opposition to authority. The other pronouncement, "do not obey a creature against his creator," again clearly limits the authority of the ruler, whatever form of ruler that may be. However, Ibn Taymiyyah – an important scholar of the Hanbali School - says in Tafseer for this verse "there is no obedience in sin"; that people should ignore the order of the ruler if it would disobey the divine law and shouldn't use this as excuse for revolution because it will spell Muslims bloods.

ACCOUNTABILITY OF RULERS

Sunni Islamic lawyers have commented on when it is permissible to disobey, impeach or remove rulers in the Caliphate. This is usually when the rulers are not meeting public responsibilities obliged upon them under Islam. Al-Mawardi said that if the rulers meet their Islamic responsibilities to the public, the people must obey their laws, but if they become either unjust or severely ineffective then the Caliph or ruler must be impeached via the Majlis ash-Shura.

Similarly Al-Baghdadi believed that if the rulers do not uphold justice, the ummah via the majlis should give warning to them, and if unheeded then the Caliph can be impeached. Al-Juwayni argued that Islam is the goal of the ummah, so any ruler that deviates from this goal must be impeached.

Al-Ghazali believed that oppression by a caliph is enough for impeachment. Rather than just relying on impeachment, Ibn Hajar al-Asqalani obliged rebellion upon the people if the caliph began to act with no regard for Islamic law. Ibn Hajar al-Asqalani said that to ignore such a situation is *haraam,* and those who cannot revolt inside the caliphate should launch a struggle from outside. Al-Asqalani used two ayahs from the Qur'an to justify this:

> "...And they (the sinners on qiyama) will say, 'Our Lord! We obeyed our leaders and our chiefs, and they misled us from the right path. Our Lord! Give them (the leaders) double the punishment you give us and curse them with a very great curse'..."

Islamic lawyers commented that when the rulers refuse to step down via successful impeachment through the Majlis, becoming dictators through the support of a corrupt army, if the majority agrees they have the option to launch a revolution against them. Many noted that this option is only exercised after factoring in the potential cost of life.

RULE OF LAW

The following hadith establishes the principle of rule of law in relation to nepotism and accountability. Narrated 'Aisha: The people of Quraish worried about the lady from Bani Makhzum who had committed theft. They asked, "Who will intercede for her with Allah's Apostle?" Some said, "No one dares to do so except Usama bin Zaid the beloved one to Allah's Apostle." When Usama spoke about that to Allah's Apostle Allah's Apostle said: "Do you try to intercede for somebody in a case connected with Allah's Prescribed Punishments?"

Then he got up and delivered a sermon saying, "What destroyed the nations preceding you, was that if a noble amongst them stole, they would forgive him, and if a poor person amongst them stole, they would inflict Allah's Legal punishment on him. By Allah, if Fatima, the daughter of Muhammad (my daughter) stole, I would cut off her hand." Various Islamic lawyers do however place multiple conditions, and stipulations e.g. the poor cannot be penalised for stealing out of poverty, before executing such a law, making it very difficult to reach such a stage. It is well known during a time of drought in the Rashidun caliphate period, capital punishments were suspended until the effects of the drought passed.

Islamic jurists later formulated the concept of the rule of law, the equal subjection of all classes to the ordinary law of the land, where no person is above the law and where officials and private citizens are under a duty to obey the same law. A Qadi (Islamic judge) was also not allowed to discriminate on the grounds of religion, race, colour, kinship or prejudice. There were also a number of cases where Caliphs had to appear before judges as they prepared to take their verdict.

According to Noah Feldman, a law professor at Harvard

University, the legal scholars and jurists who once upheld the rule of law were replaced by a law governed by the state due to the codification of Sharia by the Ottoman Empire in the early 19th century:

How the scholars lost their exalted status as keepers of the law is a complex story, but it can be summed up in the adage that partial reforms are sometimes worse than none at all. In the early 19th century, the Ottoman Empire responded to military setbacks with an internal reform movement. The most important reform was the attempt to codify Shariah. The Westernizing process foreign to the Islamic legal tradition sought to transform Shariah from a body of doctrines and principles to be discovered by the human efforts of the scholars into a set of rules that could be looked up in a book.

Once the law existed in codified form, however, the law itself was able to replace the scholars as the source of authority. Codification took from the scholars their all-important claim to have the final say over the content of the law and transferred that power to the state.

REACTION TO EUROPEAN COLONIALISM

In the 19th century European encroachment on the Muslim world came with the retreat of the Ottoman Empire, the arrival of the French in Algeria (1830), the disappearance of the Moghul Empire in India (1857), the Russian incursions into the Caucasus (1857) and Central Asia. The first Muslim reaction to European encroachment was of "peasant and religious", not urban origin. "Charismatic leaders", generally members of the ulama or leaders of religious orders launched the call for jihad and formed tribal coalitions. Sharia in defiance of local common law was imposed to unify tribes.

Examples include Abd al-Qadir in Algeria, the Mahdi in Sudan, Shamil in the Caucasus, the Senussi in Libya and in Chad, Mullah-i Lang in Afghanistan, the Akhund of Swat in India, and later, Abd al-Karim in Morocco. All these movements eventually failed "despite spectacular victories such as the destruction of the British army in Afghanistan in

1842 and the taking of Kharoum in 1885."

The second Muslim reaction to European encroachment later in the century and early 20th century was not violent resistance but the adoption of some Western political, social, cultural and technological ways. Members of the urban elite, particularly in Egypt, Iran, and Turkey advocated and practiced "Westernization". The failure of the attempts at political westernization, according to some, was exemplified by the Tanzimat reorganization of the Ottoman rulers.

Sharia was codified into law (which was called the Mecelle) and an elected legislature was established to make law. These steps took away the Ulama's role of "discovering" the law and the formerly powerful scholar class weakened and withered into religious functionaries, while the legislature was suspended less than a year after its inauguration and never recovered to replace the Ulama as a separate "branch" of government providing Separation of powers. The "paradigm of the executive as a force unchecked by either the sharia of the scholars or the popular authority of an elected legislature became the dominant paradigm in most of the Sunni Muslim world in the twentieth century."

THE MODERN POLITICAL IDEAL OF THE ISLAMIC STATE

In addition to the legitimacy given by medieval scholarly opinion, nostalgia for the days of successful Islamic empire simmered under later Western colonialism. This nostalgia played a major role in the Islamist political ideal of Islamic state, which primarily means a state which enforces traditional Islamic laws. The Islamist political program is generally to be accomplished by re-shaping the governments of existing Muslim nation-states; but the means of doing this varies greatly across movements and circumstances. Many Islamist movements, such as the Jamaat-e-Islami in Bangladesh, have found that they can use the democratic process to their advantage, and so focus on votes and coalition-building with other political parties.

Other more radical movements such as Jama'atul Mujahideen Bangladesh embrace militant Islamic ideology. In the face of the tremendous poverty, corruption and disillusionment with conventional politics, the political ideal of the Islamic state has been criticized by many espousing liberal movements within Islam and for example by Ziauddin Sardar, as being utopian and not offering real solutions.

ISLAM AS A POLITICAL MOVEMENT IN THE 20TH CENTURY

Following World War I and the dissolution of the Ottoman Empire, and the subsequent dissolution of the Caliphate by Mustafa Kemal Atatürk (founder of Turkey), many Muslims perceived that the political power of their religion was in retreat. There was also concern that Western ideas and influence were spreading throughout Muslim societies. This led to considerable resentment of the influence of the European powers. Resentment of all foreign forces in Arab lands was exacerbated when Hitler indirectly gained control of Syria via Vichy France in 1940. The Baath Party was created in Syria and in Iraq as a movement to resist and harry the British, using some elements of Nazi, Islamic, socialist doctrines, and anti-Semitic propaganda.

AFTER THE SECOND WORLD WAR

After the war, this party shifted to the Soviet Union's sphere of influence. Stalin had by then become an opponent of Zionism, having liked the Arabs initially found it compatible, and then rejected it as bourgeois, racist, and colonial. Any Arab tendency to anti-Semitism was drastically magnified after World War II when Israel was created, at literally the crossroads of all traditional Arab lands. The fact that the promise made to Arabs had been broken, while that to Jews had been kept, was often ascribed to racism. A religious focus for rhetoric became more common, and more mullahs became involved in politics.

The Palestinian Diaspora stressed social structures in Arab states, which expelled many Jews. Zionism was identified as the opponent, and some argued a coherent Islamism was required as a response. However, Islam was still not the dominant trend in resisting colonialism or even Zionism. During the 1960s, the predominant ideology within the Arab world was pan-Arabism which deemphasized religion and emphasized the creation of socialist, secular states based on Arab nationalism rather than Islam. However, governments based on Arab nationalism have found themselves facing economic stagnation and disorder. Increasingly, the borders of these states were seen as artificial colonial creations - which they were, having literally been drawn on a map by European colonial powers.

Now from Cairo to Tehran, the crowds that in the 1950s demonstrated under the red or national flag now march beneath the green banner. The targets are the same: foreign banks, nightclubs, local governments accused of complacency toward the West. The continuity is apparent not only in these targets but also the participants: the same individuals who followed Nasser or Marx in the 1960s are Islamists today.

CONTEMPORARY MOVEMENTS

Some common political currents in Islam include:

- Traditionalist fundamentalism, which accepts traditional commentaries on the Quran and Sunna and "takes as its basic principle imitation (taqlid), that is, refusal to innovate", and follows one of the five maddhah legal schools or Madh'hab (Shafiism, Malikism, Hanafism, Hanbalism) and, may include Sufism. An example of Sufi traditionalism is the Barelvi school in Pakistan.
- Reformist fundamentalism, which "criticizes the tradition, the commentaries, popular religious practices (maraboutism, the cult of saints)", deviations, and superstitions; it aims to return to the founding texts. This reformism generally developed in response to an external threat (the influence of Hinduism on Islam, for example. 18th-century examples are Shah Wali Allah in India and Abd al-Wahhab (who founded Wahhabism) in the Arabian Peninsula. A modern example may be Salafism (*Salafiyya*).

- Islamism or political Islam both follows and departs from reformist fundamentalism, embracing a return to the sharia, but adopting Western terminology such as revolution and ideology and taking a more liberal attitude towards women's rights. Contemporary examples include the Jamaat-e-Islami, Muslim Brotherhood and the Iranian Islamic Revolution.
- Liberal movements within Islam generally define themselves in opposition to Islamic political movements, but often embrace many of its anti-imperialist elements.

SUNNI AND SHIA DIFFERENCES

According to scholar Vali Nasr, political tendencies of Sunni and Shia Islamic revival differ, with Sunni fundamentalism "in Pakistan and much of the Arab world" being "far from politically revolutionary", while Shia fundamentalism is strongly influenced by Ruhollah Khomeini and his talk of the oppression of the poor and class war. Sunni fundamentalism "was rooted in conservative religious impulses and the bazaars, mixing mercantile interests with religious values."... Khomeini's version of fundamentalism engaged the poor and spoke of class war.

This cleeavage between fundamentalism as revivalism and fundamentalism as revolution was deep and for a long while coincided closely with the sectarian divide between the Sunnis - the Muslim world's traditional 'haves', concerned more with conservative religiosity - and the Shia - the longtime outsiders,' more drawn to radical dreaming and scheming." Graham Fuller has also noted that he found "no mainstream Islamist organization (with the exception of [shia] Iran) with radical social views or a revolutionary approach to the social order apart from the imposition of legal justice."

MODERN DEBATES

Once the common opposition to colonialism, corruption and racism was established as a focus, debates on political Islam became generally focused on several core questions through the 1970s:

- The status of women and integration of priorities of feminism into a renewed fiqh
- Islamic economics and the role of debt in oppression and stagnation of Muslim states
- Zionism and the response to the formation of the state of Israel and the question ofstatehood
- Self Governance in Muslims nations or in nations with significant Muslim minorities
- Control of oil revenues in the Middle East

United Nations cooperation was pivotal in this view - as was cooperation with secular forces and allies. The agenda of secular and Islamist movements during this period was all but indistinguishable. However, some rural movements were finding progress made here to be symbolic and unsatisfactory. In 1979 the political situation drastically changed, with Egypt making peace with Israel, the Iranian Revolution, and the Soviet invasion of Afghanistan - all three events had wide-ranging effects on how Islam was perceived as a political phenomenon.

PERCEPTION OF PERSECUTION

Some Muslims place the blame for all flaws in Muslim societies on the influx of "foreign" ideas including debt-based capitalism, communism, and even feminism; a return to the principles of Islam is seen as the natural cure. This is however interpreted in very many ways: socialism and Marxism as a guide to adapting Islam to the modern world was in decline by the 1980s as the USSR invaded Afghanistan and polarized attitudes against Communism and other secular variants of socialism. Capitalism was often discredited by plain corruption.

One persistent theme that both proponents and opponents of Islam as a political movement note is that Muslims are actively persecuted by the West and other foreigners. This view is of course not distinguishable from a critique of imperialism including oil imperialism, since many Muslim nations are sitting on relatively vast oil reserves. Colonialism is often identified as the force which is 'against Islam', and seems to neatly encompass British Empire experiences as well as those of modern times - the long Ottoman domination being more or less forgotten.

REACTIVE ISLAM

It was largely through reactive measures that the movement that is labeled Islamist came to be visible to the West, where it was labeled as being a distinct movement from Islam, pan-Arabism and resistance to colonization. The legitimacy of this kind of distinction is very much in doubt. Olivier Roy holds that the primary motive of all of this activity is resistance to colonialism and control of the Islamic World by outsiders. In this view, the movement called Islamist is wholly reactive and incidental, just a convenient rationale used to justify what is in fact resistance of a cultural and economic sort.

However, there are many overt similarities. Those militants who follow a version of sharia based on the classical fiqh ("jurisprudence") as interpreted by local ulema ("jurists"), were the most prominent of several competing trends in modern Islamic philosophy in the 1970s and 1980s. It was at this time that they became visible - and a concern - to the West, as they challenged the modernist dictators that the West had generally put trust in.

COLD WAR EXPLOITATION

But such cross-cultural exchanges, polite activism and moderate views were very often suppressed by the funders of more militant strains who sought to exploit them against the Soviet Union. The United States, for instance, in the 1980s supplied university-authored textbooks to the mujahedeen of Afghanistan that encouraged militant attitudes and even taught arithmetic using examples involving hand grenades and "dead infidels". There was also pressure against secular socialism in the Islamic World, and especially in Iraq, Syria and Iran, until the Iranian Revolution of 1979 proved it could well be counter-productive and led to a backlash that put regimes in place that would be hostile to the Western, secular, world.

ROLE IN TERRORISM

Some militant Islamist forces have been implicated in terrorism and have become targets in a series of military initiatives justified by the US rhetoric of "War on Terrorism", which has been adopted by Russia, Israel and other countries. This has led Muslims and the opponents of these initiatives (in the peace movement) to characterize it sometimes as actually a War on Islam. As part of this war, they claim, literally every political interpretation of Islam, from classical fiqh to Marxist to such moderate views as those of Dr. Shakir, are all being classified as part of one "enemy" movement.

MOVEMENTS DESCRIBED AS 'ISLAMIST'

What these groups have in common tends to be opposition to the United States and Israel. They vary widely in terms of the form of Islamic Law they prefer.

GLOBALIZATION

Along with many other cultural phenomena, Islamic political thought has undergone its own globalization as adherents of many different strains have come together. Even in such strictly controlled, secretive groups as Al-Qaida, there were believing Muslims of drastically varying backgrounds coming together, some of whom accepted the tactics and priorities of the group, and some not. While violent fanatics deployed by cynical leaders make highly visible attacks on Western interests and even on 'homelands', this is thought by many to be no more than backlash for an entire 20th century full of cynical attempts by German, British, and American Empires to deploy Islamic idealists as a mere tactic.

When Russia joined the Council of the Islamic Conference in 2003, it emphasized that it had a long history of successful co-existence with Muslims, and a large integrated population of Muslims (few of which are in any sense Islamist). President

Vladimir Putin, despite a long and bloody confrontation with rebels in Chechnya, offered to act as a bridge or neutral broker in dealings between Muslims and NATO, the EU and USA. This was a quite different rhetoric, a more pragmatic one likely reflecting the reality that the ex-Soviet republics of Uzbekistan, Kazakhstan, Turkmenistan, and Azerbaijan had substantial Islamic political movements - similar to those in Turkey and Pakistan, relatively modern in tone and willing to participate in the US War on Terrorism to some degree, although not as direct combatants.

Some analysts believe that the old Cold War battlelines have been redrawn, with Russia choosing new allies - those with a record of success in forcing US withdrawals from strategic territories (Beirut, Somalia and - depending on interpretation - Afghanistan and Iraq) with Muslim populations. In this view, the old Marxist alliance against colonialism is the dominant rhetoric.

Others accept the Russian pledge as sincere, and believe that Islamist movements of all stripes will eventually come to accommodation with domestic secular forces, and Islam as a global anti-corruption, anti-colonialism, and anti-racism movement, less focused on Zionism and Palestine. George W. Bush for instance has noted the real need as economic development in Muslim countries, to break the cycle of poverty that tends to feed into extremist movements. In Afghanistan, Pakistan, Turkey and Iraq, the Bush administration has worked closely with nominally Islamic forces and ruling political parties in government. It denies intensely that it is involved in a War on Islam. However, polls of Muslim nations indicate these denials are not trusted. Any accommodation will not be quick in coming.

INTERNATIONALISM

Political Islam in a strictly non-evangelical sense cannot be described as Islamist. In a strictly political sense, born out of the struggles against colonialism and the war on terror, Islamic resistance movements can be seen to be analogous to other resistance movements, such as Latin American struggles against US "imperialism". In this sense political Islam falls within the scope of internationalism, which has many other branches - Maoist, Marxist and of course Latin American. The Latin American struggles have been reported for example in the magazine 'New Internationalist' and likewise the struggles in the Islamic world have been reported in the magazine 'Islamic Internationalist'.

7

The Great Unholy Wars

Dar-al-Harb

Headlines about suicide bombers killing U.S. and coalition soldiers in Iraq and Afghanistan proliferate day by day. Attacks on civilians in non-combat zones, like last month's London subway bombings, however, cross an ethical line for all but the most radical jihadist extremists. American conservative talk show hosts and others challenge, where are the spokesmen for Islam, especially when civilians are killed? Muslim clerics have long been accused of hanging back when denunciation and condemnation should have been the order of the day.

The London bombings that killed 53 civilians produced some of the most vocal and public reactions to date from mullahs and imams, Muslim teachers who issue fatwas, regarding Islamic law and practice. Islamic leaders meeting in July in London after attacks there drew careful distinction between "the suicide bombing of those who are trying to defend themselves from occupiers, which is something different from those who kill civilians, which is a big crime," according to Sayed Mohammed Musawi, the head of the World Islamic League in London".

"It is our understanding that those who carried out the bombings in London should in no sense be regarded as martyrs," a joint statement by the London group stated. The

Toronto Star Web site reported on July 22, "For the first time, imams from across Canada joined together yesterday to issue a statement denouncing terrorism and calling upon Canadian Muslims to confront extremism."

The pronouncements stated that such attacks are prohibited and play into the hands of their "enemies." The pragmatic issue of protection (and in some minds, pre-emption) naturally follows for Western cultures victimized by other fatwas that explicitly declare jihad (holy war) against them.

This requires military, law enforcement and political leaders to "get in the heads" of terrorists. Where does one begin to understand an event like the following? A Mogadishu-style mob kills and mutilates American civilians, dragging them through the streets. Crowds chant, "Long live Islam!" and "God is great!" Was this representative of Islam or an insane riot?

Reactions vary, especially among Western Europeans and Americans. Spanish voters removed a pro-Iraq War and pro-U.S. president and catapult into office an anti-Iraq war Socialist mere hours after a devastating terrorist attack of their own on March 11, 2004. This seemed to many to signal a de facto victory for terror, a capitulation to extremist genocide that utterly ignored the aims of radical jihadists.

A U.S. commission appointed to investigate the September 2001 attacks on the World Trade Center and the Pentagon strenuously probed for "what could have been done" by the Clinton and Bush administrations to respond to terrorist threats, particularly from al Qaeda, the chief focus of the "war on terror" since 9-11. Very recently, Britain and France have changed course and cracked down on terror suspects, even deporting suspected terrorist - sympathizing imams or mullahs. Terror victims from Bali to Turkey to Saudi Arabia, the very birthplace of al Qaeda arch-terrorist Osama bin Laden, still grapple with just what possesses religious zealots to snuff out life in such a dramatic, calculated way—all in the name of Allah and their view of Islamic ideals.

UNDERSTANDING ISLAM

One common pitfall to understanding is conflating Islam with Islamism, described below. What one soon sees regarding Islam is a huge array of complex and sometimes contradictory layers amidst a religion that permeates all areas of life: political, social and religious? Islam is a "socio-cultural and religio-economic political system" according to Dr. Warren Larson—a concept largely inconceivable to Westerners, even religious ones. Understanding the terrorists requires close examination of the root claims made by the perpetrators of terror: that a purification of Islam legitimately entails a purging of the non-Muslim (infidel) cultures, particularly those of Israel and America but including the entire West. (And obviously, those inside the Dar al-Islam, or region of Islam, are not exempt if considered oppressors.)

Nothing new, the doctrine of conquering and subjugating infidels spawned a history of brutal occupation by Muslim peoples, seen as a struggle to purify the earth and guarantee submission to Allah, the ultimate value. In fact according to the Qur'an, those in the Dar al-Harb (non-Muslim world, literally, house of war) were to submit to "Islam" (literally submission), by "choice" of force. Yet, the very latest Qur'anic verse - and thus the most authoritative to most Muslims - speak of the closeness shared by Muslims and Christians. And until recently, such warfare was always limited in scope and only to true combatants.

The modern-day orientation of terrorist minorities - and they represent a miniscule but influential and growing fraction of the world's Muslims - seems to spring mainly from later passages in the holiest book of Islam, the Qur'an, and the life story of Islam's Prophet Muhammad, who received direct inspiration for the Qur'an from Allah (the sole deity, it is stressed). However, it's the definitions that distinguish terrorist jihad from the mainstream Muslim interpretations of holy war. Rutgers Religion professor James Turner Johnson writes, "The radical ideology of jihad... [makes] the use of violent means, indiscriminately and without principled limits, a binding obligation for all Muslims."

Renditions of Muhammad's life and sayings (Sunna) are found in the Hadith, deemed nearly as sacred by Muslims as the Qur'an. Another telling biographical source for Muhammad is A. Guillaume's translation of Muhammad's original biography by Ibn Ishaq, written in the second century of the Islamic era and, one century later, edited by Ibn Hisham. All those sources clearly depict Muhammad as a powerful demagogue who increasingly leveraged violence and the growing power that it gave him to endorse or participate in persecution, robbery, pillaging, execution, torture and warring on those outside of Islam- a philosophy and practice both enshrined in and mitigated by holy writ, even alongside texts that emphasize commonalities and good relations with Jews and Christians.

Many later Islamic schools of thought seek balance by emphasizing the kinder, gentler writings—which are usually, nonetheless, considered to have been abrogated by the more violent, later texts. Moderates also interpret relevance of his sayings to Muhammad's day and situation; however, the founder of Islam remains a figure who was no stranger to religiously motivated brutality. The conquests of Suleyman the Magnificent and other Muslim rulers were marked by similar treatment of vanquished foes. From the 11th-13th centuries, The Assassins, an Islamic sect, were infamous for murdering as a religious duty.

CHRISTIANITY NOT ABOVE REPROACH HISTORICALLY

In all fairness, Islam's history of conquering and holding in religious bondage those outside its beliefs is not unlike what other cultures commonly perpetrated from earliest biblical times to recent centuries. In the time of Muhammad and throughout the time of the Ottoman Empire, conquest, mass killing and religious punishment were commonplace in virtually all cultures. Thus, judging Muhammad by post-9-11 standards must be kept in perspective.

Moses has controversially been characterized as bloodier than Muhammad and Muslims invoke Old Testament genocide as harsher than Islam's vanquishments (which nonetheless were carried out against specific people for a specified time, not as a blanket doctrine). Muslims point out the Crusades, which seem a mirror image in many ways to the conquests of Christian Europe's arch-enemy, Islam. Spanish and Portuguese Catholic invaders forcibly converted Indian natives across the Americas. The inquisitions of the Catholic Church mark a time of terror compared with today's pluralistic standards. And Reformers' internecine doctrinal struggles resulted in executions. Thus, Christians have needed to pause before comparing the worst of Islam with their own history and to repent where necessary.

EXTREME ISLAMISM OR JIHADISM

Today's news media constantly invoke the term fundamentalism in reference to militant Islam, or Islamism. However, as Frog and Amy Orr-Ewing write in Holy Warriors: A Fresh Look at the Face of Extreme Islam, "Defining fundamentalism, even within Islam alone, is notoriously difficult." The authors continue, "'Islamism' is ... seen as the enemy among more liberal expressions of Islam, for both sides wants to win the battle for legitimacy and orthodoxy in the public sphere. This is also true of Islamic discourse within and with the West.

Even among emerging 'fundamentalist' groups there is also competition for the right to interpret afresh, and this can lead to greater radicalism and extremism." Johnson writes, "Bin Laden's jihad not only pits Islam against America, the West as a whole and ultimately the rest of the non-Islamic world; it also seeks to overthrow the contemporary Muslim states and mainstream views of Islamic tradition among the great majority of contemporary Muslims".

Western pundits and think tanks busily deconstruct the social, economic and educational struggles of loosely affiliated groups like al Qaeda and their adherents, but as Middle East scholar Daniel Pipes points out, "Islamism has few connections to wealth or poverty; it is not a response to deprivation." Rather, if the West is to understand extremist Islam, it must get one simple fact straight, as World culture commentator Gene Edward Veith states in Conflict of Religions: "A jihad has been declared against Americans. This means that authoritative Muslim clerics have issued a decree that killing Americans is not just a religious duty but an act that merits salvation" based on the single guaranteed method of salvation espoused in the Qur'an, martyrdom.

An important caveat: as stated in Islam and Violence, "Our point, of course, should not be taken to imply that all faithful and devout Muslims must become violent in order to be true to the teachings of Islam. We will not hesitate to say that the vast majority of the Muslim world condemns acts of terror and violence." Still, as the editors of The Economist wrote in a special survey of Islam and the West, Sept. 13th-19th, 2003), "...The problem for those who want to believe that Islam has nothing to do with Islamic terrorism is not only that the terrorists themselves say otherwise.

It is also the existence of a whole body of theory [particularly that of Syed Qutb, highly influential 20th Century Egyptian writer and revolutionary theorist, considered a martyr by followers] that is called upon to justify this activity, and which has zealous adherents." Simply put, we resonate with the writers of Islam and Violence (above) on this point: Though this has not been common practice for millions of Muslims the world over for centuries, given a plain reading, "Muslims who commit acts of violence and terror in the name of God can find ample justification for their actions based on the teachings of the Qur'an and the sayings and examples of prophet Muhammad himself." This is what the radical Islamists are doing, to a growing chorus of approval from Muslims who buy into the doctrine of jihad against the West.

Thus, in the spirit of open inquiry we seek a closer, albeit limited, look at Islam:

- What were Muhammad's and his early followers' motives and modus operandi regarding those outside the faith?

- How has Islam's doctrine of war and violence developed since then?
- What effect have various Muslim viewpoints had on modern-day adherents?
- Which of these convictions drive Islamist terrorists?

This collection seeks to allow the texts and history of Islam to speak for them as much as possible and is presented through the lens of a biblical worldview. Honest, bright people will disagree, some strenuously, but we trust in a way that can retain civil dialogue.

During the question period after my notorious YAF talk last Thursday, it came up again: one of the students asked if we weren't conferring legitimacy on Osama and Co. by calling them jihadists instead of something like *mufsidoon*: evildoers. That is just one small indication of how influential this idea has become – and of course it enjoys great influence in the State Department. Now one of its foremost proponents, a man named Jim Guirard, who called me up a few years ago and spent a great length of time trying to convince me to get on board with this idea, writes in its defense in *Accuracy in Media*. He's responding to this excellent column by Walid Phares, about which I commented at some length here.

Guirard affects a cutesy, folksy writing style, beginning with the three question marks and hapax legoumenon he uses in his title, "Is AQ-style Terrorism 'Jihadi Martyrdom' or 'Irhabi Murderdom?" Perhaps it is unsporting or invincibly crabbed of me to note such a thing, but I must say I found it incongruous that a man who has the Pentagon's ear and confers with the highest American military officials writes like a lovestruck teenage girl. With all his cuteness and misspellings, Guirard seems practically to be begging not to be taken seriously. But since he is taken seriously, and his ideas are taken seriously, they are worth dealing with again.

That's "expatriate" and "Streusand." That angry writer's complaint was that the four of us are refusing to follow his (and so many other's) current addiction to Osama bin Laden's self-sanctifying language of so-called "Jihadi Martyrdom" –

namely, the five-word al Qaeda narrative of so-called Jihad (holy war) by purported mujahideen (holy warriors) and alleged shuhada (martyrs) who are supposedly destined for Jennah (Paradise) as a reward for killing all of us kuffr (infidels) and in due course disposing of al-Shaitan al-Kabir (the Great Satan). Dr. Phares insists that this is the one and only valid framework within which to properly and sufficiently attack al Qaeda-style Terrorism.

Phares doesn't say that at all, of course. He says that the concept of *hiraba,* unlawful warfare, which Guirard says we should use to label contemporary jihadist activity, "implies that a 'genuine' war against a real enemy does exist and that these hotheaded soldiers have simply acted without orders. Hence this cunning explanation puts 'spin' on Jihad but leaves the core idea of Jihadism completely intact." Thus obligingly calling jihadism *hiraba* could leave us open to having to confront in the near future a jihad deemed genuine by those so anxious for us to relabel Osama's efforts. In other words, it doesn't get to the heart of the matter: the persistence of religious violence arising within an Islamic context. It leaves that wide open as a possibility for the future.

But Guirard doesn't deal with this point. Instead, he contents himself, like Dinesh D'Souza and so many others, with the manipulative little slur of charging that his opponent agrees with bin Laden – with all the unsavory associations that brings: they're both hotheads, hardliners, fascists at heart, doncha know? But this sidesteps the questions of why the version of Islam purveyed by Osama and the other jihadists has gained such traction within the Islamic world, and why the jihadist claim to represent "true" or "pure" Islam has so much resonance. And since Guirard and his ilk refuse to acknowledge that that is even happening, they can't formulate any worthwhile response to it.

In sharp contrast, Marine Corps LtG James Mattis has recently condemned this sort of AQ narrative as "tyranny in false religious garb." But when we, the four accused, recommend a new counter narrative which attacks the Salafi-

Wahhabi-UBL conspiracy's deceitful self-labeling, Dr. Phares berates us (as he might now General Mattis, as well?) as somehow "representing the views of classical Wahhabis and the Muslim Brotherhood". Not quite. Phares actually said: "When researched, it turns out that this theory was produced by clerics of the Wahhabi regime in Saudi Arabia and the Muslim Brotherhood, as a plan to prevent Jihad and Jihadism from being depicted by the West and the international community as an illegal and therefore sanctioned activity." It is, again, a shame that Guirard did not see fit to address that except with a sneer.

But, of course, it is Walid Phares himself, not us, who is so insistently parroting al Qaeda's patently false description of itself and its suicide mass murders as "Jihadi" (Holy Guys) defenders of Allah and the Qur'an. See, Guirard's fundamental assumption, behind the cutesy language ("'Jihadi' (Holy Guys)" indeed), is that jihad is a good thing, a holy thing, and that the jihadists have appropriated it in defiance of Islamic theology and law. And that therefore, if we start using the terms that actually apply to them and their activities – criminals, unlawful warfare, rather than jihadists and jihad – the moderate Muslim majority will feel empowered to rise up against them, and take back Islam.

It would be great if it were true. But unfortunately it's just a fantasy. The imperative to wage war against unbelievers in order to establish over them the hegemony of Islamic law wasn't invented by Al-Qaeda; it is taught by all the Sunni schools of jurisprudence and by the Shi'ites also. This doesn't mean that every Muslim takes it seriously. But it does mean that it's just whistling in the dark to think that Al-Qaeda's claim to represent Islamic purity can't draw on genuine elements of Islamic theology that encourage bellicosity. Fantasy-based policymaking is never wise.

In sharp and everlasting contrast to this de facto embrace of the enemy's self-serving description of political, cultural and religious reality, this writer's proposed counter narrative condemns the al Qaeda, al Sadr, Hizballah, Hamas and other

"Death to America" terrorists as waging Hirabah (unholy war, forbidden "war against society") by mufsiduun (evildoers, sinners and corrupters) and munafiquun (hypocrites) destined for Jahannam (Eternal Hellfire) as punishment for having become al Murtadd al Qaeda (the al Qaeda Apostasy) against Qur'anic Islam – namely, for having tried to drag all Muslims into a most unholy war against Abrahamic America and the West.

"*This writer's* proposed counter narrative..." (emphasis added). But do Muslims worldwide, whether jihadists or not, really listen to Jim Guirard's version of Islam? If there were major Islamic sects or leaders teaching this sort of thing and representing it as "Qur'anic Islam," that would be one thing. But there aren't. Likewise Kilcullen's new lexicon, in Guirard's article below, is based not on reality but on what we really wish jihad were all about:

> In his multi-faceted article, "New Paradigms For 21st Century Conflict," David Kilcullen of General David Petraeus' senior staff in Baghdad recommends five major initiatives to be taken in developing truly effective counterterrorism (COIN) strategies, operations and tactics against al Qaeda-style Terrorism (AQST).
>
> In briefest of terms, these are to (1) Develop a New Lexicon, (2) Get the Grand Strategy Right, (3) Remedy the Imbalance in Government Capability, (4) Identify New Strategic Services, and (5) Develop Capacity For Strategic Information Warfare. While others will comment in learned fashion on all five of these topics in due course, this commentary will concern only the first – the proposed New Lexicon. To make a medical analogy, this is an enemy which is not in the nature of a state-based, clearly definable tumor to be neatly cut out by a scalpel but is, instead, an ideology-based cancer which been metastasizing for several decades (particularly the last one) and is attacking far-flung elements of Western Civilization 'round the clock and seeking a "death by a thousand cuts" result.
>
> The first of Kilcullen's five steps toward an effective antidote – a worldwide chemotherapy-type counterattack

– on the raging AQST cancer is his call for "a new lexicon based on the actual, observed characteristics of [our] real enemies ..." In so doing, he clearly recognizes that in order to meet Tsun-Tzu's ancient admonition that we must "Know The Enemy," we absolutely must have a truthful common language by which to achieve that end and then to communicate such knowledge effectively to multiple audiences.

Although he does not list particulars of this proposed new lexicon, here are more than a dozen of the Arabic and Islamic words of which he would almost surely approve. They are the words, the semantic tools and weapons, we will need to break out of the habit-of-language box (largely invented by Osama bin Laden himself) which currently depicts us as us the bad guys, the "infidels" and even "the Great Satan" – and which sanctifies suicide mass murderers as so-called jihadis and mujahideen ("holy guys") and "martyrs" on their heroic way to Paradise. Importantly, the ubiquitous (It's everywhere! It's everywhere!!) word Jihad is entered four times, in order to more clearly define its several confusing and often conflicting meanings.

Irhab (eer-HAB) – Arabic for terrorism, thus enabling us to call the al Qaeda-style killers irhabis, irhabists and irhabiyoun rather than the so-called "jihadis" and "jihadists" and "mujahideen" and "shahids" (martyrs) they badly want to be called. Hirabah (hee-RAH-bah) – Unholy War and forbidden "war against society" or what we would today call crimes against humanity. Among the many al Qaeda-style crimes and sins which constitute this most "unholy war" is such willful and unrepented transgressions as those enumerated in the next section of this proposed glossary of terms.

Jihad al Akbar (gee-HAHD ahl AHK-bar) – this "Greater Jihad" is a personal and spiritual struggle or striving to become closer and more faithful to Allah and his teachings as set forth in the Qur'an. Here is the problem with this whole endeavor in microcosm: Hassan Al-Banna (founder of the Muslim Brotherhood), Abdullah Azzam (cofounder of Al-Qaeda) and others argued that the idea of jihad as a spiritual struggle as based on a weak hadith – a tradition of Muhammad that couldn't be taken as authentic. They gained many recruits by arguing this successfully among Muslims. And so now here come Kilcullen and Guirard, reminding Muslims that jihad is primarily an inner spiritual struggle. How the Muslims who have bought the argument that all that will is based on a weak hadith react? Will they lay down their arms? Or chuckle at the ignorant infidels?

Jihad al Saghir (gee-HAHD ahl Sahg-HEER) – "Lesser Jihad" can be a physical – and even a military – struggle to protect or to free Muslims and non-Muslims from oppression, but only in strict accordance with reasonable and non-terroristic standards set forth in the Qur'an, which provides that only the Caliph (or head-of-state?) can legally declare such a Jihad. Osama bin Laden is neither.... Fine. Until you realize that many Muslim authorities identify as "oppression" anything except a Sharia state.

The implications of that for the above statement are clear. And only the state authority can declare a jihad? Unfortunately, there is a difference of opinion on this question among contemporary Islamic scholars. Some argue that Muslims may wage war in order to establish that Islamic state, and then continue to wage war against unbelievers under its aegis. Others contend that the Islamic state must be established by peaceful means, and only then may Muslims wage jihad warfare. The latter position was held by Syed Abul Ala Maududi, the influential Pakistani jihad theorist who died in 1979, Sheikh Muhammad Said Ramadan Al-Buti, and Sheikh Muhammad Naasir ud-Din Al-Albani. The former view is held by Islamic scholars such as Muhammad Amarah and Khair Haykel, as well as by Azzam and, of course, other mujahedin today.

It is important to note, however, that Maududi and Al-Buti, as well as others who hold this view, don't reject the idea of jihad against unbelievers in order to establish the hegemony of Islamic law. Maududi, after all, wrote that non-

Muslims have "absolutely no right to seize the reins of power in any part of God's earth nor to direct the collective affairs of human beings according to their own misconceived doctrines." If they do, "the believers would be under an obligation to do their utmost to dislodge them from political power and to make them live in subservience to the Islamic way of life."

So in other words, this is just a disagreement about means, not about ends. ...Just for starters, imagine the khawarij (outside the religion) al Qaeda's great difficulty in winning the approval of any truly devout and faithful Muslims whatever once these genocidal irhabis (terrorists) come to be viewed by the Umma (the Muslim World) as mufsiduun (evildoers) engaged in Hirabah (unholy war) and in murtadd (apostasy) against the Qur'an's God of Abraham – and as almost surely on their way to Jahannam (Eternal Hellfire) for their Satanic ways....

Yes, that would be great. But pretending that truly devout and faithful Muslims will follow the lead of non-Muslims in defining these things is naive in the extreme. Of course, to sustain the validity of such condemnatory labels, there must be a true-to-the-Quran basis for their application to the al Qaeda, al Sadr, Hizballah, Hamas and assorted other Terrorists.

Indeed. This is readily available in the fact that at the heart of AQST's own false labels and equally false promises of a sex-orgy Paradise is a pattern of plainly satanic and cultic violation of many of the fundamental precepts of authentic Islam – including such sinful transgressions and such de facto desecrations of the Qur'an as:

- Wanton killing of innocents and noncombatants, including many peaceful Muslims

Here we go again. Define "innocent" and "noncombatant." British jihadist Anjem Chaudary says no non-Muslims are innocent. How will this stop him?

- Decapitating the live and desecrating the dead bodies of perceived enemies

- Committing and enticing others to commit suicide for reasons of intimidation

Qur'an 9:111 guarantees Paradise to those who "kill and are killed" for Allah. And that's not suicide, in the jihadist view. How will Guirard's lexicon overcome that idea?

- Fomenting hatred among communities, nations, religions and civilizations
- Ruthless warring against nations in which Islam is freely practiced
- Issuing and inspiring unauthorized and un-Islamic fatwas (religious edicts)
- Using some mosques as weapons depots and battle stations, while destroying others
- Forcing extremist and absolutist versions (and perversions) of Islam on fellow Muslims, when the Qur'an clearly says that there shall be "no compulsion in religion"

Qutb and others argue that the "no compulsion" verse does not rule out fighting until "religion is for Allah." Will Guirard's use of this verse change any jihadist minds?

- Distorting the word "infidels" to include all Christians, all Jews and many Muslims, as well – when the Qur'an calls them all "Children of the Book" (the Old Testament) and "Sons of Abraham," and calls Jesus one of Islam's five main Prophets

People of the Book, not Children of the Book. Anyway, fine, don't call them infidels. They still must be fought and subjugated, per Qur'an 9:29.

- Deliberate misreading, ignoring and perverting of passages of the Qur'an, the Hadith and the Islamic Jurisprudence (the Fiqh)

Such as the jihadists claim that the peaceful Muslims do this. Guirard claims that the jihadists do it. The real challenge is to refute the jihadist use of Islamic texts and teachings in a way that blunts the force of jihadist recruitment. Peaceful Muslims haven't done it yet. One final note. Guirard argues that what he is doing here was done effectively during the Cold War:

A look-back lesson from the Cold War argues strongly that we should have done a far better "war of words" job of challenging – rather than all too often parroting – the Soviets' and Fascist Fidel Castro's false narrative of so-called "Liberation by purported Progressive Movements and alleged Popular Fronts who were destined for heaven-on-earth People's Democracies as a reward for killing us Reaganite Fascists and disposing of American Imperialism."

Recognize the remarkable parallels? Both then and today, the deadly dangerous problem is that of "semantic infiltration," which the late, great Senator Pat Moynihan and Dr. Fred Charles Ikle- Ronald Reagan's Under Secertary of Defense for Policy, who is today still active at the Center for Strategic and International Studies- carefully defined in the early 1980s as follows:

"Simply put, semantic infiltration is the process whereby we come to adopt the language of our adversaries in describing political reality. The most totalitarian regimes in the world would call themselves 'liberation movements.' It is perfectly predictable that they should misuse words to conceal their real nature. But must we aid them in that effort by repeating those words? Worse, do we begin to influence our own perceptions by using them?"

Back then, it was a case of Leninist, Maoist and Castroite tyranny wrapped up in false "Liberationist" lingo. Today, it is the neo-Leninist, fascist-Left and pseudo-Quranic narrative of "Jihadi Martyrdom" which General Jim Mattis so correctly condemns as "tyranny in false religious garb" – while all too many of us continue the "useful idiocy" parroting. Sure. We should challenge the jihadist idea that Sharia equals justice.

And we should call it tyranny. But that is not the same thing as formulating some genuine way to counter jihadist claims to represent true Islam. Inventing our own benign little Islam and hoping that Muslims will buy it won't do that.

8

Terrorism in the West

In recent years there have been many Islamic acts of terror committed against Western countries. The bombing of the marine barracks in Lebanon; two US embassies in Africa; the bombing of the US destroyer Cole in Yemen; the attacks of September 11; The deadly explosions in Bali; the Madrid train bombings; the subway in London-these are just the most publicised attacks. All of them were openly or covertly supported by most Muslim rulers and are silently condoned by most of the Islamic communities around the world.

Several years ago US president Bush very publicly declared war on Terror. I would like to review the achievements so far: Osama bin Ladin is still alive, Sadam Hussein is making a mockery of the Western style court in Bagdad, Iran is successfully avoiding International sanctions and continuing to develop an Islamic nuclear bomb, and Saudi Arabia has been quietly financing the spread of Wahabism, using Islamic terror world wide without any punitive measures from the West. Well done, Mr. President!

The United States and European countries are not fighting Islamic expansionism. It is all just pretence and deception! They attack relatively insignificant targets like Afghanistan and Iraq and are unwilling to destroy the real nest of the Islamic hate against all the "infidels and crusaders"-Saudi

Arabia and Iran. At the same time, the tendency for covert protection of possible enemies does exist. For example, after the September 11 attack only one plane was allowed to leave USA-the one with the members of the Saudi royal family and the Bin Ladin family on board. The FBI was not allowed to interview them!

Israel has been a defender of the West against Arab terror, by successfully defeating Arab's aggression for many decades. Unfortunately, the world governments, due to deeply ingrained anti-Semitism and oil dependency, play a dangerous game by vilifying the Jewish state. Greed and apathy has also spread to Israel and is infecting the political hierarchy of the country. The corrupt political apathy prevents the IDF from effective self-defense, undermining the state security and does not allow delivering a decisive blow to the enemies of Israel.

The war of civilizations was declared a long time ago. The darkness of Islamic fundamentalism is advancing against Democracy. It is time for our leaders to realize that they are responsible for the lives of their citizens, as well as their own families. The corrupt practice of self-enrichment by politicians and big Western business is dangerous and self-destructive. Up to now, they have been ruling the world using covert manipulation-conducted by big business and petro-dollars of Arab sheiks. Our future is at stake. The time for us to wake up and say "Enough!" is right now. We can put an end to this war by taking the blindfolds off and by facing reality. When will we do it?

The conventional interpretation of "Jihad":

According to *Beliefnet*, Al-Hajj Talib 'Abdur-Rashid, imam of the *Mosque of Islamic Brotherhood* in Harlem, NY, defines three levels of jihad - personal, verbal and physical. Considering each in turn:

PERSONAL JIHAD

This is the most important form. This type of jihad, called the *Jihadun-Nafs*, is the intimate struggle to purify one's soul of evil influences – both subtle and overt. It is the struggle to cleanse one's spirit of sin. In a brochure, the *Institute of Islamic Information & Education* describes several different contexts in which The Qur'an (the Islamic Holy Book) and the Hadith (the collected sayings of Muhammad) use the word "*jihad*" to refer to personal struggles:

- Putting "Allah ahead of our loved ones, our wealth, our worldly ambitions and our own lives."
- Resisting pressure of parents, peers and society; strive against "the rejecters of faith..." (Quran 25:52)
- "...strive and struggle to live as true Muslims..."
- "Striving for righteous deeds."
- Spreading the message of Islam. "The (true) believers are only those who believe in Allah and his messenger and afterward doubt not, but strive with their wealth and their selves for the cause of Allah. Such are the truthful." (Quran, 49:15)

VERBAL JIHAD

To strive for justice through words and non-violent actions Muhammad encouraged Muslims to demand justice in the name of Allah. When asked: "'*What kind of jihad is better?*' Muhammad replied, 'A word of truth in front of an oppressive ruler!'" According to the Institute of Islamic Information and Education: "The life of the Prophet Muhammad was full of striving to gain the freedom to inform and convey the message of Islam. During his stay in Makkah [Mecca] he used non-violent methods and after the establishment of his government in Madinah [Medina], by the permission of Allah, he used armed struggle against his enemies whenever he found it inevitable."

PHYSICAL JIHAD

This relates to the use of physical force in defense of Muslims against oppression and transgression by the enemies of Allah, Islam and Muslims. Allah commands that Muslims lead peaceful lives and not transgress against anyone. If they are persecuted and oppressed, the Qur'an recommends that they migrate to a more peaceful and tolerant land: "Lo! Those who believe and those who emigrate (to escape persecution) and strive (Jahadu) in the way of Allah, these have hope of Allah's mercy..." (Quran, 2:218).

If relocation is not possible, then Allah also requires Muslims to defend themselves against oppression by "fighting against those who fight against us." The Qur'an states: "To those against whom war is made, permission is given [to defend themselves], because they are wronged - and verily, Allah is Most Powerful to give them victory." (22:39) The defensive nature of physical jihad (or "*jihad with the hand*") is frequently lost among many, Muslims, Christians, secularists and others.

In her book "*Muhammed*," author Karen Armstrong writes: "Fighting and warfare might sometimes be necessary, but it was only a minor part of the whole jihad or struggle. A well-known tradition (hadith) has Muhammad say on returning from a battle, ' We return from the little jihad to the greater jihad,' the more difficult and crucial effort to conquer the forces of evil in oneself and and in one's own society in all the details of daily life."

Other interpretations of "Jihad":

Both the Judeo-Christian *Holy Bible* and the Muslim *Holy Qur'an* are large religious books, containing a great range of material dealing with religion, spirituality, justice, laws, love, etc. And they also contain references to violence, hate, murder, war, and even genocide.

It would be quite possible to assemble passages from the Bible- particularly the Hebrew Scriptures (a.k.a. Old Testament) which describe genocide, rape, execution of non-virgin brides, murder of homosexuals, torture of prisoners, the rape of female prisoners of war, murder of a family because of the act of the father, the regulation and condoning of human slavery, and many other acts, cultural traditions, and laws which are profoundly immoral by today's religious and secular standards. If all one read of the Bible was a collection of such passages, one might conclude that the Bible is an evil document that promotes violence, unethical behavior. One might even conclude that it should be banned as hate literature.

Similarly, it is possible to scan the Bible for passages relating to humans' love of God; love of humans by God; striving for justice; supporting widows, orphans, the sick, the imprisoned; love and concern for fellow humans; spirituality; and may other acts, cultural traditions, and laws which promote a loving, moral and ethical life. If all one read of the Bible was a collection of such passages, one might conclude that the Bible is a precious document indeed – one worthy of emulating.

Which group of passages represents the real Bible? They both do! For centuries, Christians have searched for guidance on social conflicts like the abolition of human slavery, equal rights and opportunities for women, equal rights and protections for gays and lesbians, etc. Some search for specific passages in the Bible dealing with these issues.

A few concluded that slavery is an acceptable institution, that women should be oppressed and denied rights, and that gays (and perhaps lesbians as well) should be executed. Others search for passages dealing with general themes, such as love, justice, and caring for ones fellow humans, and concluded the opposite. Others have used other techniques to assess the Bible's messages. Which represents the "true" message of the Bible? They both do. And this is the reason why there are over 1,000 Christian groups in North America, all basing their beliefs and practices on the Bible, and yet teaching conflicting many beliefs about deity, humanity and the rest of the universe.

The Qur'an is similar. A small percentage of Muslims who are from the extreme, radical and violent wing of Islamic Fundamentalism, and who are "...passionate, [deeply] religious and anti-Western..." might dwell on passages or verses dealing with conflict, war, and resistance to oppression. Many conclude that the Qur'an expects them to engage in acts of terrorism, assassinations, suicide bombings, armed aggression against persons of other religions, oppression of women, executing innocent persons, etc.

Those Muslim Fundamentalists who are not extreme, violent and radical and those Muslims from mainline or liberal wings of the religion might concentrate on passages and themes of spirituality, justice, personal struggle, peace, freedom, etc.

They are consulting the same book, with a different emphasis, and achieve very different results. We see the same split among Christians as they study Islam and the Qur'an. Some emphasize the earlier passages in the Qur'an which emphasize cooperation with the Jews and Christians – the "*People of the Book.*" They tend to interpret "*Jihad*" in terms of personal struggle towards purity.

Others emphasize later passages of the Qur'an which were received during a time of conflict. They tend to interpret "*Jihad*" as holy war. They come to opposite conclusions about whether Islam is a religion of peace or war.

The Islamic Jihad Movement in Palestine known in the West as PIJ is a small Palestinian militant organization. The group has been designated as a terrorist group by the United States, the European Union, the United Kingdom, Japan, Canada, Australia and Israel. Their goal is the destruction of the state of Israel and its replacement with a Palestinian Islamic state. This group defines jihad as acts of war against Israelis. Palestinian Islamic Jihad also opposes many other Arab governments, whom they see as being insufficiently Islamic and too Western.

The PIJ's armed wing, the Al-Quds brigades, has claimed responsibility for numerous terrorist attacks in Israel, including suicide bombings. Their ability to carry out attacks on Israel has been limited since Israel's construction of the West Bank barrier and the isolation of the Gaza Strip, although they frequently threaten waves of "martyrdom operations". The group is responsible for the Qassam rocket barrages at Israeli towns that have killed and injured civilians, and cause widespread hardship in communities in Israel's south. The rockets are primarily launched from Hamas-controlled Gaza.

Islamic Jihad is significantly smaller than Hamas, and lacks the wide social network that Hamas has. The Palestinian Islamic Jihad was formed in the Gaza Strip during the 1970s by Fathi

Shaqaqi and Abd Al Aziz Awda as a branch of the Egyptian Islamic Jihad, an organization currently led by Ramadan Abdullah Mohammad Shallah. The group is also said to receive some funding from Hezbollah. The group has also clashed repeatedly with Hamas following the latter's takeover of the Gaza strip in mid-2007.

The Palestinian Islamic Jihad was created after many members of the Egyptian Muslim Brotherhood found that the organization was becoming too moderate and did not commit enough effort to the Palestinian struggle. So therefore in the late 1970s, the founders of the PIJ, Fathi Shaqaqi and Abd al-Aziz Awda created the group to fight for the sove-reignty of Palestine and the destruction of Israel. Shaqaqi and Awda conducted operations out of Egypt until 1981 when group was exiled after the assassination of President Anwar Sadat.

The PIJ continued its work in Gaza until it was exiled to Lebanon in 1987. While in Lebanon, the group was able to receive training from Hezbollah and ultimately developed a close relationship with the Lebanese organization. While in Lebanon, the PIJ adopted the use of suicide bombing and other forms of terrorism as their principle method of achieving their goals. In 1989, the PIJ moved its operation to Damascus where it remains to this day.

The group is currently based in the Syrian capital, Damascus, but there are also offices in Beirut, Tehran and Khartoum. Its financial backing is believed to come from Syria and Iran. The group operates primarily in the West Bank and Gaza Strip, but has also carried out attacks in Jordan and Lebanon. Its main strongholds in the West Bank are the cities of Hebron and Jenin. The PIJ has approximately 50 to 200 members as well as recruiting suicide bombers and volunteers. Because of its small size, the PIJ is unable to run large scale training camps so instead they rely heavily on other organizations such as Hezbollah for support.

Islamic Jihad has much in common with Hamas. They both work towards the destruction of Israel as a state as well as restoring the "true faith" to the Muslim world. The dis-tinction between the groups comes in the order of these priorities. "The Islamic Brotherhood, like many other funda-mentalist Islamic movements, sees jihad as a general duty of all Muslims and proposed that first 'proper Islam' should be established throughout the Muslim world. Only after the primary goal is achieved, violent jihad should be directed against Israel.

In contrast, the irredentist Hamas movement switched the two priorities. It maintained that first jihad should be directed at liberating all of Palestine, and then Muslims should direct their attention to the goal of restoring the 'true faith' to the rest of the Islamic world." Both groups were formed as offshoots of the Muslim Brotherhood and receive a large amount of funding from Iran. With similar goals, Hamas and the PIJ have worked together on a number of attacks on Israel including a suicide bombing in Beit-Lid in February 1995 that killed eight Israelis and wounded fifty.

Fathi Shaqaqi led the organization for two decades until his death in Malta in October 1995 by an unknown party. The Palestinian Islamic Jihad often attempts to carry out attacks against Israeli targets on the anniversary of his death, although the identity of the assassins was never determined. During the Al-Aqsa Intifada, beginning in September 2000, the PIJ committed many suicide bombing attacks against Israelis. Many of the attacks in 2001 and 2002 came from the PIJ in Jenin, headed by Mahmoud Tawallbe, Ali Sefoori and Tabeth Mardawi.

The headquarters of the PIJ in Jenin and the West Bank was seriously damaged during Operation Defensive Shield: Tawallbe was killed by an IDF Caterpillar D9 armored bulldozer while Sefoori and Mardawi were arrested by Israel security forces. On February 20, 2003, University of South Florida computer engineering professor Dr. Sami Al-Arian was arrested after being indicted on 50 terrorism related charges. US Attorney General John Ashcroft alleged at a press conference that Dr. Al-Arian is the North American head of the Palestinian Islamic Jihad. On December 6, 2005, Al-Arian was acquitted on eight of the 17 charges against him and the jury deadlocked on the rest 10–2.

Then on March 2, 2006, Al-Arian entered a guilty plea to a charge of conspiracy to help members of the Palestinian Islamic Jihad in nonviolent activities, unrelated to the PIJ. Al-Arian was sentenced to 57 months less time (about 38 months) served, and will be deported upon completion of the remainder of the sentence. Islamic Jihad is alleged to have used teens as suicide bombers. On March 29, 2004, 16-year-old Tamer Khuweir in Rifidia, an Arab suburb of Nablus was apprehended by Israeli security forces as he prepared to carry out a suicide attack. His older brother claimed he was brainwashed to do it by an Islamic Jihad cleric and demanded the Palestinian Authority investigate the incident and arrest those responsible for it.

After Shaqaqi's death, Palestinian Islamic Jihad has been led since 1995 by fellow founder Sheikh Abdullah Ramadan Shallah, aka Ramadan Abdullah Mohammad Shallah, who was then listed as a "Specially Designated Terrorist" under United States law on November 27, 1995, and subsequently was indicted on RICO charges, and consequently became one of the FBI Most Wanted Terrorists on February 24, 2006.

The PIJ's main target is Israel but they also see the United States and Western Secularism as an enemy. The PIJ "considered the United States an enemy because of its support for Israel. The PIJ also opposes moderate Arab governments that it believes have been tainted by Western secularism and has carried out attacks in Jordan, Lebanon and Egypt.

ISRAELI RESPONSE

The Israeli response has been to use targeted assassination.

MILITANT ACTIVITIES

The Palestinian Islamic Jihad has claimed responsibility for many militant activities over the years. The organization is responsible for a number of attacks including more than 30 completed suicide bombings. "On December 22, 2001, despite a declaration by Hamas to halt suicide bombings inside Israel, in response to a crackdown on militants by Yassir Arafat, PIJ vowed to continue its terror campaign. PIJ's representative in Lebanon, Abu Imad Al Rifai, told Reuters, 'Our position is to continue. We have no other choice. We are not willing to compromise.'" The Palestinian Islamic Jihad has claimed responsibility for the following attacks:

- August 1987: The PIJ claimed responsibility for a shooting that killed the commander of the Israeli military police in the Gaza Strip.
- December 1993: Killed an Israeli reservist, David Mashrati, during a public bus shooting.
- April 1994: A car bomb aboard a public bus killed nine people and injured fifty.
- January 1995: Suicide bombing attack near Netanya killing eighteen soldiers and one civilian.
- April 1995: Suicide bomb in Netzarim and Kfar-Darom. The first bomb killed eight people and injured over 30 on an Israel bus. The second attack was a car bomb that injured twelve people.
- March 1996: A Tel Aviv shopping mall is the site of another suicide bombing killing twenty and injuring seventy five.
- November 2000: A car bomb in Jerusalem at an outdoor market killed two people and injured ten.
- June 2001: Suicide bomb attack at a Tel Aviv nightclub killing twenty-one people.
- March 2002: A suicide bomber killed seven people and injured approximately thirty aboard a bus travelling from Tel Aviv to Nazareth.
- June 2002: Eighteen people are killed and fifty injured in a suicide attack at the Meggido Junction.
- July 2002: A double suicide attack killed five people and injured 40 in Tel Aviv.
- November 2002: Ambush in Hebron.
- May 2003: Three people killed and eighty-three injured in a suicide bombing at a shopping mall in Afula.
- August 2003: A suicide bomber killed twenty-one people and injured over one hundred on a bus in Jerusalem.
- October 2003: Suicide bomber killed twenty-two and

injured sixty at a Haifa restaurant.

- October 2005: A bomb detonated in a Hedera market was responsible for killing five people.
- April 2006: Suicide bomb in Tel Aviv killed eleven.
- January 2007: Both the Al-Aqsa Martyrs Brigades and the PIJ claim responsibility for a suicide bombing at an Eliat bakery that killed three.
- On June 9, 2007, in a failed assault on an IDF position at the Kissufim crossing between Gaza and Israel in a possible attempt to kidnap IDF soldiers, four armed members of the al-Quds Brigades (the military wing of Islamic Jihad) and the Al Aqsa Martyrs' Brigades (the military wing of Fatah) used a vehicle marked with "TV" and "PRESS" insignias penetrated the border fence and as-saulted a guard tower in what Islamic Jihad and the army said was a failed attempt to capture an Israeli soldier. IDF troops killed one militant, while the others escaped. The use of a vehicle that resembled a press vehicle evoked a sharp response from many journalists and news organizations. The Middle East director for Human Rights Watch, Sarah Leah Whitsonn, responded by saying, "Using a vehicle with press markings to carry out a military attack is a serious violation of the laws of war, and it also puts journalists at risk." The FPA responded by saying,
    - "Armored vehicles marked with TV are an invaluable protection for genuine journalists working in hostile environments. The FPA has long campaigned for the continued availability of armored vehicles for its members, despite official opposition in some quarters. The abuse of this recognized protection for the working journalist is a grave development and we condemn those that carried it out. Such an incident will reduce the protection offered by marked vehicles."
    - During a press conference, an Islamic Jihad spokesperson Abu Ahmed denied that they had put press markings on the jeep used in the attack and said, "The Al-Quds Brigades used an armoured jeep resembling military armoured jeeps used by the

Zionist intelligence services."

- On March 26, 2009, two Islamic Jihad terrorists were imprisoned for a conspiracy "to murder Israeli pilots and scientists using booby - trapped toy cars."

Islamic Jihad has also launched deployed its own rocket, similar to the Qassam rocket used by Hamas, called the Al Quds rocket.

HOLY WAR

As the precursor of the HAMAS movement, the Muslim Brotherhood in Gaza promoted the long-term strategy of creating the foundations of a Muslim state that would eventually become powerful enough to destroy Israel. According to the doctrines of the Brotherhood, part of the process in bringing about the ideal pan-Islamic state includes the spiritual phenomenon of an "Islamic reawakening" throughout the entire Muslim world. Only subsequent to the "Islamic reawakening" and the re-establishment of Islamic political power as the Caliphate could the destruction of the Jewish state begin as a divinely-sanctioned war between Islamic forces and those of Israel and in other words, holy war later.

Taking this position one step further, HAMAS' spiritual leader Sheik Ahmad Yasin formulated the concept that 'Palestine' should become the central battlefield for the creation of a nationalist Islamic state and in other words, holy war now. For HAMAS, the question of Israel's eventual eradication is central and absolute. HAMAS differs in view from the Muslim Brotherhood in asserting that the establishment of an Islamic state in 'Palestine' will serve as the tool for achieving their ultimate goal of creating a pan-Islamic state across the Middle East.

HAMAS' redeveloped outlook came about shortly before the Palestinian uprising in 1987 and the parallel development in Gaza of a third organization, the Islamic Jihad Movement in Palestine (IJMP). Inspired by the Islamic revolution that swept Iran in 1979, the Islamic Jihad challenged the Brotherhood by staging spectacular attacks on Israeli soldiers. Following the doctrine that Islamic land must be ruled only by Muslim 'believers', the IJMP's war on Israel differs from that of HAMAS only in its immediate goal - that a pan-Islamic empire must be created throughout the Middle East with its foundations on the ruins of Israel.

It perceives itself as the vanguard of an internationalist-oriented movement of 'believers' who have taken upon themselves the responsibility of repulsing Western influence from the Islamic world. The evil of Western influence is personified by the United States, which Ayatollah Khomayni termed "the Great Satan." Consequently Israel, as the agent of the U.S. in the region, is termed "the Little Satan." From this perspective, the Islamic Jihad sees itself as fighting a worldwide war against the West, following in the footsteps of the Prophet Muhammad. The IJMP regards itself as one part of the larger Iran-sponsored Islamic Jihad movement, which is most well known for its abduction of American and other Western hostages in Lebanon.

To compete with what was perceived as the more activist approach of the Islamic Jihad, Sheik Ahmad Yasin, then a Muslim Brotherhood leader, adjusted his own doctrine, leading to the formation of HAMAS. In 1987 he nationalized the war of the IJMP, and spoke of an Islamic Palestinian state as a stage towards his movement's final goal. Rather than insisting on the establishment of a pan-Islamic state as the prerequisite for waging holy war on Israel, Yasin changed the strategy of the Muslim Brotherhood in Gaza to that of "partial" holy war.' In this manner, Muslim Brotherhood and HAMAS activists could participate in the Palestinian uprising while at the same time remaining faithful to their notion of a cataclysmic holy war that would eventually be waged by their Caliphate. HAMAS joined Islamic Jihad in deciding that the time for its jihad is now.

Several years after the December 1979 Soviet invasion of Afghanistan, an Egyptian named Mustafa Shalabi founded a charitable organization in Brooklyn to assist the Afghani Muslim counterinsurgents. Aid to the Afghani mujahideen ("wagers of jihad") consisted of cash and supplies, but, more significantly, the recruitment of young American Muslims who were willing to join the ranks of the Afghanis. In order to prepare the American recruits for their struggle against the Soviets, some were sent for paramilitary training at a private camp in Connecticut. The organization is known simply as the "Brooklyn jihad office."

Mustafa Shalabi and a Syrian friend, Abd al-Qader Kallash, sponsored Sheik Rahman upon his arrival in New York in 1990, providing him with an apartment, a telephone and a car and driver. Not long afterward, a dispute broke out in the Muslim community. The sheik and his followers wanted to transform the jihad office into a conduit for Al-Jihad in Egypt, while their opponents wanted the organization to remain as it was. Responding to his opponents, Sheik Rahman denounced Shalabi as "dishonest" and a "bad Muslim."

The area mosques had letters signed by the sheik posted in them pronouncing a ban on any dealings with Shalabi. Fearing for the safety of himself and his family, Shalabi sent his wife to Egypt and made preparations for himself to go to Afghanistan. Several days after seeing his wife off to Egypt, Shalabi was found shot and knifed to death. Sheik Rahman asserts that he "never knew" Shalabi. More recently, Ezzat al-Sheemy, a founder of Brooklyn's Abu Bakr Mosque, decided to establish an alternative summer Arabic language and culture program as a counter-weight to the educational program provided by the mosque.

El-Sheemy asserts that the mosque's school is "run by radicals bent on 'brainwashing' children into becoming militants." In July of 1992, Al-Sheemy was warned by the sheik's followers in the mosque that Sheik Rahman had "approved the use of violence against him and certain teachers - unless he ceded control of the program to Abu Bakr at once." Justifying his reaction to the threats, Al Sheemy explained, "They told me I'd end up like Mustafa Shalabi, so I gave in." Sheik Rahman also denies any connection to this incident.

More recently, Sheik Rahman has denied that he was in any way involved in the World Trade Center bombing. He denied knowledge of any of the suspects, including Mahmud Abu Halima, who once served as his driver. When asked about his long-term goals in the United States, Sheik Rahman assured a reporter that he will "show all Americans that they'll never be happy if they don't follow Islam."

AFTERWORD: TERROR AT THE TWIN TOWERS

On February 26 1993, a powerful explosion tore through the foundations of the World Trade Center in Lower Manhattan, killing six people, including a woman who was seven months pregnant, and injuring over 1000. Fifty thousand people were evacuated from the damaged buildings. The blast left a crater 200 by 100 feet wide and five stories deep, and caused the ceiling of the mezzanine of the adjacent Port Authority Trans-Hudson (PATH) train station to collapse. An FBI expert on explosives described the blast as "the largest improvised explosive device that's been in the U.S. since we started doing forensic explosive investigations in 1925."

Explosives experts estimate that the bomb which caused the explosion weighed approximately 1000 pounds, and the price of the chemicals used to make it cost slightly more than $400. Several days after the explosion occurred, police and federal officials made their first arrest in the case. Tracing the VIN (vehicle identification number) found on a piece of metal at the site of the explosion, investigators were led to Mohammed Salameh, a 25-year-old illegal alien from Jordan who allegedly rented the yellow Ford Econoline van which was used in the bombing.

Salameh, together with the two other suspects who were arrested - Nidal Ayyad and Ibrahim Elgabrowny - all participated in demonstrations on behalf of El Sayyid Nosair. A fourth suspect who fled this country, Mahmud Abu Halima, is believed to be head of a HAMAS terrorist cell. Halima is believed to have fled to Pakistan. The bombing of the World Trade Center marks a turning point in the United States' confrontation with terrorist organizations. Previously, American citizens overseas have been targets of terror groups, particularly Middle Eastern ones, leaving U.S. territory virtually unscathed - until now.

The challenge to the United States and other countries which face this threat is twofold. It must protect the security of its citizens from terrorists who abuse the rights granted to them in a free society. At the same time it must preserve those same rights which democratic nations cherish. Islam makes it obligatory upon Muslims to stand by the oppressed regardless of their race, color, religion or affiliation and say no to the oppressor and ask him to respond to the voice of reason and justice.

As regards the question you posed, we would like to cite for you the fatwa issued by the eminent Muslim scholar, Sheikh 'Atiyyah Saqr, former Head of Al-Azhar Fatwa Committee that reads:

Jihad is one of the words that have been misused due to misunderstanding its true meaning. The word "Jihad" is derived from the Arabic word "Jahd" which means fatigue or the word "Juhd" which means effort. A Mujahid is he who strives in the Cause of Allah and exerts efforts which make him feel fatigued. The word "Jihad" means exerting effort to achieve a desired thing or prevent an undesired one. In other words, it is an effort that aims at bringing about benefit or preventing harm.

Jihad can be observed through any means and in any field whether material or moral. Among the types of Jihad are struggling against one's desires, the accursed Satan, poverty, illiteracy, disease, and fighting all evil forces in the world. There are many religious texts that refer to these types of Jihad. Among the forms of Jihad is defending life, property or honor. Those who die while engaging in Jihad are considered to be martyrs, as confirmed by Hadith. Jihad is also done to avert aggression on home countries and on all that is held sacred, or in order to face those who try to hinder the march of the call of truth.

In Islamic Shari'ah, Jihad in the Cause of Allah means fighting in order to make the Word of Allah most high, and the means for doing so is taking up arms in addition to preparation, financing and planning strategies. A large number of people are supposed to take part in Jihad including farmers, craftsmen, traders, doctors, engineers, workers, security men, preachers, writers and all those who directly or indirectly participate in the battle. This type of Jihad was a major concern of Muslims in the beginning of the formation of the Islamic community, and a lot of verses of the Glorious Qur'an and the Hadith advocated and encouraged it.

Almighty Allah says: (March forth, whether you are light (being healthy, young and wealthy) or heavy (being ill, old and poor) and strive with your wealth and your lives in the Cause of Allah.) Jihad is considered an individual duty (Fard 'Ein), on all Muslims who are capable and fit to fight, in the event of being invaded by the enemy, and is considered a collective duty (Fard Kifayah) in the event of not being invaded. However, if the Imam (leader) calls to Jihad, people must respond to his call. This is evident from Allah's Saying, (O you who believe! What is the matter with you, that when you are asked to march forth in the Cause of Allah (i.e. Jihad) you cling heavily on the earth?), and the Hadith narrated by Al-Bukhari and Muslim, "When you are called to Jihad, then go forth."

A question arises: is taking up arms the only means to spread Islam? Fighting originally had two main objectives: the first one was to ward off an actual or an anticipated aggression, and the second one was to clear the hurdles in the path of Da'wah (call for Islam). The battles of Badr, Uhud, Al-Khandaq and others are examples of staving off actual aggression and some of them were fought in order to aid the oppressed. Almighty Allah says: (But if they seek your help in religion, it is your duty to help them…).

The conquest of Makkah was undertaken for the purpose of staving off an expected aggression after the Quraish had violated its covenant with the Prophet (peace and blessings of Allah be upon him) in Al-Hudaybyah; this was also the case of the expedition of Tabuk and other expeditions. It also cleared the obstacles placed in the path of Islam by enabling the Muslims to leave Madinah and spread the call to Islam all over the world because Islam is a universal message.

Since Jihad was legalized in Islam and the Prophet (peace and blessings be upon him) said that he was sent by Allah to wage war against disbelief and that his sustenance was "tied" to his spear, as related by Ahmad on the authority of Ibn `Umar, then we have to understand that Islam advocated acquiring the highest degree of power, and the reason for this is that Islam, at that time, was a newly rising power and was expected to be "attacked" by the already existing powers to prevent it from competing with them over power – a conflict that is common to all ages.

Therefore, the new entity had to be defended in order to prove its strength and deliver its message. If Islam were a local temporary call, taking up arms would be just for the purpose of defense, but Islam is a universal call that had to reach the whole world. However, the only means at that time was traveling, which was, and still is fraught with dangers; so taking up arms was necessary to prevent the enemies from standing in the path of the Islamic call. While arms were necessary to remove the hurdles in the past, their sole mission now is to defend Islam against those who want to harm it and harm those who embrace it.

As for spreading Islam, there are several means that spare people the trouble of traveling, such as newspapers, books, the Internet and other means that have known no boarders, although they may be controlled to some extent. However, radio stations have become of such power and prevalence that they can reach people while being at home or even in bed, and they can neither be prevented by any authority, nor held back by any door or border. The superficial understanding of the legality of fighting contained in the verses of the Glorious Qur'an and the Prophet's hadiths may give the impression that Islam has been spread by force and that if it had not been for force, Islam would not have existed or become predominant in many countries or embraced by such a large number of people. But how could this be said about Islam which is the religion of mercy?

Allah Almighty says: (But if the enemy inclines towards peace, do thou also incline towards peace and trust in Allah.).The Prophet also says: "O people! Do not wish to face the enemy (in a battle) and ask Allah to save you (from calamities) but if you should face the enemy, then be patient and let it be known to you that Paradise is under the shades of swords." The call to Islam is not meant to be imposed on anyone; people are completely free to make their choice. In fact, creeds can never propagated by a dagger. Allah Almighty says to Noah: (Shall We compel you to accept it when you are averse to it?). Allah says to Muhammad (peace and blessings be upon him): (Wilt thou compel mankind against their will to believe!); many other verses convey the same meaning.

While there are texts that explicitly indicate the absolute order to fight, there are others that restrict it to whether it is for the purpose of staving off an aggression, preventing an expected aggression or making it a punishment for violating a covenant. Allah Almighty says: (Fight in the cause of Allah those who fight you, but do not transgress limits.). And says: (But if they violate their oaths after their covenant and taunt you for your faith, fight thee the chiefs of unfaith.). In fact, the previous verse specifies the meaning of the verses: (And fight the pagans all together as they fight you all together.), and slay them wherever ye catch them."

As for those who call for taking up arms to change the current state of the Islamic communities, we have previously said that any means of reform based on violence will not achieve its goals. In addition to this, exercising power requires extensive preparation and planning including a careful study of all existing circumstances before taking such a step, i.e. calling arms. However, this should not be understood as undermining the importance of Jihad in its general sense. Jihad will continue till the end of days in all its forms and through its entire means.

This is evident from the Hadith narrated by Abu Dawud: "Jihad will continue from the day I was sent by Allah till the last people of my nation fight against the Antichrist (Dajjal), it will neither be stopped by oppression nor abstention". This Hadith denotes the continuance of Jihad in all fields including armed Jihad, is an integral element; this fact is evident from referring to fighting against the Antichrist.

DIPLOMATIC IMMUNITY AND ETHICS OF WAR

According to the Islamic Holy Book - the Quran, God has bestowed honour on every individual irrespective of skin colour, race, nationality, etc. Freedom is one of the great favours of God and its deprivation is a great misery. Under the Islamic dispensation, no one can be made a captive without a just cause. Prisoners can only be taken in the event of a regular declared war or battle and not for any other reason or under any other pretext.

The Holy Quran specifically states:

It does not behove a Prophet that he should have captives until he engages in regular fighting in the land. If you take captives, except in regular fighting, you will be regarded as desiring the goods of this world, while ALLAH desires for you the Hereafter. And ALLAH is Mighty, Wise (8:68)

This verse cuts at the root of not only slavery practice in years gone by but also demolishes any supposed justification of modern day hostage-taking and hijacking of innocent people not involved in actual combat.

In his farewell address the Holy Prophet of Islam gave special instructions regarding good treatment which should be meted out to prisoners. The Holy Prophet said:

O men, you still have in your possession some prisoners of war. I advise you, therefore, to feed them and to clothe them in the same way and style as you feed and clothe yourselves. To give them pain or trouble can never be tolerated.

More specific commandments on the ethics of war and treatment of prisoners are contained in the fifth verse of the forty-seventh chapter of the Quran. This comprehensive verse can be paraphrased as follows:

"When engaged in a regular battle, it should be fought bravely and relentlessly. War can be continued till peace and freedom of conscience are established. Prisoners are to be taken judiciously. Free men cannot be deprived of their liberty without a just and reasonable cause. When war is over, prisoners should be released as an act of favour or on taking ransom or by negotiating a mutual exchange."

In the history of Islam all these methods have been used for releasing prisoners. A novel method to get release was that the educated prisoners could teach reading and writing to those who were illiterate, in lieu of ransom. These verse further strikes at the roots of those who would justify modern day terrorism in the name and under the banner of Islam. Envoys are privileged people in the Islamic system. They enjoy full personal immunity. They are not subject to political ransom, no matter how worthy the cause may be, and to kidnap them is a heinous crime. They must not be killed, molested or maltreated. There are numerous instances from the Holy Prophet's life which illustrate the application of these principles.

Thus Islamic scriptural commandments and the precepts of the Holy Prophet of Islam concerning diplomatic immunity are free from ambiguities. In a nutshell, taking hostages and maltreating envoys and private citizens in any shape and form is totally foreign to the teachings and doctrines of Islam. In other words, the philosophy of Islam totally rejects terrorism.

CONCEPT OF JIHAD IN ISLAM

Through the actions of some elements, the western world visualizes a wrong concept of *Jihad* (Holy War). The word *Jihad* conjures up the vision of a marching band of religious fanatics with savage beards and fiery eyes, brandishing swords and attacking the infidels. *Jihad* in Islamic terminology means to make an effort, to endeavour and to strive in a noble way. Over the centuries this meaning of *Jihad* has been obliterated or at least diluted. The critical juncture in the Islamic world requires reviving and recapturing the true and pristine meaning of *Jihad*.

Jihad can be divided into two broad categories. First is *Jihad-e-akbar*. This is *Jihad* against one's own person to curb sinful inclinations, i.e., purification of self. This is the most difficult *Jihad* and hence in terms of rewards and blessings is the highest category of *Jihad*. The second is *Jihad-e-asghar*. This is *Jihad* of the sword. This is communal *Jihad* and presupposes certain specific conditions. The Quran speaks of fighting only against those who first attack Muslims and this is the very condition laid down in other verses of the Holy Quran as well. The so-called *verse of the sword* in the Islamic scripture is often taken out of context as if it inculcates an indiscriminate massacre of all unbelievers.

The Quranic words such as *kill whatever you find them* apply only in cases where the enemy has first attacked Muslims and apply to those unbelievers and enemies who break their oaths and firm agreements. They do not apply to unprovoked wars and battles. To interpret these verses in any other manner would be a travesty of the lofty ideals of Islam. There is not a single instance in the life of the Holy Prophet where he offered the alternative of the sword or Islam to anyone. The Western media and even some scholars sometimes ignore the distinction between these two aspects of *Jihad*.

It must be remembered that the Holy Quran does not make *Jihad*, the *holy war*, in context of an article of faith. The sayings and traditions of the Holy Prophet render it into a formula for active struggle that invariably and incorrectly tended towards a militant expression. Modern day terrorism is contrary to the purview of the real spirit of the Islamic *Jihad*. The presentation of Islam as a crude and barbaric religion which gives itself the right to cause unwarranted human and material suffering and destruction under the guise of Divine authority is not the kind of Islam we find in the Holy Quran and in the precepts of the Holy Prophet Muhammad (peace and blessings of Allah be upon him!)

PEACE AND INTERNATIONAL RELATIONS IN ISLAM

Among the attributes of God, the Holy Quran mentions that He is the Source of peace and the Bestower of security (59:23). The establishment of peace and maintenance of security must, therefore, be the constant objective of all Muslims and non-Muslims alike. Every pursuit and activity which disturbs peace is severely condemned in Islam. We find specific injunctions in the Holy Quran:

And create not disorder in the earth after it has been set in order. ... (7:57; 11:86; 29:37)

Mischief and wickedness are condemned in several other

verses and Muslims are commanded to work wholly for peace. Islam draws attention to factors which tend to disturb or destroy peace and order, and deprecates them. Domination of one group by another in the domestic sphere, or of one people by another in the international sphere is a potent cause of disturbance of peace and is therefore strongly condemned. Economic exploitation of one people or country by another inevitably leads to domination by the exploiters, and develops into a potential threat to peace. The Holy Quran prohibits such exploitation and an economy based on exploitation cannot be beneficial in its consequences, nor can it endure.

Islam visualizes an association of strong and stable states allied together in the pursuance of peace, freedom of conscience and the promotion of human welfare. Treaties or covenants between nations may have to be drawn up which should be done in a straightforward language and should not be evaded or repudiated under the temptation of securing some advantage. In case of difficulties and disputes, it is the duty of Muslims to bring about a peaceful settlement and adjustment. The Holy Quran teaches that God has sent His revelation to all people from time to time.

Many of prophets of the Old Testament are mentioned by name and so is Jesus who with other prophets is honoured and revered by all Muslims. Indeed, the Quran requires belief in the truth of all these prophets. Islam is thus unique and distinct in requiring an affirmation in all prophets wherever they appeared and therefore it seeks to bring about reconciliation between the followers of different faiths and to establish a basis of respect and honour among them. The Quran says:

Surely, those who believe and the Jews and the Christians and the Sabians - whichever party from among these truly believes in ALLAH and the Last Day and does good deeds, shall have their reward with their Lord, and no fear shall come upon then nor shall they grieve (2:63).

The same message is repeated in 5:70. The basic unity of the followers of all faiths is emphatically stressed in the Holy Quran and the creation of discord and disunity by terrorism or otherwise has no place in Islam. In the domain of international relations, religion and inter-religious relations occupy an important position. Unfortunately, comparatively little attention is paid to this aspect of human relations. It is assumed that religion is a private matter for each individual and should, therefore, have no direct connection with the political, social aspects of life.

This assumption is not justified. Islam being an egalitarian religion is not just a personal faith, but all-encompassing codes of values and conduct. Islam is and will be a vital factor in human relations and there is a good ground of hope that it might progressively become more effective in promoting unity and accord rather than continue to be required on the part of religious and political leaders to achieve that goal. I must conclude by saying that whether peace or war, acts of terrorism are not only condemned in Islam but are also pointedly declared alien to the teachings of Islam which in fact means peace through the submission to the Will of God, the Lord of all human beings. Only through conformity to Divine laws can we hope to achieve the ideal of a secure world free of terrorism.

Islam means the religion of peace. A person following Islam will find that he or she is surrounded by noble teachings, the aim of which is to establish peace between man and Allah, the Creator of all; between man and man; and between man and the rest of Allah's creation. How does such a religion deal with the issue of terrorism? And what does the word terrorist mean? Dictionaries will define a terrorist as one who systematically uses violence and intimidation to achieve political ends - or one who controls or forces others to do something by violence, fear or threats. All these definitions are covered by two words in the Holy Qur'an, the sacred book of Islam: Fitnah and Ikrâh.

In the Holy Qur'an, God begins to deal with the issue of terrorism by teaching Muslims never to become terrorists in the first place. Two of the very first verses of our Holy Book say: 'Al-Fitnatu ashad-du minal qatl' – meaning that in the sight of Allah, 'persecution, or making people constantly fear for their lives, is much worse than killing'. And also: 'Lâ ikrâha fid-dîn' – 'There shall be no compulsion in religion', that is to say, that no one has the right to force others into complying with their demands or compelling others to follow their line of thinking.

Allah Almighty warns the believers again and again that they should never abandon Him, the source of all goodness. Allah Almighty reminds us that it is those who have abandoned Him and thrown away all good, and divested themselves of every shred of human decency, that are the ones who will eventually resort to terrorizing others, forcing them into complying with their demands. The believers are repeatedly reminded that they would lose Allah Almighty's love and His favors if they ever began to behave in that way.

But Islam does not content itself with these injunctions strongly forbidding Muslims from ever becoming terrorists. It also makes sure that the believers are made into highly moral, excellently behaved people, by inculcating those lofty human values that can turn them into people who sincerely love humankind without distinction of religion, race or social status. Islam no doubt encourages the logical and rational discussion of views with people of all creeds in a calm and dispassionate way, with the only aim that truth prevails over error and falsehood. But it also reminds us that it is error and falsehood as such that are to be hated and detested.

The people who unfortunately hold on to error are never to be hated. That is why the motto of the Ahmadiyya Muslim Community is 'Love for all, hatred for none.' In Islam, an amazingly powerful emphasis is laid on developing love for mankind and on the vital importance of showing mercy and sympathy towards every creature of Allah Almighty, including human beings and animals. For indeed, love and true sympathy is the very antidote of terrorism. It is related by 'Ayesha, may Allah be pleased with her, the talented wife of the Holy Prophet Muhammad, may peace and blessings of Allah be upon him, that some desert Arabs came to him one day and asked: 'Do you kiss your children?' He answered: 'Yes.' They said: 'We never kiss them.'

The Prophet (sa) said: 'What can I do if your hearts have been stripped of compassion?' He also said that Allah Almighty has no mercy for him who has no mercy for his fellow beings. The measure of compassion shown by the Holy Prophet (sa) cannot but amaze anyone who knows how rough and violent was the society into which he had been born. Abu Qatâdah may Allah be pleased with her, relates that the Messenger of Allah told him: 'It happens that I stand up to lead the prayer, having in mind to lengthen it. Then I hear the cry of an infant and I shorten the prayer fearing lest I should cause inconvenience to its mother.'

Far from inciting hatred and aggressiveness in its followers, Islam keeps on enjoining kindness and sympathy for all. The Holy Prophet Muhammad may peace and blessings of Allah be upon him, said: 'Charity is incumbent upon every human limb every day on which the sun rises. To bring about reconciliation between two contestants is charity. Helping a person mounts his animal or to load his baggage on to it is charity. A good word is charity. Every step taken toward the mosque for prayer is charity. To remove anything from the street that causes inconvenience is charity.'

He incessantly admonished Muslims to behave well towards their neighbors, saying: 'That one will not enter Paradise whose neighbor is not safe against his mischief.' He also declared: 'By Him in Whose Hands is my life, you will not enter Paradise unless you believe, and you will not truly believe unless you love one another. Shall I tell you something whereby you will love one another? Multiply the greeting of peace among yourselves.' One day he found a mother bird beating her wings on the ground in distress. He asked his companions: 'Who has done this?' They said: 'We took her young ones out of her nest.' The Holy Prophet (sa) said: 'Restore them to her. No mother must be tormented on account of her child.'

On another occasion, he found one of his companions setting fire to an anthill. He immediately told them to put out the fire saying: 'No one has the right to torment others with fire.' As Allah Almighty says in the Holy Qur'an that the true believers are: 'those who suppress their anger and forgive people', likewise, the Holy Messenger of Allah, Muhammad, may peace and blessings of Allah be upon him, said: 'Allah is Gentle and loves gentleness in all things. Make things easy and do not make them hard. And cheer people up and do not repel them.'

It is clear that the true believers and all other good, honest people are always on the receiving end of terrorism, never on the delivering end. Whenever such tendencies appear in society by which the peace is being disturbed and people cannot live their lives without fear, Muslims are enjoined to counter them first of all by reasoning with those responsible for the disturbance. The Holy Qur'an says:

Call unto the way of your Lord [that is the way of justice and goodness] with wisdom and goodly exhortation, and argue with them in a way that is best. *(Ch.16: v.126)*

And the Qur'an repeatedly tells us to seek help from Allah Almighty with patience and prayer. But if reasoning with those people bent on wickedness and praying for them fails to bring about a change in their ways, then Allah Almighty says, again at the end of Chapter 16, verse 127:

'Then if you desire to punish the oppressors, punish them to the extent you have been wronged.'

Allah Almighty commands the Muslims that when things get out of hand, they should join forces to restore peace by use of reasonable force. They have been enjoined by the Holy Prophet Muhammad, may peace and blessings of Allah be upon him, to join forces if need be with followers of other faiths to do so. Thus, in the famous document known as the Treaty of Medina, The Messenger of Allah declared:

Article 1:

This is the treaty of Muhammad, the Prophet (the Messenger of Allah) between the Believers and Muslims of the Quraish and the people of Yathrib, and between those who follow them and join them in fighting (the common enemy).

Article 2:

And it is that they constitute an Ummah Wâhidah (One Nation) separate from other people.

Article 25:

And also that the Jews of the tribe of 'Auf constitute an Ummah Wâhidah with the Believers - even though the Jews will follow their own religion and the Muslims will follow their own - and this will include both their friends and themselves. (Quoted from Reuben Levy in 'Sociology of Islam, part I, pages 279-282)

Here, all the inhabitants of the city of Yathrib, or Medina, were called upon to join in fighting the forces that were terrorizing the citizens. Muslims have been made to promise that they will help defend the followers of other faiths from unjust and cruel attacks as well. For example, in his charter for all time to come addressed to all Christians living as citizens under Muslim rule, the Holy Prophet Muhammad, may peace and blessings of Allah be upon him, states:

I promise that any monk or wayfarer who will seek my help on the mountains, in forests, deserts or habitations, or in places of worship, I will repel his enemies with my friends and helpers, with all my relatives and with all those w ho profess to follow me and will defend them, because they are my covenant. And I will defend the covenanted against the persecution, injury and embarrassment of their enemies in lieu of the poll tax they have promised to pay. If they prefer to defend their properties and persons themselves, they will be allowed to do so and will not be put to any inconvenience on that account.

No bishop will be expelled from his bishopric, no monk from his monastery, no priest from his place of worship, and no pilgrim will be detained in his pilgrimage. None of their churches and other places of worship will be desolated or destroyed or demolished. No material of their churches will be used to build mosques or houses for the Muslims; any Muslim doing so will be regarded as recalcitrant to Allah and His Prophet. Monks and Bishops will be subject to no tax or indemnity whether they live in forests or on rivers, in the East or in the West, in the North or in the South. I give them my word of honor. They are on my promise and covenant and will enjoy perfect immunity from all sorts of incon-veniences. Every help shall be given them in the repair of their churches. They shall be absolved of wearing arms. They shall be protected by the Muslims. Let this document not be disobeyed till Judgment Day." (Quoted from Balâdhar)

In Islam, every effort is thus made to protect the peace of not only the Muslims, but also of the followers of other faiths. Allah Almighty says:

And if Allah did not defend some men by means of others, there would surely have been pulled down mon-asteries, churches, synagogues and mosques wherein the name of Allah is oft remembered. (Ch.22: v.41)

However, Muslims have been warned by the Holy Founder of Islam, Muhammad, the Messenger of Allah, may peace and blessings of Allah be upon him, that when they enter the territory of those who have been terrorizing and harshly persecuting them, they should not lose all sense of perspective and justice, and be tempted to start acting savagely, like the terrorists themselves. The worst crime of ungratefulness would be that committed by a people who, having forgotten that they had just been subjected to terrible cruelties, start meting out the same, if not worse, cruelties to others. The Prophet ordered:

'You will meet those who remember Almighty Allah in their houses of worship. Have no dispute with them, and give no trouble to them. In the enemy country, do not kill any women or children, or the blind, or the old. Do not pull down any tree; nor pull down any building.' (Quoted from Halbiyyah, Vol.3).

So the only Jihad permitted in Islam is the war of the oppressed against the oppressor, the war waged to protect the peace of all people irrespective of their religion or creed. Tactics used today such as suicide bombing, etc. are absolutely out of the question for true followers of Islam. Allah Almighty says:

And kill not your own selves. Surely Allah is Merciful to you. (Ch.4: v. 30)

...and cast not yourselves into ruin with your own hands... (Ch.2: v.196)

Islam strictly forbids the killing of innocent, non-aggressive people...no hostility are allowed except against the aggressors. (Ch.2: v.194)

These three verses alone are sufficient to prevent Muslims from crashing airplanes into buildings, or from sending suicide bombers to blow up innocent civilians. Once the evildoers have ceased misbehaving and have been justly punished for their crimes, then Allah Almighty says:

And fight them until there is no more persecution, and religion is freely professed for Allah. But if they desist, then remember that no hostility is allowed except against the aggressors. (Ch.2: v.194)

To sum up, Islam advocates three steps against terrorism:

1. To give an excellent moral upbringing to all Muslims, so that they become upright, just, moral, kind and loving people, thereby ensuring that they never disrupt the peace of others.
2. Whenever the peace is disrupted, to reason and argue with the evildoers, and sincerely pray for them, to make them change their ways.
3. If all reasoning fails, then to join forces with all good people to combat the mischief-mongers until peace has been restored, but always keeping the dictates of justice in view.

It is our belief that not only Islam, but no true religion, whatever its name, can sanction violence and bloodshed of innocent men, women and children in the name of Allah Almighty. Terrorists may use religious or political labels, but no one should be deceived by their wily ways and treacherous guiles. They have nothing to do with religion. They are the enemies of peace. They must be combated at every level as advocated by Islam, the religion of peace.

Bibliography

Abraham, A. J. *Islamic Fundamentalism and the Doctrine of Jihad.* Lima, OH: Wyndham Hall Press, 2002.

AbuKhalil, As'ad. *Bin Laden, Islam, and America's New 'War on Terrorism'*. Open Media Pamphlet Series. New York: Seven Stories Press, 2002.

Aho, James. *Politics of Righteousness: Idaho Christian Patriotism.* Seattle, WA: University of Washington Press, 1995.

Alexander, Yonah. *European Terrorism Today & Tomorrow.* Brassey's Terrorism Library. Washington, DC: Brassey's, 1992.

Alexander, Yonah. *Middle East Terrorism: Selected Group Profiles.* Washington, DC: Jewish Institute for National Security Affairs, 1994.

Al-Khattar, Aref M. *Religion and Terrorism: An Interfaith Perspective.* Westport, CT: Praeger, 2003.

Anderson, Chris. *The Billy Boy: The Life and Death of LVF Leader Billy Wright.* Edinburgh: Mainstream, 2002.

Anderson, Sean. *Terrorism: Assassins to Zealots.* Lanham, MD: Scarecrow Press, 2003.

Anti-Defamation League, *Extremism on the Right: A Handbook.* New York: Anti-Defamation League, 1988.

Appleby, R. Scott. *Ambivalence of the Sacred: Religion, Violence, and Reconciliation.* Lanham, MD: Rowman & Littlefield Publishers, 2000.

Bar, Shmuel. *Warrant for Terror: Fatwas of Radical Islam and the Duty of Jihad.* Hoover Studies in Politics, Economics, and Society. Lanham, MD: Rowman & Littlefield, 2006.

Bartholomeusz, Tessa J. *Buddhist Fundamentalism and Minority Identities in Sri Lanka*. New York: State University of New York Press, 1998.

Barton, Greg. *Indonesia's Struggle: Jemaah Islamiyah and the Soul of Islam*. Sydney, Australia: University of New South Wales Press, 2004.

Cateura, Linda Brandi. *Voices of American Muslims: 23 Profiles*. New York: Hippocrene Books, 2005.

Catholic Institute for International Relations, *Guatemala, Never Again*. Maryknoll, NY: Orbis Books, 1999.

Davies, Barry. *Terrorism: Inside a World Phenomenon*. London: Virgin Books, 2003.

Devji, Faisal. *Landscapes of the Jihad: Militancy, Morality, Modernity*. Ithaca, NY: Cornell University Press, 2005.

Emerson, Steven. *Worldwide Jihad Movement: Militant Islam's Target the West*. Jerusalem, Israel: Institute of the World Jewish Congress, 1995.

Esposito, John L. *Islam: The Straight Path*. 3rd edition. New York: Oxford University Press, 1998.

Esposito, John L. *The Islamic Threat: Myth or Reality?*. New York: Oxford University Press, 1992.

Esposito, John L. *The Oxford Dictionary of Islam*. New York: Oxford University Press, 2003.

Esposito, John L. *Unholy War: Terror in the Name of Islam*. New York: Oxford University Press, 2002.

Etzioni, Amitai. *How Patriotic is the Patriot Act? Freedom Versus Security in the Age of Terrorism*. New York: Routledge, 2004.

Fandy, Mamoun. *Saudi Arabia and the Politics of Dissent*. New York: Palgrave, 2001.

Farah, Douglas. *Blood From Stones: The Secret Financial Network of Terror*. New York: Broadway Books, 2004.

Gardell, Mattias. *Gods of the Blood: The Pagan Revival and White Separatism*. Durham, NC: Duke University Press, 2003.

Gerges, Fawaz A. *The Far Enemy: Why Jihad Went Global*. New York: Cambridge University Press, 2005.

Habeck, Mary R. *Knowing the Enemy: Jihadist Ideology and the War on Terror*. New Haven, NY: Yale University Press, 2006.

Hiro, Dilip. *War Without End: The Rise of Islamist Terrorism and Global Response*. New York: Routledge, 2002.

Howard, Russell D. *Defeating Terrorism: Shaping the New Security Environment*. Guilford, CT: McGraw-Hill, 2004.

Huband, Mark. *Warriors of the Prophet: the Struggle for Islam*. Boulder, CO: Westview Press, 1999.

Hudson, Rex A. *Who Becomes a Terrorist and Why: The 1999 Government Report on Profiling Terrorists*. Guilford, CT: Lyon Press, 2002.

Jaber, Hala. *Hezbollah: Born with a Vengeance*. New York: Columbia University Press, 1997.

Jacquard, Roland. *In the Name of Osama bin Laden: Global Terrorism & the bin Laden Brotherhood*. Durham, NC: Duke University Press, 2002.

Jaimoukha, Amjad M. *The Chechens: A Handbook*. New York: Routledge Curzon, 2005.

Karawan, Ibrahim. *Islamic Impasse*. New York: Oxford University Press, 1997.

MacArthur, John. *Terrorism, Jihad, and the Bible: A Response to the Terrorist Attacks*. Nashville, TN: W Publishing Group, 2001.

Miniter, Richard. *Losing Bin Laden: How Bill Clinton's Failures Unleashed Global Terror*. Washington, DC: Regnery, 2003.

Mishal, Shaul. *The Palestinian Hamas: Vision, Violence, and Coexistence*. New York: Columbia University Press, 2000.

Napoleoni, Loretta. *Modern Jihad: Tracing the Dollars Behind the Terror Networks*. Sterling, VA: Pluto Press, 2003.

Noorani, A. G. *Islam & Jihad: Prejudice versus Reality*. New York: Zed Books, 2002.

Nusse, Andrea. *Muslim Palestine: The Ideology of Hamas.* Amsterdam: Harwood Academic Publishers, 1998.

O'Ballance, Edgar. *Islamic Fundamentalist Terrorism, 1979-95: The Iranian Connection.* Washington Square, NY: New York University Press, 1997.

O'Ballance, Edgar. *Islamic Fundamentalist Terrorism: 1979-95.* Basingstoke: Macmillan, 1997.

Ojeda, Auriana. *Islamic Fundamentalism.* San Diego, CA: Greenhaven Press, 2003.

O'Kane, Rosemary. *Revolutionary Reign of Terror: the Role of Violence in Political Change.* Brookfield, VT: Elgar, 1991.

Rana, Muhammad Amir. *A to Z of Jehadi Organizations in Pakistan.* Lahore: Mashal Books, 2004.

Randal, Jonathan C. *Osama: The Making of a Terrorist.* New York: Knopf, 2004.

Rapoport, David C. *The Rationalization of Terrorism.* Frederick, MD: University Publications of America, 1982.

Scheuer, Michael. *Through Our Enemies Eyes: Osama bin Laden, Radical Islam, and the Future of America.* Rev. ed., 2nd ed.. Washington, DC: Potomac Books, 2006.

Taheri, Amir. *Holy Terror: Inside the World of Islamic Terrorism.* Bethesda, MD: Adler & Adler, 1987.

Venske, Ben. *The al-Qaeda Threat: An Analytical Guide to al-Qaeda's Tactics & Targets.* Alexandria, VA: Tempest Publishing, 2003.

Venzke, Ben. *The al-Qaeda Threat: An Analytical Guide to al-Qaeda's Tactics & Targets.* Alexandria, VA: Tempest, 2003.

Waardenburg, Jacques. *Muslims and Others: Relations in Context.* New York: Walter de Gruyter, 2003.

Wiktorowicz, Quintan. *Global Jihad: Understanding September 11.* Falls Church, VA: 2002.

Zacharias, Ravi K. *Light in the Shadow of Jihad.* Sisters, OR: Multnomah Publishers, 2002.

Index